ON THE JOB
IN THE
BIG APPLE

NORMA IRIS PAGAN MORALES

ISBN 978-1-959895-08-4 (paperback)
ISBN 978-1-959895-07-7 (eBook)

Printed in the United States of America

DEDICATION

This book is dedicated to all members
of the New York City Police Department.
Thank you for your service.

OVERVIEW

The New York City Police Department had its origin in trying to find a better way to control the rising crime rate as early as the mid-19th century.

As you begin reading, you will understand how the crime, in the city that never sleeps, was brought on by the massive population growth which caused primarily by poor Irish immigrants from Ireland beginning in the 1820's.

You will learn how New York City implemented the London, England policing model of a full-time professional police force in 1845. This was done with the establishment of the Municipal Police, replacing the inadequate, outdated night watch system which had been in place since the 17th century with the founding of the Dutch colonial city of New Amsterdam.

The Municipal Police were impatiently replaced by a Metropolitan Police. Other local police were consolidated.

As you keep reading, you will be amazed how I took you to the past and back to the present time. It was not easy collecting stories about this great second to none organization, but it was not impossible.

TABLE OF CONTENTS

CHAPTER 1

FIRST SETTLEMENT. 1609-1626

To understand the development of our second to none organization, I will take you into an imaginary journey in time....

In September 1609, the ship Half-Moon, impatiently sailed the American coast. This ship was looking for a shorter route from Europe towards India.

The sailors had no idea that they were heading to the mouth of a great lonely river. This river was flowing silently out from the heart of an unknown continent.

The Half-Moon was a small and clumsy yacht operated by Dutch and English sailors. They were commanded by an English adventurer known as Hendrik Hudson. His craft and crew were all typical of that era. They were eager to sail and love adventures.

They were explorers who were too anxious to sail under any flag that promised them glory and profit. They didn't care or wonder at what cost of hardship or danger.

This was the age of strong and brave seamen that came from England and the Netherlands. It was a period when the greatest deeds were done on the ocean by these rough heroes of cut-glass and compass. They won honor by exploring the unknown seas.

These men took possession of unknown lands, no less than by their ability in the ugly water-fights which have made their names immortal.

Their small ships dared the dangers of the most distant oceans and shattered the sea-might of every rival naval power. They led their lives of stormy danger and looked forward unmoved to inevitable death.

For more than a quarter of a century, Spain and Portugal had not only taken the lead in but had almost monopolized all ocean exploration and intercontinental settlement. They conquest and were indeed, the most daring navigators to be found in their ranks.

The Italians also served during that time but were competitors with Portugal and Spain. Even at the beginning of the seventeenth century they were still the only peoples who had permanently occupied any portion of the New World. Their massive possessions included all tropical, sub-tropical, and south-temperate America.

By this time, there were more than one hundred fights among the Italians, Portuguese and Spaniards. Also, the sea beggars and sea travelers of Holland and England had destroyed the navies of the Spanish king. England and Holland won from those who fought for his flag the mastery of the ocean.

Let me tell you that Spain was still powerful; but it was a power that was declining. There were always races on who was going to plant their flag for their country.

Northern Europe established their standards in the New World. They stood toward the Spaniards and Spanish Americans as aggressors. Their blows had to be blocked and returned. Sometimes they were returned with good effect, but the Spanish people have always been on the defensive, fearing, not a threatening invasion.

Yet, though the career of Spain as a conquering power was thus cut short. Two expecting centuries passed before Spain lost any considerable portion of land. Spain land held when the ships of the English colonists first sighted the shores of America.

It seemed, and was, perfectly possible in the seventeenth century, that the nineteenth century would see flourishing Dutch and Swedish states firmly seated along the Hudson and the Delaware.

So, it came about that the English colonists and their American descendants had to tame a wild and stubborn continent. They also had to take many of the reasonable portions of the domain which the English-speaking Americans inherit, from the hands of other intruders of European blood.

Many cities of the Union bear testimony by their early history to this fact. Albany, Detroit, and Santa Fe´ are but three out of many towns wherein the English gained what the Dutch, the French, or the Spaniards had spread.

The history of New York deserves to be studied for more than one reason. It is the history of the largest English-speaking city which the English conquered but did not find. Most of the population, composed as it is and ever has been of many shifting strains, has never been English.

Again, for the past hundred years, it is the history of a wonderfully prosperous trading-city. New York is the largest city in the world in which the democratic plan has been faithfully. This plan has been tried for so long that the trial, had made some exceptional advantages.

It also had made some usually exceptional disadvantages. It is of immense interest alike for the measure in which it has succeeded and for the measure in which it has failed.

Henry Hudson, on coming to the river to which his name was afterward given, did not at first know that it was a river at all. He believed and hoped that it was some great arm of the sea, that in fact it was the Northwest Passage to India. Hudson and so many other brave men died in vainly trying to discover the short passage to India.

For a week he lay in the lower bay. Then, for a day, he shifted his anchorage into what is now New York Harbor. His boats explored the surrounding shoreline. He found many Indian villages, and the neighborhood seemed well populated.

The savages gathered to see the white strangers, and eagerly traded off their tobacco for the knives and beads of the Europeans. Of course, there were arguments between the rough, brutal sailors and the changeable, suspicious, unfaithful red men.

Once a boat's crew was attacked by two canoes, loaded with warriors, and a sailor was killed by an arrow which pierced his throat. Yet overall, their relations were friendly, and the trading and exchanging went on unchecked.

Hudson soon found that he was off the mouth of a river, not a passage. He spent three weeks exploring it. He went sailing up till the rapid water warned him that he was at the head of navigation, near the present site of Albany.

Henry Hudson also found many small Indian tribes scattered along the banks, and frequently kept on good terms with them, giving their chiefs trinkets of various kinds, and treating them for the first time to a taste of "fire-water," the terrible curse of their race ever since.

Hudson was well received when he visited the bark dwellings. His hosts always received him by giving him feasts. The dishes included not only wild bird, but also fat dogs, killed by the squaws, and skinned with mussel shells.

The Indians, who had made some progress in agriculture, brought to the ship quantities of corn, beans, and pumpkins from the great heaps drying beside their villages. Their fields great rich soil for planting.

Hudson had to be constantly on his guard against his new-found friends. Once he was attacked by a party of hostile warriors whom he beat off, killing several of their number. However, what far outweighed such danger in the gain-greedy eyes of the trade-loving adventurers, was the fact that they saw in the possession of the Indians great stores of rich furs. The European merchants prized furs as they did silks, spices, ivory, and precious metals.

Having reached the head of navigation, the Half-Moon turned its bluff bows southward, and drifted down stream with the rapid current until it once more reached the bay.

The brilliant fall weather had been varied at times with misty days and nights; and during the Half-Moon's inland voyage its course had lain through scenery singularly wild, grand, and lonely.

The Half-Moon had passed the long line of frowning, battlemented rock-walls that we know by the name of the Palisades. It had threaded its way round the bends where the curving river sweeps in and out among bold peaks.

By now, the ship had sailed in front of the Catskill Mountains. Perhaps even so, as early in the season, it was crowned with shining snow.

From the ship decks, the lookouts scanned with their watchful eye's dim shadowy wastes, stretching for countless leagues on every hand. All the land was covered trees. It looked like one huge forest, where red hunters who had never seen a white face followed wild beasts, upon whose kind no white man had ever gazed.

Early in October, Hudson set out on his homeward voyage to Holland, where the news of his discovery excited much interest among the daring merchants, especially among those whose minds were bent on the fur-trade.

Several ships were sent across the newly found bay and river. They were sent to exchange with the savages and to explore and report further upon the country.

The most well-known of these sea-captains who followed Hudson, was Adrian Block.

During that time, he was anchor off Manhattan Island when lost his ship by fire. He at once started building another ship. He was a man of great resource and always succeeded. He made his fortune for himself.

Block built and launched a forty-five-foot yacht which he christened the Restless. The Restless was a fit name for the bay of one of these daring, ever-roaming adventurers.

This primitive pioneer ship was the first ever launched in our waters. Its tip was the first whichever wrinkled the waters of the Sound. The first trading and exploring ships did well, and the merchants saw that great profits could be made from the Manhattan fur-trade.

The explores, at that time, were determined to establish permanent posts at the head of the river and at its mouth. The main fort was near the mouth of the Mohawk, but they also built a few cabins at the south end of Manhattan Island.

They left half a dozen of their employees with Hendrik Christiansen. Christiansen was the head man over both posts.

The great commercial city of New York therefore, had its origin, not unfittingly, in a cluster of traders' huts.

This obscure beginning was to spring one of the mightiest cities of any age. It was marvelous alike for its wonderfully rapid growth and its splendid material prosperity.

From the outset the new town, it intended to be the largest in the New World. It was even the largest the whole world. It took its place among those communities which owe their existence and growth primarily to commerce.

Their whole character and development for good and evil being more profoundly affected by commercial than by any other influences. Even in its very beginning, the direction in which the great city on Manhattan Island should develop was foreshadowed, and its course outlined in advance.

Christiansen was soon killed by an Indian. For two or three years his fellow-traders lived on Manhattan Island. They lived at the remoter outposts of the fur-trade in the far northwest of this continent.

Some kept decent and straight; others grew almost as filthy and savage as the red men the forest. They hunted, fished, and wasted; sometimes they killed their own game. Other, times they got it by exchange from the Indians, together with tobacco and corn.

Now and then they argued with the surrounding savages. Generally, they kept on good terms with Indians. In exchange for rum and trinkets, they gathered innumerable bundles of valuable furs, mostly of the beaver, which swarmed in all the streams.

Also, they gathered otters. There were many more northern kinds of things, such as the raven and the fish.

For a long time, furs were piled in the holds of three or four small boats whose yearly or half yearly arrival from Holland formed the chief relief to the repetitiveness of the fur-traders' existence.

The merchants who first sent over boats and built a trading-post, joined with others to form the "New Netherland Company". this was a time when settlement and conquest were undertaken more often by great trading companies than by either the national government or by individuals.

The Netherlands government granted the New Netherland Company the monopoly of the fur-trade with the newly discovered territory for three years from 1615 and renewed the grant for a year at a time until 1621.

There was more powerful competitor being in the field in those days.

Some companies were simple trading corporation. They made no effort to really settle the land. The fur-trade proved profitable, and the post on Manhattan Island was continued.

In 1621, the great West India Company was chartered by the States-general. It was given the monopoly of the American trade. It was by this company that the city was really founded. The first settlement was intended to be permanent.

All the magnificent territory discovered by Hudson was granted it under the name of the New Netherlands. The company was one of the three or four huge commercial corporations of imperial power that played no small part in shaping the world's destiny during the two centuries immediately preceding the present.

All these changes of fur trades and rules were in the constitution and history archetypical of the time. The great trading-city of America was really founded by no one individual, nor yet by any national government, but by a great trading corporation.

It created, however, the fight and to bear rule no less than to carry on commerce. The merchants who formed the West India Company were granted the right to exercise powers such as belong to sovereign States, because the task to which they set themselves was one of such incredible magnitude and danger that it could be done only on such terms.

By the way, all the above mentioned were soldiers and sailors no less than traders. It was only merchants of iron will and restless daring who could gain the golden harvests in those hazardous sea-fields, where all save the strongest surely died. The paths of commerce were no less dangerous than those of war.

The West India Company was formed for trade, and for colonizing the world's waste spaces and it was also formed to carry on fierce war against the public enemy, the King of Spain.

Let me remind you that it made war or peace as best suited it. it also gave governors and judges to colonies and to conquered lands. It formed cities, and built forts, it hired mighty admirals to lead to battle and rob, the ships of its many fleets.

Some of the most successful and heroic feats of arms in the history of the Netherlands were performed by the sailors in the pay of this company.

Steel in their hands brought greater profit than gold. The fortunate stockholders of Amsterdam and Zealand received enormous dividends from the sale of the spoil of the ruined cities of Brazil, and of the captured treasure-ships which had once formed part of the Spanish "silver fleet."

During the early part of the seventeenth century, the Atlantic coast from Acadia to Florida became scattered with settlements of dozen different European nations.

At irregular pauses along this extended seaboard, the French, the English, the Dutch, the Swedes, as well as the Spaniards. They built little forts and established small trading-towns.

When the English had fairly begun to take over the land in New England and Virginia, the Dutch still held the Hudson, and the Swedes the mouth of the Delaware.

Acadia was still French, and Florida Spanish. It was altogether uncertain which one of these races would prove champion over the others, or whether anyone would.

There was at least a good chance that the Spaniards would hold their own land. North America, like moderate Europe, would be held by many nations, differ from one to the other in language, in religion, and in blood.

We have grown so accustomed to regarding America north of the Rio Grande as the natural heritage of the English-speaking peoples that we find it hard to realize how uncertain seemed the prospect during the period when colonization began.

None could predict which power would win the struggle. The fate of America was bound up in wars in which her future was hardly, if at all, considered.

Let me remain you that if Gustavus Adolphus had not fallen on the field of Lützen. He found as he hoped, a great Scandinavian kingdom surrounding the Baltic.

The fleets were as powerful as her armies. It may well be that the fame and terror of the Swedish name. It would have protected peace and prosperity to the long-haul Swedish colonists.

Also, if the Dutch fleets would have been a bit stronger, the Dutch diplomats would have prized Manhattan. The New Netherlands might never have become New York.

During this mess fighting and trading, the company had little time to think of colonizing. Nevertheless, in 1624 some families of protestant Walloons were sent to the Hudson in the ship New Netherland. A few of them stayed on Manhattan Island.

The following summer, several more families arrived. The city may be said to have been really founded. The residents on Manhattan Island, after 1624, were permanent settlers and simple short-lived fur traders.

Finally, in May 1626, the director, Peter Minuit, a Westphalian, was appointed by the company as first governor of the colony. He arrived at the harbor in his ship the Sea-Mew. He led a band of true colonists.

These men brought with them their wives and little ones. They also brought their cattle and their house-hold goods. These colonists settled down in the land with the purpose of holding it for themselves and for their children's children.

CHAPTER 2

TIMELINE OF EVENTS

1600 thru 2001

Let's begin with Manhattan

Manhattan 1609-1634

Henry Hudson's unexpected journey:
This legendary explorer found the river that would carry his name.
The island of Manhattan was growing. It rose from a Dutch settlement to the world capital. It acquired the nickname
"The Growingest Island"

Brooklyn 1635

Brooklyn the second creation
A growing city transformed into a bustling borough.

The Bronx 1639

The Bronx's tale: New York's link to the mainland was fashionable from the very beginning.

Queens 1642

The history of Queens: it was once-rustic getaway evolved into New York City's most diverse borough.

New York City Metropolitan Police in 1845

One of the first major tests of the effectiveness of the newly formed New York City Metropolitan Police in 1845 was the Astor Place Riot 1849.

During this era, the city police officers wore a badge but were not required to wear full regulation uniforms until 1854.

Municipal and Metropolitan Police in 1857.

New York City Municipal and Metropolitan police officers fought each other in front of the New York City Hall for control over the police force in the New York City Police Riot of 1857.

The newly formed New York City Metropolitan Police replaced the former Municipal Police in 1857.

Staten Island 1661

Staten Island became a part of NYC – despite nearly joining New Jersey.

The New York City Draft Riots of 1863

New York City Metropolitan Police attacking American Civil War draft rioters.

Regulation Uniforms for police officers 1871

The regulation uniforms of the New York City Metropolitan Police in 1871

The Tompkins Square Riot 1874

New York City Police Department mounted policeman striking unarmed civilians with batons during the Tompkins Square Riot of 1874

Cleaning up corruption in the force 1895

New York City Police Commissioner Theodore Roosevelt in 1895 who tried to cleanup police corruption within the New York City Police Department

Manhattan 1898

The birth of NYC: the contrasting cities combined to form 'Greater New York'
New York City was the capital of the world.

Long Island City 1899

The story of the newsies' two-week strike against publishers Pulitzer, Hearst
NYC at the turn of the century: A metropolis brimming with hope and promise.

Manhattan 1900

NYC introduced the nation to auto expos as car sales exploded
Teddy Roosevelt's Road from 'damned cowboy' to first NYC-born president.

Albany 1901

Tammany Hall 1901
Richard, The Boss, Croker: the corrupt Tammany Hall leader became 'Master of the City'.

Manhattan 1902

Ulysses S. Grant's wife was laid to rest in tomb beside the only president buried in NYC.

Lower East Side 1902

The kosher beef riots: NYC housewives led weeks-long protest over costly meats.

Manhattan 1903

The murder of Andrew Haswell Green, the 'father of Greater New York'

East River 1904

Tragedy in the East River: The General Slocum disaster

Coney Island 1904

Coney Island: Brooklyn beach getaway became an iconic theme park.

Manhattan 1904

The opening of the subway: A long-awaited transit system became a NYC institution.

Times Square 1904

Times Square takes center stage: From empty, dirt roads to 'crossroads of the world.'

Tammany Hall 1905

Media entrepreneur William Randolph Hearst ran for mayor, eyed presidency.

The Bronx 1906

The protest over Ota Benga, an African man displayed with apes at the Bronx Zoo.

Long Island 1907

The case of 'Typhoid Mary', the first carrier of the disease in the U.S.

Wall Street 1907

J.P. Morgan and the Panic of 1907: One financier proved mightier than Wall Street.

Broadway 1907

An ambitious couple Flo Ziegfeld and Anna Held launched the famed Ziegfeld Follies on Broadway

Ellis Island 1907

Coming to NYC: Millions of immigrants made a dangerous trip across Atlantic for a better life.

Manhattan 1908

Evelyn Nesbit, Stanford White and the first Trial of the Century

Washington Heights 1908

The Bonehead': A Giants rookie's pushed Cubs to the National League title

Upstate New York 1908

NYC suffragettes challenged a police prohibition to launch <u>the first women's march.</u>

Police Officers saved children 1908

New York City Police Department police officers protecting children from a fallen electrical wire in Brooklyn in 1908.

New York City Police Headquarters 1909-1973

Former New York City Police Department headquarters was located at Centre and Broome Streets from 1909 thru 1973

Manhattan 1909

NYPD mob cop Joe Petrosino: The Italian American crime fighter who fought the Black Hand.

Manhattan 1910

Halley's Comet and doomsday panic came to town

Hudson River 1910

Glenn Curtiss and the Hudson Flyer: The pioneering pilots made the unsafe flight across NY

Tammany Hall 1910

The story of William Gaynor, the only New York mayor ever gunned down in office.

Greenwich Village 1911

Triangle Shirtwaist Factory fire: One of NYC's worst disasters improved workers' rights.

New York City 1912

Titanic rescue: The Carpathia saved hundreds of survivors from the notorious sunken ship

Broadway 1912

The sparkling king: Diamond Jim Brady's big appetite for jewels and food

Albany 1913

William Sulzer was the first and still the only NY governor to be impeached.

Lower Manhattan 1913

Inside NYC's Woolworth Building, the once-tallest skyscraper in the world

Upstate 1915

NYPD officer Charlie Becker became the first American cop to get the death penalty.

Manhattan 1916

Polio panic: NYC was home to world's first outbreak and officials blamed poor immigrants.

Union Square 1917

A mobile music distribution entity, Tin Pan Alley became the commercial center of song publishing.

Greater New York 1917

The Catskill Aqueduct solved New York City's water shortage.

Brooklyn 1917

Planned Parenthood founder Margaret Sanger was arrested for opening first birth control clinic in U.S.

NYPD 1918

Capt. Edyth Totten and women police standby the New York City Police Department_

New York City 1919

The day the heroes of World War I were welcomed in NYC

New York City 1920

Dry times in NYC: New Yorkers brewed and boozed despite Prohibition.

Long Island 1920

Airmail in America: sky-high delivery on Long Island changed mail service forever.

New York City 1920

The 1920 Wall Street bombing: Authorities blamed agitators for the deadly explosion amid the first Red Scare

New York City 1920

The history of traffic lights

Port Authority 1921

History of the Port Authority: N.Y. and N.J. joined forces to solve chaos at nation's foremost gateway.

Harlem 1922

The rise and fall of Marcus Garvey, once the most powerful man in Harlem

The Bronx 1923

Babe Ruth beat a long slump to come back as baseball's homerun king.

New York City 1925

A Utah hick founded the 'sophisticated' New Yorker magazine

New York City 1925

Rumhounds Izzy Einstein and Moe Smith turned Prohibition arrests into comedy.

New York City 1925

From fill-in to star: A morning exercise host John B. Gambling became NYC's first radio personality.

Uptown 1926

Daddy' and Peaches Browning: The scandalous marriage between an elderly baron and a 15-year-old schoolgirl

Downtown 1926

Olympic champ Gertrude Ederle became first woman to swim English Channel.

Midtown 1926

Thousands swarmed NYC's streets for 'Latin Lover' Rudolph Valentino's funeral

Broadway 1927

Mae West's arrest for onstage filthiness made her a star

Greater New York 1927

NYC innkeeper, Raymond Orteig, drove Charles Lindbergh to fly nonstop across Atlantic

Manhattan 1927

The day New York City threw Charles Lindbergh a tickertape parade for increasing nonstop to Paris in the Spirit of St. Louis

Brooklyn 1928

The death and extravagant funeral of Al Capone associate Frankie Yale

Harlem 1928

Black Belt: Harlem became the center of the black world

Long Island 1929

Master builder, Robert Moses led the creation of Long Island's Jones Beach

Manhattan, Westchester 1930

The unsolved mystery of Judge Joseph Force Crater's disappearance

Long Beach, LI 1931

The peculiar, scandalous death of socialite Starr Faithfull

Manhattan 1931

Hooverville cropped up in NYC among the Great Depression

Five Boroughs 1931

Five Families: The modern Mafia came to be.

Five Boroughs 1932

Inside Mayor Jimmy, Beau James, Walker's mighty downfall
Little Flower: The rise of Fiorello LaGuardia — NYC's first Italian American mayor

Harlem 1934

Harlem's Apollo Theatre turned into the Mecca of black show business.

Manhattan 1934

The scandalous custody battle between the Whitney's and the Vanderbilt's over 'Little Gloria'

The Bronx 1934

Richard Hauptmann was executed for the kidnapping, killing Charles Lindbergh's child in 'Crime of the Century.'

Manhattan 1934

Buckets of Bones: Child cannibal Albert Fish's account of his grisly slaying of 10-year-old Gracie Budd

Five Boroughs 1935

How Harlem's Col. Hubert, Black Eagle, Julian soared to glory at home and in Ethiopia

Five Boroughs 1936

The shocking way Thomas Dewey locked up mobster Charles, Lucky, Luciano

Manhattan 1936

From Rail to Rubber: The bus replaced the streetcar on New York City's streets

Manhattan 1937

Cops raided NYC's Minsky's Travesty for 'incorporated filth.'

Chinatown 1937

Solidarity in Chinatown: Thousands of Chinese took to NYC streets in unity as Japan invaded homeland.

Turtle Bay 1937

The 'Beekman Hill maniac': The story of sculptor Robert Irwin's Easter weekend killing spree.

Manhattan 1938

Jazz at Carnegie Hall The night Benny Goodman brought the sounds of 'youth, freedom' to the iconic venue.

Manhattan, Brooklyn, Long Island 1938

The story of Douglas 'Wrong Way' Corrigan's 'accidental' flight across the Atlantic

Manhattan, Long Island 1938

The story of Joe Louis' brutal, shock defeat of German Max Schmeling for the world heavyweight title

Manhattan 1938

The Jumper: The day a young man's suicidal standoff transfixed Midtown Manhattan

Five Boroughs 1938

The 'War of the Worlds' broadcast sparked a Mars attack panic in NYC.

Manhattan 1939

A murderous crime boss, Louis Lepke, surrendered to gossip columnist Walter Winchell and the FBI

Manhattan 1939

Fritz Kuhn and American Nazis brought anti-Semitic passion to New York City before WWII

Flushing 1939

The New York World's Fair: The 'World of Tomorrow' came to NYC

Brooklyn, Queens 1939

Mayor LaGuardia championed building the biggest and best-equipped airport in the nation.

The Bronx 1939

The day Lou Gehrig, struck by ALS, declared himself the 'luckiest man on the face of the Earth.'

Brooklyn 1940

The Brooklyn-Battery Tunnel became the final link in Robert Moses' plan for New York.

Boroughs 1940

Gathering for war: The draft came to New York.

Brownsville, East New York 1941

The Canary that Couldn't Fly: Abe Reles and Murder Incorporated

Polo Grounds 1941

The panic after Pearl Harbor: NYC on the point of WWII

Manhattan 1942

The Normandie blaze: Fire cleaned the world's largest ocean liner

Amagansett, LI 1942

A team of incompetent German agents failed a WWII sabotage mission in NYC.

Midtown 1942

Young Frank Sinatra took the world by storm during a week at the Paramount Theatre.

Wall St. 1943

The unsolved murder of famous anarchist Carlo Tresca

Five Boroughs 1943

Tammany Hall scandal: Crime boss Frank Costello and the judge

Manhattan 1943

The real Flip Corkin: The true story behind the war hero in the Daily News funny pages

Williamsburg 1943

Betty Smith's 'A Tree Grows in Brooklyn' became a literary sensation

Coney Island 1944

The blaze that brought down Coney Island's Luna Park

Midtown 1945

Incident on the 79th Floor: The story of the Empire State Building bomber crash

Times Square 1945

A jubilant city celebrates: Scenes from New York City on V-J Day

Five Boroughs 1945

Navy Day: New York City welcomed the American armada home from the war

Midtown 1946

William Zeckendorf and the deal that brought the UN to New York

Long Island 1947

Levittown and the suburban dream of postwar New York

Harlem 1947

Palace of Junk: The tragic death of Harlem's housebound Collyer Brothers

Brooklyn 1947

Jackie Robinson's debut with the Brooklyn Dodgers erased the color line

Five Boroughs 1948

Russian defector Oksana Kasenkina's leap for freedom

Five Boroughs 1948

New York City and the television boom

Manhattan 1949

The Barrio Congressman: Vito Marcantonio and the Puerto Rican migration

Five Boroughs 1949

The Communist councilman: The trial and conviction of Benjamin Davis

Midtown 1949

The story of Birdland, 'the Jazz Corner of the World'

Five Boroughs 1950

Independence Day, 1950: A mystery killing and a threat of war

Five Boroughs 1950

The Fugitive Mayor: William O'Dwyer's abrupt exit from City Hall

Brooklyn 1950

NYPD corruption scandal: the Harry Gross affair

Five Boroughs 1951

Dope menace: New York's panic over teen drug addiction

The Five Boroughs 1951

Duck and cover: New York's first citywide drill for the A-bomb

The Five Boroughs 1951

Hope and heartbreak: The long wait of New York City's families for missing soldiers in Korea

The Bronx 1952

Christine Jorgensen's transformation from transgender G.I. to tabloid star

Union Square 1953

The story behind the execution of Julius and Ethel Rosenberg

Brooklyn 1953

Longshoremen and the mob: When violence and corruption ruled the Brooklyn waterfront

East Village 1954

The vagabond poet and his wife: The murder of Maxwell and Ruth Bodenheim

Manhattan 1954

No Harm in Horror: Congress investigated whether comic books were poisoning young minds

Manhattan 1955

Not so funny papers: The feud between two comic strip creators over the origins of 'Li'l Abner'

The Five Boroughs 1956

A New York brewery teamed up with ad agency Young & Rubicam to change TV advertising forever

Washington Heights 1956

Why Do Fools Fall in Love?': The Teenagers and the rise of rock 'n' roll

Manhattan 1956

An acid attack on a New York journalist sparked an 'all-out war' on the mob.

Manhattan 1957

Mob justice: A year of violence in gangland

Brooklyn 1957

The story behind the Brooklyn Dodgers' moves to Los Angeles

Brooklyn 1958

Bobby Fischer: The rise to stardom of Brooklyn's young chess wizard

Manhattan 1959

The Cape Man murders shook New York City

Manhattan 1959

Showbiz scandals: The TV quiz show and radio payment controversies

Park Slope 1960

Red Snow: Brooklyn's United Airlines crash disaster

The Five Boroughs 1961

Robert F. Wagner and the construction of modern New York City

Greenwich Village 1961

Jane Jacobs fought 'urban renewal' in the West Village and won

Queens 1962

The story of the not-so-amazing' Mets' abysmal first season

Greenwich Village 1962

Greenwich Village and the birth of the folk movement

Manhattan 1963

End of a landmark: The demolition of Old Penn Station

The Five Boroughs 1963

Stopping the Presses: New York's newspaper strike

Kew Gardens 1964

The murder of Kitty Genovese rattled the conscience of New York City

The Five Boroughs 1964

Freedom Riders and riots: NYC's long hot summer at the height of the Civil Rights Movement

Upper West Side 1964

Two surf bums pulled off a daring jewel heist from NYC's American Museum of Natural History

Turtle Bay 1964

The story of an attempted bazooka attack on the United Nations

New York City policemen 1964

New York City policemen having a confrontation with African American protesters during the Bedford–Stuyvesant riot of 1964, an extension of the Harlem Riot in Harlem, New York City

Jamaica 1964

Mania: The Beatles take New York City

Washington Heights 1965

The day Malcolm X was assassinated in Harlem

The Five Boroughs 1966

Shutdown: John Lindsay, Michael Quill, and the NYC transit strike of 1966

Building the World Trade Center 1966

Construction of the World Trade Center towers began in 1966.

Alphabet City 1967

The Summer of Love: Everything was peace and love until the cops showed up.

The Five Boroughs 1968

The teacher's union shut down NYC schools for two months over racially charged community control.

Flatiron 1968

Flower child feminist and failed playwright Valerie Solanas shot Andy Warhol.

Manhattan 1968

Master builder' Robert Moses lost his grip on New York City power

Harlem 1968

You thought I was gone, baby, but I'm back!': Adam Clayton Powell Jr. returned to New York City.

Greenwich Village 1969

Cops raid the Stonewall Inn, riots ensue, and a gay pride movement is born.

The Five Boroughs 1969

A blizzard became a political storm for New York City Mayor John Lindsay

Manhattan 1969

Norman Mailer and Jimmy Breslin made headlines with 'odd couple' NYC political campaign.

Greenwich Village 1970

The Weathermen: Some of the city's wealthiest children bombed Manhattan homes in an anti-war protest.

Midtown 1971

Muhammad Ali and Joe Frazier meet in the Madison Square Garden boxing ring for an epic battle.

Brooklyn 1971

Small-time mob boss Joe Colombo's great civil rights crusade

Manhattan 1971

The north tower of the World Trade Center was completed in 1970; the south tower was completed in 1971.

Midtown 1971

There's a New Game in Town': Off-Track Betting comes to New York City.

Manhattan 1973

The World Trade Center – including the Twin Towers and four other buildings – officially opened in 1973.

Manhattan 1973

Martha Mitchell, the outspoken wife of Nixon's attorney general, brought southern candor to Washington

Manhattan 1974

Death Wish': In crime-ridden NYC, audiences broke box-office records cheering for a movie vigilante

Manhattan 1975

Running on empty: New York City faced the consequences of financial finagling.

The Five Boroughs 1976

New York City celebrated its bicentennial while on the brink of financial ruin.

Queens 1977

Son of Sam terrorized NYC during the summer of 1977.

The Five Boroughs 1977

When riots raged amid the New York City blackout of 1977.

Lower Manhattan 1977

The Human Fly: The day George Willig climbed the south tower of NYC's World Trade Center

Manhattan 1979

The story of Nelson Rockefeller's death and the spin that kept the sexy truth out of the headlines.

Manhattan 1979

When Pope John Paul II visited New York City.

Manhattan 1980

The early history of the Guardian Angels and their controversial New York City subway patrols

Manhattan 1980

The day John Lennon was gunned down at the Dakota in Manhattan.

The Bronx 1981

New York City's rap scene in the early 1980s

Manhattan 1981

Norman Mailer's friendship with an ex-convict-turned-author ended in murder.

Manhattan 1982

Blunt New York City mayor Ed Koch and poetic Mario Cuomo battled for the governor's office

Brooklyn 1983

The Brooklyn Bridge's 100th birthday: a centennial celebration 200 years in the making

Manhattan 1983

A 50-foot inflatable King Kong atop the Empire State Building on the movie's 50th anniversary. It sounded like a god idea

Bronx 1984

The Wedtech scandal: The fraudulent 'success story' in the South Bronx

Manhattan 1984

The story of Bernhard Goetz, the subway vigilante

Queens 1984

The political downfall of vice-presidential candidate Geraldine Ferraro

Lower West Side 1985

How the 'Soot Lady' and striped bass defeated the Westway development project.

Flushing, Queens 1986

Corruption scandal: Donny Manes and the public trough

Wall Street 1986

Ivan Boesky and the end of the '80s Wall Street boom

Flushing, Queens 1986

Gotta Believe: The 'Amazing' Mets' and the 1986 World Series

Islip, Long Island 1987

Trash Fight: The long voyage of New York's unwanted garbage barge

South Bronx 1987

Second Spring: The rebirth of the South Bronx

East Harlem 1988

The crack scourge swept New York City

Manhattan 1988

The Bess Myerson affair: a divorce, a judge's daughter and a courtroom drama

Manhattan 1989

Even you can get it': Alison Gertz and the new face of AIDS.

Manhattan 1993

Terrorist attack killed six, injured over 1000 at World Trade Center

1996

TWA Flight 800 crashed, killed 230; New York Yankees won World Series.

1998

New York Yankees won World Series.

1999

New York Yankees won World Series.

World Trade Center September 11, 2001

During 9-11, the temporary New York City Police Department headquarters was at 106 Liberty St; set up near the World Trade Center on September 11, 2001.

Two New York City Police Department officers at the World Trade Center site five weeks after the September 11 attacks.

New York City Police Department K-9-unit officers with a search and rescue dog were at the World Trade Center site after the September 11 attacks in 2001.

CHAPTER 3

GIOVANNI
DA VERRAZZANO

Giovanni da Verrazzano was the first explorer to arrive in New York in 1524. He served under the French crown. Giovanni da Verrazzano named the area New Angoulême. This area was inhabited by the Algonquins and Iroquois Native Americans.

New York City remains one of the most wanted out destinations in the world. From its elegant NYC jazz clubs to the amazing adventures in NYC at night.

There remain many sights to see and things to do in the <u>City That Never Sleeps!</u>

While you may picture New York City as an urban center and concrete jungle, it is also one of the world's most diverse areas and melting pots of different people, experiences, and stories which make it an exciting place to visit.

New York City wasn't always the image of <u>hustle</u> and <u>bustle</u> that much of the world knows it to be today. Within this complex city lays a rich historical backdrop populated with complicated cultures and people.

In my stories, you will dive into the history of this unique city. This is before the rise of the amazing things to do in NYC. You can experience and see how learning more about its rich past can help you love it even more today…

The history of New York City can be traced back to the origins of the United States, with the earliest version of the <u>City That Never Sleeps</u> beginning when it was first settled by Dutch traders in the early 1600 and 1700s.

Back then the city was far from its glorious stamp as a eager cultural center but rather acted as a key trading point for the Americas and inhabitants interested in dealing with the "new world."

Let's go through history step-by-step…

First starting with the British taking over the city from the Dutch. Changing the name, it had.

New Amsterdam was change to the name we know it to be today, New York. Despite being a regional focus for the British, the revolutionary government by George Washington also set up a base near Brooklyn to leverage power away from Britain.

This same location can still be visited to watch playful re-enactments of pre-revolutionary America, perfect for the history <u>buffs</u> out there.

After the revolutionary war, New York grew into an important center for cotton production as well as other industrialized sectors. This gave way to the development of the Erie Canal, which supported trade and boosted the city's ability to attract investment even more. From here on out, New York was on its way to being a political, economic, and cultural powerhouse in America.

I am taking you now to the past so that you will understand the present…

The second navigator to explore the bay in the service of the Dutch was Henry Hudson in 1609. He gave his name to the Hudson River.

The Dutch were the first Europeans to settle in the area, building Fort Nassau in 1614, the first European settlement in the area today known as New York.

In 1626, Peter Minuit, Governor of the Dutch West India Company bought the island of Manhattan from Native Americans for 24 dollars and founded a colony called New Amsterdam. The colony developed a profitable fur trade in the region with the Native American tribes.

In 1674, because of the Treaty of Westminster, the island of Manhattan was passed to the English, who renamed it New York in honor of the Duke of York. A few years later, King James II established the Dominion of New England, comprising all the neighboring colonies.

With the presence of the British, New York became an important and prosperous commercial port.

In 1754 Colombia University was founded, which is today one of the most prestigious in the world.

During this era, there were lots of conflicts in New York. Throughout the eighteenth century, the English settlers and the French fought for the control of Manhattan, conflicts in which the pilgrims managed to involve the different Native tribes in their causes.

New York played an important role in the American War of Independence, witnessing several battles. In 1775, fighting broke out between independent militia, and the British.

A year later, the United States was voted independent. However, the State of New York did not ratify the Federal Constitution until 1788.

In 1789, Congress assembled in New York which elected George Washington as President. NYC became the Federal Capital for a year until it was moved to Washington D.C.

During the 1820's, New York became the center of the abolitionist movement. Furthermore, in 1863, New York witnessed the Draft. Week, violent disturbances took place to condemn a new

51

law passed by Congress to draft men to fight in the ongoing American Civil War. The economic growth and immigration transformed the city, making New York City the largest town in the States in 1835.

Up until 1898, New York was made up of only Manhattan. Later, the districts of Brooklyn, Queens, The Bronx, and Staten Island became part of the city. This was made possible thanks to the construction of many of its famous bridges and Subway in 1904.

Let's see what happened in New York during the Twentieth Century...

During the twentieth century, New York grew enormously. The Statue of Liberty observed the arrival of millions of immigrants. It became the hub of European, Asian and Latin-American immigration.

After World War II, New York became the world's most important city with great economic, Wall Street, political, UN Headquarters, and cultural relevance. New York replaced Paris as the mecca of art and culture.

The tragic terrorist attacks that took place in New York on 11 September 2001, had far-reaching consequences in the States and in the rest of the world, establishing new security standards both in the city and worldwide.

CHAPTER 4

BROOKLYN, NY

The first settlement in Brooklyn were the Dutch farmers. In 1636 was soon followed by other settlements in Flatlands, Wallabout, the Ferry, Gravesend, and, in 1645, Breuckelen. It is also spelled Breucklyn, Breuckland, Brucklyn, Broucklyn, Brookland, and Brookline.

The present spelling became fixed about the close of the 18th century. Later settlements included New Utrecht, 1650, Flatbush 1651, Bushwick, and Williamsburg 1660.

The American Revolutionary War Battle of Long Island was fought in Brooklyn on August 27, 1776. The remains of the American army leaving for Brooklyn Heights overlooking the East River.

Early in the 19th century, Brooklyn became the world's first modern commuter suburb. Brooklyn Heights was transformed into a wealthy residential community.

The most populous section of Brooklyn was incorporated in 1816 as a village and in 1834 as a city.

Williamsburg and Bushwick were occupied in 1855. Other communities were absorbed until the city of Brooklyn became neighboring with Kings County in 1683.

By the 1880s Brooklyn had become one of the country's most important manufacturing centers. Its busy port was handling more capacity than its fellow worker in Manhattan.

Sugar refining was the city's largest single industry, but Brooklyn was also the site of ironworks. The ironclad battleship Monitor of Civil War fame was constructed at the Continental Iron Works in Greenpoint.

Petroleum refineries, slaughterhouses, and many factories were in Brooklyn. Clocks, cigars, beer, insulated wiring, electrical signs, packaged coffee, and even teddy bears were all produced in Brooklyn.

All the above mentioned did not begin declining as a manufacturing hub until the 1950s, when manufacturers began relocating to less expensive locales.

Ranked among the most populous cities in the United States during the last four decades of the 19th century, Brooklyn had its own Academy of Music 1859 and Historical Society 1863.

In the late 1860s Frederick Law Olmsted and Calvert Vaux, the architects of Manhattan's Central Park, designed a system of parks and parkways for Brooklyn on a scale theretofore unseen in the United States.

Parkways, the term coined by Olmsted and Vaux, radiated from 526-acre Prospect Park, 1870s, stretching southward as far as Coney Island. Grand Army Plaza, featuring the John H. Duncan Memorial Arch, was later added as the park's primary entrance.

Notwithstanding these civic milestones, the construction of John Roebling and Washington Roebling's Brooklyn Bridge to Manhattan, completed 1883 effectively ruined Brooklyn's independent existence, as business interests craved closer ties to the metropolis.

Overcoming the opposition of the local Democratic machine, Brooklyn accepted consolidation by a margin of only 277 votes and became a part of Greater New York in 1898.

Yet, despite their economic and political subordination to Manhattan, Brooklynites maintained a fiercely independent identity that was supported by pride in their hometown Major League Baseball team.

The Dodgers, who played in intimate Ebbets Field and whose Jackie Robinson broke the Major League's color barrier.

Significantly, Brooklyn had also been a magnet for Black Americans relocating from the South during the Great Migration. The departure of the Dodgers for Los Angeles in 1957 was a huge blow to civic pride that corresponded with the onset of the decline of the local economy as the United States began transitioning to the postindustrial era.

Between 1954 and 1990 manufacturing output in Brooklyn was cut in half. Furthermore, the Brooklyn dockyards fell into disuse, and in 1966 the Brooklyn Navy Yard was closed.

CHAPTER 5

QUEENS NY

Queens was one of the original twelve counties of the English province of New York, established in 1683.

After the capture of the Dutch colony of New Netherland by the English in 1664 and 1674, this province became New York, encompassing a much larger area than New York. the present state of New York, transformed into an English, later British, crown colony.

The original Queens County covered the area of present-day borough of Queens and present-day County Nassau. The capital was Jamaica. Originally, there were five townships: Flushing, Vlissingen, Jamaica, Rustdorp, Hempstead, Heemstede, Newtown, Middelburgh and Oyster Bay. North Hempstead seceded from Hempstead in 1784.

In 1870, the northwestern part of Newtown near Manhattan split off as Long Island City.

On January 1, 1898, western Queens County, including Flushing, Jamaica, Long Island City, and Newtown, and including the Rockaway Peninsula, which belonged to Hempstead, was incorporated into New York City. The local councils in this part and the county council were abolished. On January 1, 1899, present-day

County Nassau was formed, encompassing the remaining area of Hempstead, North Hempstead, and Oyster Bay.

Queens has a total of fourteen neighborhoods and each neighborhood has its own identity. Residents of the neighborhoods hardly identify themselves as New Yorkers, but as residents of their neighborhood.

Flushing is one of Queens' largest neighborhoods and has a large and growing Asian community. The community consists of Chinese, Koreans, and South Asians. The Asians mainly live in the east, near the border of Nassau County.

The neighborhood has traditionally known Italian Americans, Latino Americans, and Greeks. The intersection of Main Street, Kissena Boulevard and 41st Avenue is considered the center of Flushing and acts as the center for Flushing Chinatown, also known as 'Chinese Manhattan'.

This community is one of the largest Chinatowns and is home to more than 30,000 Chinese-born Chinese.

Howard Beach, Whitestone & Middle Village, these neighborhoods are home to many Italian Americans.

Ozone Park and South Ozone Park, these two neighborhoods are home to many Italians, Spaniards, and Guyanese.

Rockaway Beach, this neighborhood has a high Irish American population.

Astoria, in the northwest, is originally a neighborhood where most Greeks live outside of Greece.

Today there are many Hispanic Americans and Italian Americans. The neighborhood also has growing communities of immigrants from the Middle East, the Balkans, and many young people from Manhattan. Near the Long Island City border is a large homeless shelter project, Queensbridge. Long Island City is also located in this district.

Maspeth and Ridgewood, these two neighborhoods are home to many Eastern European immigrants, including Poles, Romanians, and other Slavic peoples. Ridgewood also has a large Hispanic population.

Jackson Heights and Elmhurst, these two neighborhoods are home to many Spaniards, Tibetans, and South Asian peoples. Jackson Heights is known as 'Little Colombia' due to the impact of the Colombians in the area. Jackson Heights also has the second largest LGBT community in New York City.

Woodside, this neighborhood has a high American-Filipino population and is also known as 'Little Manila'. Many Irish Americans also live there. Most Filipino Americans live in Hollis and Queens Village.

Richmond Hills, also known as 'Little Guyana', is known for its large population of Guyanese immigrants. There are also many Punjabis living in the district. That is why the district is also known as 'Little Punjabi'.

Rego Park, Forest Hills, Kew Gardens and Kew Gardens Hill, these neighborhoods originally housed many Jews, originally the Jews came from Germany and Eastern Europe. But today there are also Jews from Israel, Iran, and the former Soviet Union.

More and more Asians are also coming to live in these neighborhoods, especially Chinese.

Jamaica Estates, Jamaica Hills, Hillcrest, Fresh Meadows and Hollis Hills, these neighborhoods are also home to many Jews and Asians.

Jamaica, this neighborhood is home to many African Americans, Caribbean, and Central Americans. Middle-class African Americans mainly live in this neighborhood. In addition to this neighborhood, many African Americans also live in Saint Albans, Queens Village, Cambria Heights, Springfield Gardens, Rosedale, Laurelton, and Briarwood.

Bellerose and Floral Park, these two neighborhoods originally housed Irish Americans, but today have a high population of Asians and Indians

Corona and Corona Heights, also known as Little Italy, was originally an Italian neighborhood with a high population of African Americans. Between 1920 and 1960 these neighborhoods were very close. Today, these neighborhoods have the highest concentration of Spaniards.

CHAPTER 6

THE BRONX

The Bronx is a borough of New York City, parallel with Bronx County, in the U.S. state of New York.

It is south of Westchester County; north and east of the New York City borough of Manhattan, across the Harlem River; and north of the New York City borough of Queens, across the East River.

The Bronx has a land area of 42 square miles, 109 km2, and a population of 1,472,654 in the 2020 census.

If each borough were ranked as a city, the Bronx would rank as the ninth-most-crowded in the U.S. Of the five boroughs, it has the fourth-largest area, fourth-highest population, and third-highest population density.

It is the only borough of New York City not primarily on an island. With a population that is 54.8% Hispanic as of 2020, it is the only majority-Hispanic county in the Northeastern United States and the fourth-most-populous nationwide.

The Bronx is divided by the Bronx River into a hillier section in the west, and a flatter eastern section. East and west street names are divided by Jerome Avenue. The West Bronx was annexed to New York City in 1874, and the areas east of the Bronx River in 1895.

Bronx County was separated from New York County in 1914. About a quarter of the Bronx's area is open space, including Woodlawn Cemetery, Van Cortlandt Park, Pelham Bay Park, the New York Botanical Garden, and the Bronx Zoo in the borough's north and center.

The Thain Family Forest at the New York Botanical Garden is thousands of years old; it is New York City's largest remaining tract of the original forest that once covered the city. These open spaces are primarily on land reserved in the late 19th century as urban development progressed north and east from Manhattan.

The word "Bronx" originated with Faroese-born or Swedish-born Jonas Bronck, who established the first settlement in the area as part of the New Netherland colony in 1639.

European settlers displaced the native Lenape after 1643. In the 19th and 20th centuries, the Bronx received many immigrant and migrant groups as it was transformed into an urban community, first from European countries, particularly Ireland, Germany, Italy, and Eastern Europe.

Later from the Caribbean region, particularly Puerto Rico, Trinidad, Haiti, Guyana, Jamaica, Barbados, and the Dominican Republic, as well as African American migrants from the southern United States, Panama, Honduras, West Africans, and South Asians.

The Bronx contains the poorest congressional district in the United States, the 15th. There are, however, some upper income, as well as middle-income neighborhoods such as Riverdale, Fieldston, Spuyten Duyvil, Schuylerville, Pelham Bay, Pelham Gardens, Morris Park, and Country Club. Parts of the Bronx saw a steep decline in population,

Public housing, and quality of life in the late 1960s, throughout the 1970s and 1980s, and into the early 1990s, ending in a wave of arson in the late 1970s.

The South Bronx experienced severe urban decay. The borough began experiencing new population growth starting in the late 1990s and continuing to the present day.

The Bronx was called <u>Rananchqua</u> by the native Siwanoy band of Lenape, also known historically as the Delawares, while other Native Americans knew the Bronx as Keskeskeck. It was divided by the Aquahung River.

The origin of Jonas Bronck, c.1600–43, has been contested. Documents indicate he was a Swedish-born immigrant from Komstad, Norra Ljunga parish, in Småland, Sweden, who arrived in New Netherland during the spring of 1639.

Bronck became the first recorded European settler in the present-day Bronx and built a farm named "<u>Emmaus</u>" close to what today is the corner of Willis Avenue and 132nd Street in Mott Haven.

He leased land from the Dutch West India Company on the neck of the mainland immediately north of the Dutch settlement of New Haarlem, on Manhattan Island, and bought additional tracts from the local tribes.

He eventually accumulated 500 acres, 200 ha, between the Harlem River and the Aquahung, which became known as Bronck's River or the Bronx, River. Dutch and English settlers referred to the area as Bronck's Land.

The American poet William Bronk was a descendant of Pieter Bronck, either Jonas Bronck's son or his younger brother, but most probably a nephew or cousin, as there was an age difference of 16 years.

Great deal of work on the Swedish claim has been undertaken by

Brian G. Andersson, former Commissioner of NYC's Dept. of Records, who helped organize a 375th Anniversary celebration in Bronck's hometown in 2014.

The Bronx is referred to with the definite article as "The Bronx", both legally and colloquially. The County of Bronx does not place

"The" immediately before "Bronx" in formal references, unlike the coextensive Borough of the Bronx, nor does the United States Postal Service in its database of Bronx addresses, the city and state mailing-address format is simply "Bronx, NY".

The region was apparently named after the Bronx River and first appeared in the "Annexed District of The Bronx" created in 1874 out of part of Westchester County.

It was continued in the "Borough of The Bronx", which included a larger annexation from Westchester County in 1898. The use of the definite article is attributed to the style of referring to rivers.

A time-worn story explanation for the use of the definite article in the borough's name stems from the phrase "visiting the Broncks", referring to the settler's family.

The capitalization of the borough's name is sometimes disputed. Generally, the definite article is lowercase in place names "the Bronx" except in official references. The definite article is capitalized "The Bronx" at the beginning of a sentence or in any other situation when a normally lowercase word would be capitalized.

However, some people and groups always refer to the borough with a capital letter, such as Bronx Borough Historian Lloyd Ultan, The Bronx County Historical Society, and the Bronx-based organization Great and Glorious Grand Army of The Bronx, arguing the definite article is part of the proper name.

In particular, the Great and Glorious Grand Army of The Bronx is leading efforts to make the city refer to the borough with an uppercase definite article in all uses, comparing the lowercase article in the Bronx's name to "not capitalizing the 's' in 'Staten Island.'"

The Bronx's development is directly connected to its strategic location between New England and New York, Manhattan. Control over the bridges across the Harlem River plagued the period of British colonial rule.

The King's Bridge, built in 1693 where Broadway reached the Spuyten Duyvil Creek, was a possession of Frederick Philipse, lord of Philipse Manor.

Local farmers on both sides of the creek resented the tolls, and in 1759, Jacobus Dyckman and Benjamin Palmer led them in building a free bridge across the Harlem River.

After the American Revolutionary War, the King's Bridge toll was abolished.

The territory now contained within Bronx County was originally part of Westchester County, one of the 12 original counties of the English Province of New York. The present Bronx County was included in the town of Westchester and parts of the towns in Yonkers, Eastchester, and Pelham.

In 1846, a new town was created by division of Westchester, called West Farms.

The town of Morrisania was created, in turn, from West Farms in 1855.

In 1873, the town of Kingsbridge was established within the former borders of the town of Yonkers, roughly corresponding to the modern Bronx neighborhoods of Kingsbridge, Riverdale, and Woodlawn Heights, and included Woodlawn Cemetery.

Among famous settlers in the Bronx during the 19th and early 20th centuries were author Willa Cather, tobacco merchant Pierre Lorillard, and inventor Jordan L. Mott, who established Mott Haven to house the workers at his iron works.

The consolidation of the Bronx into New York City proceeded in two stages. In 1873, the state legislature annexed Kingsbridge, West Farms, and Morrisania to New York, effective in 1874; the three towns were soon abolished in the process.

The whole territory east of the Bronx River was annexed to the city in 1895, three years before New York's consolidation with Brooklyn, Queens, and Staten Island. This included the Town of Westchester, which had voted against consolidation in 1894 and parts of Eastchester and Pelham. The nautical community of City Island voted to join the city in 1896.

On January 1, 1898, the consolidated City of New York was born, including the Bronx as one of the five distinct boroughs, at the same time, the Bronx's territory moved from Westchester County into New York County, which already included Manhattan and the rest of pre-1874 New York City.

On April 19, 1912, those parts of New York County which had been annexed from Westchester County in previous decades were newly constituted as Bronx County, the 62nd and last county to be created by the state, effective in 1914.

Bronx County's courts opened for business on January 2, 1914. This same day that John P. Mitchel started work as Mayor of New York City.

Marble Hill, Manhattan was now connected to the Bronx by filling in the former waterway, but it did not become part of the borough or county.

The history of the Bronx during the 20th century may be divided into four periods.

A prosperous period during 1900–29, with a population growth by a factor of six from 200,000 in 1900 to 1.3 million in 1930. The Great Depression and post-World War II years saw a slowing of growth leading into an eventual decline.

The mid to late century were hard times, as the Bronx changed during 1950–85 from a predominantly moderate-income to a predominantly lower-income area with high rates of violent crime and poverty in some areas. The Bronx has experienced an economic and developmental revival starting in the late 1980s that continues into today.

The Simpson Street elevated station was built in 1904 and opened on November 26, 1904. It was listed in the National Register of Historic Places on September 17, 2004, reference #04001027.

The Bronx was a mostly rural area for many generations, with small farms supplying the city markets. In the late 19th century, however, it grew into a railroad suburb.

Faster transportation enabled rapid population growth in the late 19th century, involving the move from horse-drawn street cars to elevated railways and the subway system, which linked to Manhattan in 1904.

The South Bronx was a manufacturing center for many years and was noted as a center of piano manufacturing in the early part of the 20th century.

In 1919, the Bronx was the site of 63 piano factories employing more than 5,000 workers.

At the end of World War I, the Bronx hosted the rather small 1918 World's Fair at 177th Street and DeVoe Avenue.

The Bronx suffered rapid urban growth after World War I. Extensions of the New York City Subway contributed to the increase in population as thousands of immigrants came to the Bronx, resulting in a major boom in residential construction.

Among these groups, many Irish Americans, Italian Americans, and especially Jewish Americans settled here. In addition, French, German, Polish, and other immigrants moved into the borough.

As evidence of the change in population, by 1937, 592,185 Jews lived in the Bronx 43.9% of the borough's population, while only 54,000 Jews lived in the borough in 2011. Many synagogues still stand in the Bronx, but most have been converted to other uses.

Bootleggers and gangs were active in the Bronx during Prohibition, 1920–33. Irish, Italian, Jewish, and Polish gangs smuggled in most of the illegal whiskey, and the oldest sections of the borough became poverty disturbed.

Enright declared that speakeasies were home to "the vicious elements, bootleggers, gamblers and their friends in all walks of life" cooperating to "evade the law, escape punishment for their crimes, or to deter the police from doing their duty."

Between 1930 and 1960, moderate and upper income Bronxites, predominantly non-Hispanic Whites, began to relocate from the borough's southwestern neighborhoods. This migration has left a mostly poor African American and Hispanic, largely Puerto Rican, population in the West Bronx.

One significant factor that shifted the racial and economic demographics was the construction of Co-op City, built to house middle-class residents in family-sized apartments.

The high-rise complex played a significant role in draining middle-class residents from older tenement buildings in the borough's southern and western fringes. Most predominantly non-Hispanic White communities today are in the eastern and northwestern sections of the borough.

From the early 1960s to the early 1980s, the quality of life changed for some Bronx residents. Historians and social scientists have suggested many factors, including the theory that Robert Moses' Cross Bronx Expressway destroyed existing residential.

Another factor in the Bronx's decline may have been the development of high-rise housing projects, particularly in the South Bronx. Neighborhoods and created instant slums, as put forward in Robert Caro's biography The Power Broker.

Yet, another factor may have been a reduction in the real estate listings and property-related financial services offered in some areas of the Bronx, such as mortgage loans or insurance policies. This process was known as redlining. Others have suggested a "planned shrinkage" of municipal services, such as firefighting.

There was also much debate as to whether rent control laws had made it less profitable or more costly for landlords to maintain existing buildings with their existing tenants than to abandon or destroy those buildings.

In the 1970s, parts of the Bronx were troubled by a wave of arson. The burning of buildings was predominantly in the poorest communities, such as the South Bronx.

One explanation of this event was that landlords decided to burn their low property-value buildings and take the insurance money, as it was easier for them to get insurance money than to try to refurbish a dilapidated building or sell a building in a severely distressed area.

The Bronx became identified with a high rate of poverty and unemployment, which was mainly a persistent problem in the South Bronx.

There were cases where tenants set fire to the building, they lived in so they may qualify for emergency relocations by city social service agencies to better residences, sometimes being relocated to other parts of the city.

Out of 289 census tracts in the Bronx borough, seven tracts lost more than 97% of their buildings to arson and abandonment between 1970 and 1980; another forty-four tracts had more than 50% of their buildings meet the same fate.

By the early 1980s, the Bronx was considered the most destroyed urban area in the country, particularly the South Bronx which experienced a loss of 60% of the population and 40% of housing units. However, starting in the 1990s, many of the burned-out and run-down tenements were replaced by new housing units.

Since the late 1980s, significant development has occurred in the Bronx, first stimulated by the city's Ten-Year Housing and community members working to rebuild the social, economic, and environmental infrastructure by creating affordable housing. Groups affiliated with churches in the South Bronx erected the Nehemiah Homes with about 1,000 units.

The grass roots organization Nos Quedamos' endeavor known as Melrose Commons began to rebuild areas in the South Bronx. Plains Road Line, 2 and 5 trains, began to show an increase in riders.

Chains such as Marshalls, Staples, and Target opened stores in the Bronx. More bank branches opened in the Bronx as a whole, rising from 106 in 1997 to 149 in 2007, although not primarily in poor or minority neighborhoods, while the Bronx still has fewer branches per person than other boroughs.

In 1997, the Bronx was designated an All-America City by the National Civic League, acknowledging its comeback from the decline of the mid-century.

In 2006, The New York Times reported that "construction cranes have become the borough's new visual metaphor, replacing the window decals of the 1980s in which pictures of potted plants and drawn curtains were placed in the windows of abandoned buildings."

The borough has experienced substantial new building construction since 2002. Between 2002 and June 2007, 33,687 new units of housing were built or were under way and $4.8 billion has been invested in new housing.

In the first six months of 2007 alone total investment in new residential development was $965 million and 5,187 residential units were scheduled to be completed.

A lot of the new development is jumping up in formerly vacant lots across the South Bronx.

In addition, came a revitalization of the existing housing market in areas such as Hunts Point, the Lower Concourse, and the neighborhoods surrounding the Third Avenue Bridge as people buy apartments and renovate them. Several boutique and chain hotels opened in the 2010s in the South Bronx.

New developments are underway. The Bronx General Post Office on the corner of the Grand Concourse and East 149th Street is being converted into a marketplace, boutiques, restaurants and office space with a USPS concession.

The Kingsbridge Armory, often cited as the largest armory in the world, is scheduled for redevelopment as the Kingsbridge National Ice Center.

Under consideration for future development is the construction of a platform over the New York City Subway's Concourse Yard adjacent to Lehman College. The construction would permit approximately 2,000,000 square feet, 190,000 m2, of development and would cost US$350–500 million.

Despite significant investment compared to the post war period, many worsened social problems remain including high rates of violent crime, substance abuse, overcrowding, and substandard housing conditions.

The Bronx has the highest rate of poverty in New York City, and the greater South Bronx is the poorest area.

CHAPTER 7

STATEN ISLAND

Staten Island is a borough of New York City, parallel with Richmond County, in the U.S. State of New York. Located in the city's southwest portion, the borough is separated from New Jersey by the Arthur Kill and the Kill Van Kull and from the rest of New York by New York Bay.

With a population of 495,747 in the 2020 Census, Staten Island is the least populated borough but the third largest in land area at 58.5 sq mi, 152 km2.

A home to the Lenape Indigenous people, the island was settled by Dutch colonists in the 17th century. It was one of the 12 original counties of New York state. Staten Island was consolidated with New York City in 1898.

It was formally known as the Borough of Richmond until 1975, when its name was changed to Borough of Staten Island. Staten Island has sometimes been called "the forgotten borough" by inhabitants who feel neglected by the city government.

The North Shore, especially the neighborhoods of St. George, Tompkinsville, Clifton, and Stapleton is the island's most urban area. It contains the designated St. George Historic District and the St.

Paul's Avenue-Stapleton Heights Historic District, which feature large Victorian houses. The East Shore is home to the 2+1/2-mile, 4-kilometer, F.D.R. Boardwalk, the world's fourth-longest boardwalk.

The South Shore, site of the 17th-century Dutch and French Huguenot settlement, developed rapidly beginning in the 1960s and 1970s and is now mostly suburban. The West Shore is the island's least populated and most industrial part.

Motor traffic can reach the borough from Brooklyn by the Verrazzano-Narrows Bridge and from New Jersey by the Outterbridge Crossing, Goethals Bridge and Bayonne Bridge.

Staten Island has Metropolitan Transportation Authority, MTA, bus lines and an MTA rapid transit line, the Staten Island Railway, which runs from the ferry terminal at St. George to Tottenville.

Staten Island is the only borough not connected to the New York City Subway system. The free Staten Island Ferry connects the borough to Manhattan across New York Harbor. It provides views of the Statue of Liberty, Ellis Island, and Lower Manhattan.

As in much of North America, human habitation appeared on the island rapidly after the Wisconsin glaciation. Archaeologists have recovered tool evidence of Clovis culture activity dating from about 14,000 years ago.

This evidence was first discovered in 1917 in the Charleston section of the island. Various Clovis artifacts have been discovered since then, on property owned by Mobil Oil.

The island was abandoned later, possibly because of the cutting out of large mammals on the island. Evidence of the first permanent Native American settlements and agriculture are thought to date from about 5,000 years ago, although early archaic habitation evidence has been found in multiple locations on the island.

Rossville points are distinct points that define a Native American cultural period from the Archaic period to the Early Woodland period, dating from about 1500 to 100 BC. They are named for the

Rossville section of Staten Island, where they were first found near the old Rossville Post Office building.

Skeletons unearthed at Lenape burial ground in Staten Island, the largest pre-European burial ground in New York City.

At the time of European contact, the island was inhabited by the Raritan band of the Unami division of the Lenape.

In Lenape, one of the Algonquian languages, Staten Island was called Aquehonga Manacknong, meaning "as far as the place of the bad woods", or Eghquhous, meaning "the bad woods".

The area was part of the Lenape homeland known as Lenapehoking. The Lenape were later called the "Delaware" by the English colonists because they inhabited both shores of what the English named the Delaware River.

The island was mixed with Native American foot trails, one of which followed the south side of the ridge near the course of present-day Richmond Road and Amboy Road.

The Lenape did not live in fixed campsites but moved seasonally, using slash and burn agriculture. Shellfish was a most important of their diet, including the Eastern oyster, Crassostrea virginica, abundant in the waterways throughout the present-day New York City region.

Evidence of their habitation can still be seen in shell dunghills along the shore in the Tottenville section, where oyster shells larger than 12 inches, 305 mm, are sometimes found.

Burial Ridge, a Lenape burial ground on a hill overlooking Raritan Bay in Tottenville, is the largest pre-European burial ground in New York City. Bodies have been reported uncovered at Burial Ridge from 1858 forward.

After conducting independent research, which included excavating bodies buried at the site, ethnologist and archaeologist George H. Pepper was contracted in 1895 to conduct paid archaeological research at Burial Ridge by the American Museum of

Natural History. The burial ground today is unmarked and lies within Conference House Park.

The first recorded European contact on the island was in 1520 by Italian explorer Giovanni da Verrazzano who sailed through The Narrows on the ship La Dauphine and anchored for one night.

The Dutch did not establish a permanent settlement on Staten Eylandt for many decades. Its name derived from the Staten General, the parliament of the Republic of the Seven United Netherlands.

From 1639 to 1655, Cornelis Melyn and David de Vries made three separate attempts to establish one there, but each time the settlement was destroyed in conflicts between the Dutch and the local tribe.

In 1661, the first permanent Dutch settlement was established at Oude Dorp, Dutch for "Old Village", by a small group of Dutch, Walloon, and French Huguenot families, just south of the Narrows near South Beach.

Many French Huguenots had gone to the Netherlands as refugees from the religious wars in France, suffering persecution for their Protestant faith, and some joined the emigration to New Netherland. At one point nearly a third of the residents of the Island spoke French.

The last vestige of Oude Dorp is the name of the present-day neighborhood of Old Town adjacent to Old Town Road.

Staten Island was not spared the bloodshed that culminated in Kieft's War. In the summer of 1641 and in 1642, Native American tribes laid waste to Old Town.

At the end of the Second Anglo-Dutch War in 1667, the Dutch ceded New Netherland to England in the Treaty of Breda, and the Dutch Staten Eylandt, anglicized as "Staten Island", became part of the new English colony of New York.

In 1670, the Native Americans surrendered all claims to Staten Island to the English in a deed to Governor Francis Lovelace. In 1671, to encourage an expansion of the Dutch settlements, the

English resurveyed Oude Dorp, which became known as 'Old Town' and expanded the lots along the shore to the south.

These lots were settled primarily by Dutch families and became known as Nieuwe Dorp meaning 'New Village', which later became anglicized as New Dorp.

Captain Christopher Billopp, after years of distinguished service in the Royal Navy, came to America in 1674 in charge of a company of infantry.

The following year, he settled on Staten Island, where he was granted a patent for 932 acres, 3.8 km2, of land.

According to one version of an oft repeated but apocryphal tale, Captain Billopp's seamanship secured Staten Island to New York, rather than to New Jersey: the island would belong to New York if the captain could sail around, it in one day, which he did.

This story is most likely untrue, due to conflicting information on the time Christopher Billopp took to complete the race and whether he received a personal prize or not.

Mayor Michael Bloomberg spread the myth by referring to it at a news conference in Brooklyn on February 20, 2007.

Reliable historical documentation of the event is extremely rare, however, and most historians conclude that it is entirely untrue.

In 1683, the colony of New York was divided into ten counties. As part of this process, Staten Island, as well as several minor neighboring islands, was designated as Richmond County. The name derives from the title of Charles Lennox, 1st Duke of Richmond, an illegitimate son of King Charles II.

In 1687 and 1688, the English divided the island into four administrative divisions based on natural features: the 5,100-acre, 21 km2, manorial estate of colonial governor Thomas Dongan in the northeastern hills known as the "Lordship or Manor of Cassiltown", along with the North, South, and West divisions.

These divisions later developed into the four towns of Castleton, Northfield, Southfield, and Westfield.

In 1698, the population was 727. The government granted land patents in rectangular blocks of 80 acres, 20,000 m2, with the most desirable lands along the coastline and inland waterways.

By 1708, the entire island had been divided up in this fashion, creating 166 small farms and two large manorial estates, the Dongan estate and 1,600 acres, 6.5 km2, parcel on the southwestern tip of the island belonging to Christopher Billopp.

The first county seat was established in New Dorp in what was called Stony Brook at the time.

In 1729, the county seat was moved to the village of Richmond Town, located at the headwaters of the Fresh Kills near the center of the island. By 1771, the island's population had grown to 2,847.

Staten Islanders were solidly supportive of the Crown, and the island played a significant role in the American Revolutionary War. General George Washington once called Islanders "our most inveterate enemies."

As support of independence spread throughout the colonies, residents of the island were so uninterested that no representatives were sent to the First Continental Congress, the only county in New York to not send anyone. This had economic implications in the months up through 1776, where New Jersey towns such as Elizabeth port, Woodbridge, and Dover instituted boycotts on doing business with islanders.

On March 17, 1776, the British forces under Sir William Howe evacuated Boston and sailed for Halifax, Nova Scotia. From Halifax, Howe prepared to attack New York City, which then consisted entirely of the southern end of Manhattan Island.

General George Washington led the entire Continental Army to New York City in anticipation of the British attack. Howe used the strategic location of Staten Island as a staging ground for the invasion.

Over 140 British ships arrived over the summer of 1776 and anchored off the shores of Staten Island at the entrance to New York

Harbor. The British soldiers and Hessian mercenaries numbered about 30,000.

Howe established his headquarters in New Dorp at the Rose and Crown Tavern, near the junction of present New Dorp Lane and Richmond Road. There are the representatives of the British government reportedly received their first notification of the Declaration of Independence.

In August 1776, the British forces crossed the Narrows to Brooklyn and outclassed the American forces at the Battle of Long Island, resulting in the British control of the harbor and the capture of New York City shortly afterwards.

Three weeks later, on September 11, 1776, Sir William's brother, Lord Howe, received a delegation of Americans consisting of Benjamin Franklin, Edward Rutledge, and John Adams at the Conference House on the southwestern tip of the island on the former estate of Christopher Billopp.

The Americans refused a peace offer from Howe in exchange for withdrawing the Declaration of Independence, and the conference ended without an agreement.

On August 22, 1777, the Battle of Staten Island occurred between the British forces and several companies of the 2nd Canadian Regiment fighting alongside other American companies.

The battle was uncertain, though both sides surrendered over a hundred troops as prisoners. The Americans finally withdrew.

In early 1780, while the Kill Van Kull was frozen over, Lord Stirling led an unsuccessful Patriot raid from New Jersey on the western shore of Staten Island. It was disgusted in part by troops led by British Commander Francis Rawdon-Hastings, 1st Marquess of Hastings.

In June 1780, Wilhelm von Knyphausen, commander of Britain's Hessian auxiliaries, led many raids and a full assault into New Jersey from Staten Island with the aim of defeating George Washington and the Continental Army.

Although the raids were successful in the Newark and Elizabeth areas, the advance was halted at Connecticut Farms, Union, and the Battle of Springfield.

British forces remained on Staten Island for the remainder of the war. Most Patriots fled after the British occupation, and the attitude of those who remained was mainly Loyalist.

Even so, the islanders found the demands of supporting the troops to be heavy. The British army kept headquarters in neighborhoods such as Bulls Head.

Many buildings and churches were destroyed for their materials, and the military's demand for resources resulted in an extensive logging by the end of the war.

The British army again used the island as a production ground for its final evacuation of New York City on December 5, 1783…

After their departure, many Loyalist landowners, such as Christopher Billop, the family of Canadian historian Peter Fisher, John Dunn, who founded St. Andrews, New Brunswick, and Abraham Jones, fled to Canada, and their estates were subdivided and sold.

Staten Island was occupied by the British longer than any single part of the Thirteen Colonies. Historic Richmond Town Museum complex is in the heart of Staten Island.

On July 4, 1827, the end of slavery in New York state was celebrated at Swan Hotel, West Brighton. Rooms at the hotel were reserved months in advance as local abolitionists, including prominent free blacks, prepared for the festivities. Speeches, pageants, picnics, and fireworks marked the celebration, which lasted for two days.

From 1800 to 1858, Staten Island was the location of the largest quarantine facility in the United States. Angry residents burned down the hospital compound in 1858 in a series of attacks known as the Staten Island Quarantine War.

In 1860, parts of Castleton and Southfield were made into a new town, Middletown. The Village of New Brighton in the town of Castleton was incorporated in 1866.

In 1872 the Village of New Brighton annexed all the remainder of the Town of Castleton and became coterminous with the town. An 1887 movement to make Staten Island a city came to nothing.

The towns of Staten Island were dissolved in 1898 with the consolidation of the City of Greater New York, as Richmond County became one of the five boroughs of the expanded city.

Although consolidated into the City of Greater New York in 1898, the county sheriff of Staten Island maintained control of the jail system, unlike the other boroughs, which had gradually transferred control of the jails to the Department of Correction.

The jail system was not transferred until January 1, 1942. Staten Island is the only borough without a New York City Department of Correction major detention center.

The construction of the Verrazzano-Narrows Bridge, along with the other three major Staten Island bridges, created a new way for commuters and tourists to travel from New Jersey to Brooklyn, Manhattan, and areas farther east on Long Island.

The network of highways running between the bridges has effectively carved up many of Staten Island's old neighborhoods. The bridge opened many areas of the borough to residential and commercial development, especially in the central and southern parts of the borough, which had been largely undeveloped.

Staten Island's population doubled from 221,991 in 1960 to 443,728 in 2000. Nevertheless, Staten Island remained less developed than the rest of the city.

Throughout the 1980s, a movement to separate from the city steadily grew in popularity, notably championed by longtime New York state senator and former Republican Party mayoral nominee John J. Marchi.

The campaign reached its peak during the mayoral term of David Dinkins, 1990–1993, after the U.S. Supreme Court invalidated the New York City Board of Estimate, which had given equal representation to the five boroughs.

Dinkins and the city government opposed a non-binding withdrawal referendum, contending that the vote should not be permitted by the state unless the city issued a home rule message supporting it, which the city would not. Governor Mario Cuomo disagreed, and the vote went forward in 1993.

Ultimately, 65% of Staten Island residents voted to withdraw, through the approval of a new city charter making Staten Island an independent city, but implementation was blocked in the State Assembly.

In the 1980s, the United States Navy had a base on Staten Island called Naval Station New York. It had two sections: a Strategic Homeport in Stapleton and a larger section near Fort Wadsworth, where the Verrazzano-Narrows Bridge enters the island.

The base was closed in 1994 through the Base Realignment and closure process because of its small size and the expense of basing personnel there.

Fresh Kills and its rivers are part of the largest tidal wetland ecosystem in the region. Its creeks and wetlands have been designated a Significant Coastal Fish and Wildlife Habitat by the New York State Department of Environmental Conservation. It opened along Fresh Kills as a "temporary landfill" in 1947, the Fresh Kills Landfill was a source of trash for the city of New York.

The landfill, once the world's largest man-made structure, was closed in 2001, but it was briefly reopened for the trash from Ground Zero following the September 11 attacks in 2001.

It is being converted into a park. Plans for the park include a bird-nesting island, public roads, boardwalks, soccer and baseball fields, bridle paths, and a 5,000-seat stadium.

Today, freshwater, and tidal wetlands, fields, stick woods, and a coastal oak maritime forest, as well as areas dominated by non-native plant species, are all within the boundaries of Fresh Kills.

CHAPTER 8

PRIMITIVE POLICING

For nearly the first 200 years of its life, New York City had no police force.

Life was savage in those early days. They didn't even have the electricity. Policing was primitive. There were no squad cars you were a macher if you had a horse and no walkie-talkies. A constable called for backup by shaking the rattle on his stick.

That's according to John DeCarlo, a former police chief and now director of the master's program in criminal justice at the University of New Haven. He said those first eight officers carried not only rattles but lanterns with tinted glass that caused them to glow green and identify them to the public at night in an era of no streetlights.

"Not the Green Lantern with the fancy superhero ring but actual green lanterns that patrolmen took on their rounds," DeCarlo explained. "And when they returned to the watch house, they'd hang their green lantern on a hook outside."

DeCarlo said those constables also abide in the lives of New Yorkers as an obscure visual reference. "The eight points on police officers' hats in the modern NYPD are an homage to the first eight members of the night watch," he said.

Their duties gradually expanded to collecting fines, recovering stolen property, and banging their sticks on the table when the proceedings in a courtroom got out of hand. But as one scholar of policing puts it, "Few paid any attention to them."

There, embedded in that one line, are two of the larger themes in the story of New York law enforcement: the thanklessness of the job and chronic tensions with the public.

William Bratton, who has done two stints as the city's police commissioner, 1994 to 1996 and 2014 to 2016, gave a couple of reasons for that tension. "It's a challenge from the beginning of time that people don't like being told what to do or to have their behavior corrected, it's human nature," he observed. "But in a democracy, what we decide on is norms of behavior, and police support those norms of behavior."

As the late police historian Thomas Repetto told WNYC, that changed when veterans of the Civil War returned to New York and reorganized the department. "After the Civil War, a lot of police departments and other organizations began to adopt uniforms and the rank structure," he said. They also started carrying deadly weapons. This is how John DeCarlo describes the result, which is with us to this day: "Cops aren't military, but we function in a paramilitary environment."

In other words, police have a lot of power to "enforce norms of behavior."

Bratton is fine with that. He's been arguing for decades that when officers use their power wisely, crime goes down and the city thrives. But he's quick to add that the power can be abused first, by cops with their hands out. "There's an issue with corruption," he said. "Every twenty years, New York seems to have a corruption crisis."

Remember those early constables who'd recover stolen property? Sometimes they'd demand payment from the victim before handing it over.

DeCarlo says it took the NYPD until 1894 to officially call out the problem by sanctioning the first in a long line of investigative bodies, this one called the Lexow Committee. "Lexow formed to investigate corruption in the department," he said. "They uncovered small stuff like taking free meals and taking payment for not ticketing the vehicles in front of a restaurant." Big stuff, too, like "counterfeiting, extortion, election fraud and brutality."

Then, in 1920, came Prohibition and its shadow industry of bootlegging, which required a lot of cops-on-the-take to function. By the time Fiorello LaGuardia became mayor in 1934, it was simply assumed that criminals would try to corrupt the police.

LaGuardia found it necessary to advise new patrolmen at their swearing-in ceremony in 1942 on how to avoid temptation. With rising agitation, he told them, "You don't have to be an experienced detective to recognize a punk or a tinhorn. Stay away from them. And if you see 'em on your beat, sock ' em in the jaw!"

Fiorello LaGuardia saluting in a black and white photo with two other men in overcoats .

Mayor Fiorello La Guardia saluting police officers, circa 1939-1940; businessman Harvey Gibson is on the far right.

Bratton says that in 1994, when he first became commissioner, he tried a more refined form of crime prevention that was no less controversial. "Policing through most of its history until the 1990s was focused on responding to crime and almost not dealing with disorder," he said. "That was certainly the case in the 1970s and 1980s, and that's why it got so bad. 1990 was the worst crime year in the history of the country and the history of New York."

His department famously introduced "broken windows" policing. Cracking down on crimes of disorder such as prostitution, public urination, and jumping subway turnstiles. He contends that a lot of New Yorkers were clamoring for just such improvements to the quality of street life. "Where, after all, do the calls for help come from?" he asked before answering his own question. "They come from residents who want the police to come in and deal with the chaos around them." Critics say the program's excesses led to harassment, unjust arrests, and a stop-and-frisk regime that over time spun out of control. The approach led to the city's historic drop in crime.

Meanwhile, quietly, a small group of terrorists was putting New York at the top of their list of go-to targets. Their intentions were revealed with a bang in 1993, when a bomb blew up at the World Trade Center and killed six people. Bratton said that prior to the attack, the department hadn't prioritized counterterrorism. "The NYPD's intelligence unit was largely a dignitary protection unit," he said.

New York's Joint Terrorism Task Force, a collaboration between the FBI and NYPD, caught the bombers and the courts sent them to prison. Bratton says that gave the department a false sense of security. "They basically solved the World Trade Center bombing and they thought that was it, that they had eliminated that problem," he said.

On September 11, 2001, you didn't see police officers running the other way, they were rushing toward it," Bratton said. "And time and again you will see that. Cops can be relied on to go toward the danger." By any measure, the NYPD fulfilled its promise that day and served with distinction. In the process, twenty-three officers lost their lives.

Yet, as Bratton admits, the department is human and therefore weak. "That doesn't make all of them heroes because they do have those issues about corruption, certainly the concerns around racism, the concerns around brutality, oftentimes coupled with racism." His formula for productive policing is to maintain order legally, compassionately, and consistently.

CHAPTER 9

THE FIRST BLACK POLICE OFFICER IN NYPD

On June 28, 1911, Samuel Battle, badge number 782, became the first Black police officer in the NYPD.

On that day, Police Commissioner Rhinelander Waldo told him, "You will have some difficulties, but I know you will overcome them." Thus, began Battle's four-decade-long career.

Along the way, Battle pushed through the ranks of the NYPD, navigated the dark waters of Tammany Hall politics, and became a founding citizen of Black Harlem.

Battle also pushed for equality in all the city's civil services, including mentoring Wesley Williams, the first Black firefighter in the New York Fire Department.

Battle's career was never easy. He faced discrimination and threats even before taking the civil service exam.

Battle's first day at the Twenty-Eighth Precinct was no different. He was greeted with silence, mockery. A cot in the precinct's flag storage loft instead of the dormitory was he place.

Years later Battle would recount his feelings to Langston Hughes, his autobiographer for a time, about enduring such abuse:

Sometimes, lying on my cot on the top floor in the silence, I would wonder how it was that many of the patrolmen in my precinct who did not yet speak English well, had no such difficulties in getting on the police force as I, a Negro American, had experienced...My name had been passed over repeatedly. All sorts of discouragements had been placed in my path. And now, after a long wait and a lot of stalling, I had finally been given a trial appointment to their ranks and these men would not speak to me. Native-born and foreign-born whites on the police force all united in looking past me as though I were not a human being. In the loft in the dark, with the Stars and Stripes, I wondered! Why?

Realizing that his story was the story of race in New York across the first half of the century, Battle commissioned a biography to be written by Langston Hughes, the preeminent voice of the Harlem Renaissance. But their 80,000-word collaboration failed to find a publisher and remained unpublished.

Using Hughes's manuscript, which is quoted liberally throughout this book, as well as his own archival research and interviews with survivors, Pulitzer Prize-winning journalist Arthur Browne explores the desegregation of the New York Police Department through the extraordinary life of Samuel Battle in "One Righteous Man: Samuel Battle and the Shattering of the Color Line in New York."

CHAPTER 10

FIRST HISPANIC DEPUTY COMMISSIONER IN NYPD

Rafael Piñeiro born 1949 is the First Deputy Commissioner of the New York City Police Department. He is highest ranking Hispanic American member of the NYPD.

In November 2013, he was supposed to be on Mayor-elect Bill de Blasio's short list to replace Ray Kelly as NYPD Commissioner.

Piñeiro was born in Valencia, Spain. He immigrated with his family from Cuba to the United States of America when he was 12.

After graduating from the New York Institute of Technology with a Bachelor of Science in Behavioral Science, he was appointed to the NYPD in June 1970 after graduating at the top of his New York City Police Academy class and receiving the Chief of Personnel's Award for the highest combined academic and physical fitness scores.

According to his official biography, he was promoted up the ranks to Deputy Chief in 1991 and Assistant Chief in 1994.

When he was promoted to Deputy Chief, he was the Commanding Officer of the Police Commissioner's Office and later the Executive Officer of Patrol Borough Bronx.

As Assistant Chief he served as Executive Officer Housing Bureau and was the Commanding Officer of the following commands: Patrol Borough Bronx, Criminal Justice Bureau, Management Information Systems Division, Personnel Bureau.

In 1995, he founded the National Law Enforcement Explorer Academy. He served as executive officer of the 17th Precinct, commander of the 41st Precinct.

In 2002, he was appointed Chief of Personnel and became the longest serving Chief of Personnel in NYPD history. He was elevated to First Deputy Commissioner in 2010.

His awards and decorations include the Police Combat Cross, the Department's second highest award for valor, which he received for confronting a gun handling suspect who had robbed a convenience store.

In 2010 he became the first Hispanic American ever appointed as First Deputy Commissioner of the New York City Police Department.

Rafael Piñeiro serves at the chief executive assistant and advisor to the Police Commissioner in the management and administration of the Police Department and assumes the duties and responsibilities of the Police Commissioner in his absence.

He maintains responsibility for the highest levels of policy formation, program development and decision making in the NYPD. He is also responsible for four major commands responsible for critical aspects of agency operations: the Personnel Bureau, Support Services Bureau, Criminal Justice Bureau, and Office of Labor Relations.

The First Deputy Commissioner is the highest-level representative of the Police Commissioner and serves on his behalf as executive liaison to the city, state and federal criminal justice and law enforcement agencies and represents the Police Commissioner at meetings and conferences conducted to address and resolve high level policy, program, and procedural issues with agency-wide ramifications.

Piñeiro graduated with a Juris Doctor from Brooklyn Law School, holds a Master of Public Administration from New York University's Robert F. Wagner Graduate School of Public Service a graduate of the inaugural class of the Police Management Institute at Columbia University.

In 1995, he attended the Kennedy School of Government at Harvard University as a Pickett Fellow in Criminal Justice. He is married to Sheila Ahern.

Even before the 2013 New York City mayoral election, Piñeiro was referenced as a potential replacement for NYPD Police Commissioner Ray Kelly.

During a televised debate, de Blasio's opponent, Joe Lhota, stated Piñeiro would be his pick to replace Kelly were he elected.

After de Blasio indicated during the campaign that he would seek a new Commissioner for the NYPD, the NYPD Hispanic Society held a press conference along with the New York Dominican Officers Organization and National Latino Officers Association advocating for Rafael Pineiro to be considered and given an opportunity to be interviewed based on his credentials and qualifications.

The Hispanic Society President Detective Dennis Gonzalez stated that he would be the first Hispanic American to ever serve as Police Commissioner.

In his statement, Gonzalez stated is this, "a tale of two cities, one white and one black, Latinos not included", apparently referencing the fact that Pineiro was not being recognized in the mainstream media but non-Hispanics were.

In November 2013, he formally met with Mayor-elect de Blasio during the annual New York Hispanic legislative conference "Somos El Futuro" in Puerto Rico to discuss the NYPD transition.

Much like Kelly, whom de Blasio stated he would not be reappointing, Piñeiro rose through the ranks of the NYPD from a beat cop to the highest level of its hierarchy.

Other candidates who met with de Blasio included former NYPD Commissioner Bill Bratton and current NYPD Chief of Department Philip Banks III. Bratton was ultimately appointed on December 5, 2013.

CHAPTER 11

SCHOELLKOPF POWER STATION

The Schoellkopf Power Station was built on land owned by Jacob F. Schoellkopf above the Niagara Gorge near the American Falls, 1,600 feet, 490 m, downriver from Rainbow Bridge.

Understanding the growing need for electricity and the role of harnessing the Falls, Schoellkopf purchased the land for the hydraulic canal on May 1, 1877, for $71,000.

After Schoellkopf Sr.'s death in 1903, his sons took over the operation of the power business.

In 1918, Schoellkopf's Niagara Falls Hydraulic Power and Manufacturing Company merged with the Niagara Falls Power Company, which was owned by Edward Dean Adams.

Much of the site is, as of 2014, occupied by the Maid of the Mist tour boat company as a maintenance area and off-season boat storage yard.

The power station remains form a part of a fully accessible tourist attraction associated with Niagara Falls State Park and relates to its Niagara Gorge hiking trail.

In 1853 construction of a "Hydraulic Canal" was begun, intended to bring water from the Niagara River above the falls to the river bluff below the falls.

The original 1874 plant did not produce electricity but used water turbines to power belts and drive shafts for nearby mills.

In 1882 Schoellkopf partnered with Charles Brush who had come to Niagara Falls with a dynamo and 16 carbon arc lights which were used on the streets of Niagara Falls, New York.

The first dynamo had a capacity of 1,800 horsepower and ran up to 1904 when it was abandoned in favor of Station No. 2. It was also known as the Quigley Pulp - Lower Mill and the Cliff Paper - Lower Mill.

In 1898 a second much larger hydroelectric plant was built at the base of the bluff, immediately in front of Schoellkopf's original 1874 plant, and reached a capacity of 34,000 hp before being shut down in 1921.

Station No. 3a was completed by 1914 and housed 13 10,000-hp turbines. Station No. 3b began construction in 1918 and contained three generators totaling 112,500 hp. Station No. 3c was completed by 1924 with a capacity of 210,000 hp.

As the old hydraulic canal was already operating at capacity a new tunnel was constructed to supply the new station.

Schoellkopf Station No. 3a, 3b and 3c outside of the picture on the right is Station No. 2.

On June 7, 1956, water began seeping into the back of the plant from the wall built against the bluff, causing the wall to crack.

At 5 p.m. that day, Station No. 3c and then Station No. 3b flooded and collapsed into the Niagara River, destroying two thirds of the plant and the six generators that produced more than 300,000 horsepower.

The grid lost 400,000 kilowatts of power and damage was estimated at $100m.

The remains of the Plant either toppled into the gorge or were razed soon after. Station 3A was damaged but remained in operation at reduced volume until 1961. The collapse led to the passage of the 1957 Niagara Redevelopment Act.

Station No. 3a was demolished in 1962 as part of Robert Moses's work to beautify the American side of the Falls. The energy lost by the 1956 collapse was replaced by the Robert Moses Niagara Power Plant, which was commissioned in 1961.

The only permanently extant part of the Schoellkopf site is the stone wall, known as Power Station No. 3, which was built during beautification efforts in 1908-10. That wall was listed on the National Register of Historic Places in February 2013. However, depending on the seasonal flow of the river, it's sometimes possible to see the twisted steel girders and even a generator turbine that fell into the river.

CHAPTER 12

PEARL STREET STATION

Pearl Street Station was the first commercial central power plant in the United States. It was located at 255–257 Pearl Street in the Financial District of Manhattan, New York City, just south of Fulton Street on a site measuring 50 by 100 feet, 15 by 30 m.

The station was built by the Edison Illuminating Company, under the direction of Francis Upton, hired by Thomas Edison

Pearl Street Station was fired by coal. It began with six dynamos, and it started generating electricity on September 4, 1882, serving an initial load of 400 lamps at 82 customers.

By 1884, Pearl Street Station was serving 508 customers with 10,164 lamps. The station was originally powered by custom-made Porter-Allen high-speed steam engines designed to provide 175 horsepower at 700 rpm,529but these proved to be unreliable with their sensitive governors.

They were removed and replaced with new engines from Armington & Sims that proved to be much more suitable for Edison's dynamos. :527 Pearl Street Station was also the world's first cogeneration plant.

While the steam engines provided grid electricity, Edison made use of the thermal byproduct by providing steam heating to local manufacturers and nearby buildings on the same Manhattan block.

Pearl Street Station served what was known as the "First District" bounded clockwise from north by Spruce Street, the East River, Wall Street, and Nassau Street.

The district, so named because of its importance in the history of electric power, contained several other power stations such as the Excelsior Power Company Building.

The station burned down in 1890, destroying all but one dynamo that is now kept in the Greenfield Village Museum in Dearborn, Michigan.

In 1929, the Edison Company constructed three scale working models of the station. When a button was pushed, a motor turned the engines, generators, and other equipment in the model.

A set of lamps connected to labelled buttons identified the various areas of the building. Cut-outs in the side of the model building allowed examination of the boilers on the first level, reciprocating steam engines and dynamos on the reinforced second level, and the control and test gear on the third and fourth levels.

The models were constructed to a scale of one-half inch to the foot and were 62 inches long, 34 inches high and 13 inches wide. The models still exist and are on display at the Smithsonian Institution's National Museum of American History in Washington, D.C.; at the Consolidated Edison Learning Center in Long Island City, New York; and at the Henry Ford Museum in Dearborn, Michigan.

Up to 31 people worked on constructing the models which took about 6 months to complete.

CHAPTER 13

EARLY NYPD "BADGES"
1800-1845

If you ask a police historian when the earliest police badge was issued in the City of New York, the answer will likely be that it was in 1845. This was the time the "Municipal Police, or Day and Night Watch" was created.

Ask the police historian what was used prior to 1845, and you will likely get a blank stare...

The 1845 badge, made of copper, was in the form of an eight-pointed star. The obverse bore the Seal of the City of New York the city and the word "POLICE."

Badges were necessary as a form of identifying individual officers because uniforms had not yet been prescribed, adopted, or worn.

The language "badges or emblems of office" comes from official records of the common council. It is referring to clothing, hats, caps, helmets, copper badges, and poles of office.

The word "office" is used interchangeably with "authority" by many sources.

An example of a pre-1845 badge of authority, are boards of office. The use of batons of office was likely carried to this country by the British, where the length and decoration of the staff portrayed the authority vested in the holder.

For example, ranking British police officials carried, and carry to this day, a small staff called a "tipstaff," to represent their office and authority. Some tipstaffs contain a compartment where a document denoting the office, officer, and the authority of their office is stored.

In New York City, during the eighteenth and nineteenth centuries, poles of office were routinely provided by the city to elected and appointed officials as a symbol of office and authority.

According to various official city records, batons or staves were "worn" and not carried.

The Minutes of the Council, dated December 28, 1807, disclosed that staves were to be "painted and numbered; and to be delivered to the several Constables and Marshals correspondent with their respective numbers." It is not known if these numbers were unique identifiers or something other.

For discussion here, there were two law enforcement entities in the city prior to 1844; the Police-Office and the Watch Department.

The titles of officers in the Police-Office were, in part, Constables, Marshals, Bell Ringers, in towers throughout the city, looking for fires, Dock Masters, Lamp, Street. Lighters, and Health Wardens.

In 1811, High Constable Jacob Hayes requested that the Common Council direct the Superintendent of Repairs to replace several staves that were "out of repair."

The City Watch was governed by the Mayor, Recorder, Alderman, and Judges of the Supreme Court. The titles under the Watch Department were Captain, Assistant Captain, and Watchman.

To date, no mention of staves of office for the City Watch, or Watch Department, was found.

The public also found use for the constables' staves...

In February 1837, due to the near doubling of the price per barrel of flour, a riot, dubbed the Flour Riot, took place. A mob marched to Hart & Co.'s warehouse located at Washington and Courtlandt Streets.

The attack violently entered the warehouse and threw hundreds of barrels of wheat and flour out of the windows and onto the streets. The flour on the street rose to a depth of two to three feet.

The mayor and constables at the scene were unable to disperse the rioters. Rioters threw flour at the mayor and "treated the staves of office with quite as little respect. They broke the staves over the constables' backs."

In 1844, an act of the New York State Assembly, which was later adopted by the city, replaced the Police-Office, and formed the "Municipal Police, or Day and Night Watch."

Another source disclosed that "The duty of marshals and constables to attend at fires, with their staves of office, etc., was abolished by the acts passed in 1844," abolishing the watch department and office of marshal."

It is important to note that the officers under the patronages of the Police-Office had duties relating to fires. From observing fires and ringing bells, to taking control of the scene and the investigation of cause and origin was their jobs.

The initial titles under the new Municipal Police Department were Mayor, Chief of Police, Chief's Clerks, Special Justices and their Clerks, Captains, Assistant Captains, Sergeants, Policemen, Constables, and Doormen.

In May 1845, the Board of Alderman directed that "The Chief of Police, Captain, Assistant Captains, Sergeants of Police, and Policemen, shall carry a suitable emblem or device, by which they may, when necessary, make themselves known."

While direct evidence has not yet been found that the resulting "suitable emblem or device" was the eight-pointed copper star, it is most likely that it was, because the "star" was adopted and worn.

In 1845, George W. Matsell was appointed by New York Mayor William F. Havermeyer as the first Chief of Police of the Day and Night Watch, Municipal Police.

Under Matsell, the eight-pointed copper star and a uniform was adopted to identify officers. The force was informally referred to as the "star police."

Staves remained in service after 1845...

In 1851, the Board of Alderman approved an expenditure of $137.50 for "Staves for Police Officers." In 1854, Police Justices were supplied with "suitable stars and staves of offices." In 1855, the Clerk of the Common Council issued, to new board members, "the usual batons, staves and stars of office."

Let me remind you of the following....

In 1844, the Municipal Police, or Day and Night Watch was created. The city ruled that the police officers "shall carry a suitable emblem or device, by which they may, when necessary, make themselves known." It is believed that the suitable emblem or device was the copper eight-pointed star worn by the Municipal Police from 1845-1854 without uniforms and from 1854-1857, with uniforms.

The staff with the carved eight-pointed star above was worn/carried by the Municipal Police from approximately 1844 to 1857.

CHAPTER 14

THE HISTORY OF NEW YORK TRAFFIC LIGHTS

Traffic signals were not always practical in New York City.

Are you tired of cars and bikes running the red lights? How about no lights at all? That's the kind of traffic system New York had until 1920, when a series of tall bare-bones towers went up down the middle of Fifth Avenue, flashing red and green lights to the growing offensive of automobiles.

Two years later they were replaced with formidably elegant bronze and stone towers, lavish contributions to the Beautiful City, but destroyed within a decade, victims of increasing traffic.

The Library of Congress has a website of digitized photographs and early movies of New York, called American Memory.

If you look at the half dozen movies set in New York it is clear that, except for a few police officers, traffic regulation amounted to "hey, watch out!"

Automobiles complicated the everything. Safety became an increasing concern...

In 1913, <u>The New York Times</u> reported on the city's "Death Harvest". This was the actual headline. From 1910 and 1912 for three different types of vehicles, the number killed by wagons and carriages, down in two years to 177 from 211: and streetcars, down to 134 from 148. Automobile fatalities nearly doubled, to 221 from 112. Ninety-five percent of the dead, according to The Times, were pedestrians.

Let me inform you that in 2013, 156 pedestrians were killed by automobiles.

Influential retailers on Fifth Avenue no doubt felt sympathy, but what hurt them at the cash register was traffic congestion. The pressure grew on the avenue. It could take 40 minutes to go from 57th to 34th Street.

There had been an experimental traffic light in 1917, but it was short-lived. Thus, it was in 1920 that the first permanent traffic lights in New York went up, the gift of Dr. John A. Harris, a millionaire physician fascinated by street conditions.

His design was a homely wooden shed on steel, from which a police officer changed signals, allowing one to two minutes for each direction.

Although the meanings we attach to red and green now seem like the natural order of things, in 1920 green meant Fifth Avenue traffic was to stop so crosstown traffic could proceed; white meant go. Most crosstown streets and Fifth Avenue were still two-way.

The doctor's signals were so well received that in 1922 the Fifth Avenue Association gave the city, at a cost of $126,000, a new set of signals, seven ornate bronze 23-foot-high towers placed at intersections along Fifth from 14th to 57th Streets.

Designed by Joseph H. Freelander, they were the most elegant street furniture the city has ever had. It was a time when elevating public taste through civic beauty was considered a fit goal for government effort.

In 1923 the magazine Architecture opined that "To understand the beautiful is to create a love for the beautiful, to widen the boundaries of human pride, enjoyment and accomplishment."

Dr. Harris's towers would have looked at home in a railway freight yard; Freed lander's towers were fitting adornments for the noblest of New York's public spaces, like the forecourt of the New York Public Library or the Plaza at 59th Street.

For reasons unstated, the towers were not placed in the center of the intersections, but several feet north or south of the crosswalks. Crosstown drivers could barely see them.

The new lights supposedly reduced that trip from 57th to 34th to 15 minutes. Soon, traffic lights were like laptops in classrooms: everyone was in favor of them.

Most of the big avenues got traffic lights, of much simpler design, and mounted on corners.

In 1927 the present system of red, yellow, and green was generally recognized, but The Times said the yellow caution light had been abandoned in New York because it was a "temptation to motorists to rush through intersections."

Cars continued to flood the streets and within a few years the police decided that Friedlander's spectacular traffic towers were blocking the roadway.

It took some convincing, but the Fifth Avenue Association came around to taking them down.

In 1929 Freelander was called back to design a new two-light traffic signal, also bronze, to be placed on the corners. These were topped by statues of Mercury and lasted until 1964.

A few of the Mercury statues have survived, but Friedlander's 1922 towers have completely vanished.

In retrospect, the automobile appears as the opening wedge to a new kind of city. Pedestrians were zoned off the streets, to which they had formerly free access.

The speed of automobiles, not horse-drawn vehicles, became the metric. Street cars, held hostage to their fixed routes, were often stalled by traffic. The streets themselves became covered with regulation after regulation. They were also covered with signs, lights, arrows and pillars, none of which were ever as elegant as the 1922 Fifth Avenue traffic towers.

CHAPTER 15

BUCKLE UP FOR SAFETY

Seatbelts were invented by an English engineer, George Cayley, to use on his glider, in the mid-19th century.

In 1946, C. Hunter Shelden opened a neurological practice at Huntington Memorial Hospital in Pasadena, California. In the early 1950s, Shelden made a major contribution to the automotive industry with his idea of retractable seat belts. This came about from his care of the high number of head injuries coming through the emergency room.

He investigated the early seat belts with primitive designs that were implicated in these injuries and deaths.

Nash was the first American car manufacturer to offer seat belts as a factory option, in its 1949 models.

They were installed in 40,000 cars, but buyers did not want them and requested dealers to remove them.

The feature was "met with insurmountable sales resistance" and Nash reported that after one year "only 1,000 had been used" by customers.

Ford offered seat belts as an option in 1955. These were not popular, with only 2% of Ford buyers choosing to pay for seatbelts in 1956.

To reduce the high level of injuries Shelden was seeing, he proposed, in late 1955, retractable seat belts, recessed steering wheels, reinforced roofs, roll bars, automatic door locks, and passive restraints such as air bags.

Subsequently, in 1966, Congress passed the National Traffic and Motor Vehicle Safety Act, requiring all automobiles to comply with certain safety standards.

Glenn W. Sheren, of Mason, Michigan, submitted a patent application on March 31, 1955, for an automotive seat belt and was awarded US Patent 2,855,215 in 1958.

This was a continuation of an earlier patent application that Sheren had filed on September 22, 1952.

However, the first modern three-point seat belt the so-called CIR-Griswold restraint used in most consumer vehicles today was patented in 1955 U.S. Patent 2,710,649 by the Americans Roger W. Griswold and Hugh DeHaven.

Saab introduced seat belts as standard equipment in 1958. After the Saab GT 750 was introduced at the New York Motor Show in 1958 with safety belts fitted as standard, the practice became commonplace.

Vattenfall, the Swedish national electric utility, did a study of all fatal, on-the-job accidents among their employees. The study revealed that most fatalities occurred while the employees were on the road on company business.

In response, two Vattenfall safety engineers, Bengt Odelgard and Per-Olof Weman, started to develop a seat belt. Their work was presented to Swedish manufacturer Volvo in the late 1950s and set the standard for seat belts in Swedish cars.

The three-point seatbelt was developed to its modern form by Swedish inventor Nils Bohlin for Volvo, who introduced it in 1959 as standard equipment.

In addition to designing an effective three-point belt, Bohlin demonstrated its effectiveness in a study of 28,000 accidents in Sweden.

Unbelted occupants sustained fatal injuries throughout the whole speed scale, whereas none of the belted occupants were fatally injured at accident speeds below 60 mph. No belted occupant was fatally injured if the passenger compartment remained intact. Bohlin was granted U.S. Patent 3,043,625 for the device.

The first compulsory seat belt law was put in place in 1970, in the state of Victoria, Australia, requiring their use by drivers and front-seat passengers. This legislation was enacted after trialing Hemco seatbelts, designed by Desmond Hemphill ,1926–2001, in the front seats of police vehicles, lowering the incidence of officer injury and death.

Mandatory seatbelt laws in the United States began to be introduced in the 1980s and faced opposition, with some consumers going to court to challenge the laws. Some cut seatbelts out of their cars.

The Federal Motor Vehicle Safety Standard № 208, FMVSS 208, was amended by the NHTSA to require a seat belt/starter interlock system to prevent passenger cars from being started with an unbelted front-seat occupant.

This mandate applied to passenger cars built after August 1973, i.e., starting with the 1974 model year. The specifications required the system to permit the car to be started only if the belt of an occupied seat were fastened after the occupant sat down, so pre-buckling the belts would not defeat the system.

The interlock systems used logic modules complex enough to require special diagnostic computers. They were not entirely dependable. An override button was provided under the hood of equipped cars, permitting one, but only one, "free" starting attempt each time it was pressed. However, the interlock system provoked severe backlash from an American public who largely rejected seat belts.

In 1974, Congress acted to prohibit NHTSA from requiring or permitting a system that prevents a vehicle from starting or operating with an unbelted occupant, or that gives an audible warning of an unfastened belt for more than 8 seconds after the ignition is turned on.

This prohibition took effect on 27 October 1974, shortly after the 1975 model year began.

In response to the Congressional action, NHTSA once again amended FMVSS 208, requiring vehicles to come with a seat belt reminder system that gives an audible signal for 4 to 8 seconds and a warning light for at least 60 seconds after the ignition is turned on if the driver's seat belt is not fastened.

This is called a seat belt reminder, SBR system. In the mid-1990s, the Swedish insurance company Folksam worked with Saab and Ford to determine the requirements for the most efficient seat belt reminder. One characteristic of the optimal SBR, according to the research, is that the audible warning becomes increasingly penetrating the longer the seat belt remains unfastened.

The seat belt, also known as a safety belt, is a vehicle safety device designed to secure the driver or a passenger of a vehicle against harmful movement that may result during a collision or a sudden stop.

The seat belt reduces the likelihood of death or serious injury in a traffic collision by reducing the force of secondary impacts with interior strike hazards, by keeping occupants positioned correctly for maximum effectiveness of the airbag, if equipped, preventing occupants being ejected from the vehicle in a crash or if the vehicle rolls over.

When in motion, the driver and passengers are traveling at the same speed as the vehicle. If the vehicle suddenly stops or crashes, the occupants continue at the same speed the vehicle was going before it stopped.

A seatbelt applies an opposing force to the driver and passengers to prevent them from falling out or contacting the interior of the car, especially preventing contact with, or going through, the windshield. Seatbelts are considered primary restraint systems, PRSs, because of their vital role in occupant safety.

An analysis conducted in the United States in 1984 compared a variety of seat belt types alone and in combination with air bags. The range of fatality reduction for front seat passengers was broad, from 20% to 55%, as was the range of major injury, from 25% to 60%.

More recently, the Centers for Disease Control and Prevention has summarized these data by stating "seat belts reduce serious crash-related injuries and deaths by about half." Most seatbelt malfunctions are a result of there being too much slack in the seatbelt at the time of the accident.

It has been suggested that although seat belt usage reduces the probability of death in any given accident, mandatory seat belt laws have little or no effect on the overall number of traffic fatalities because seat belt usage also did not prevent safe driving behaviors, thereby increasing the total number of accidents. This idea, known as compensating-behavior theory, is not supported by the evidence.

In case of vehicle rollover in a US passenger car or SUV, from 1994 to 2004, wearing seat belt reduced the risk of fatalities or incapacitating injuries and increased the probability of no injury:

CHAPTER 16

THE FIRST TRAFFIC RELATED UNIT IN THE NYPD

By the end of the 19th Century, traffic in New York City was largely uncontrolled. This was a very important era in the New York City Police Department. You are going to see why...

There were carriages and wagons dashing everywhere. Runaway horses added to the chaos with alarming frequency...

Getting across a busy street could be a real challenge. The constant hazard to pedestrians led in the 1860's to the formation of the first traffic-related unit in the NYPD, <u>the famous Broadway Squad"</u>.

The officers of the Broadway Squad were the largest and most imposing in the Department. The minimum height was six feet. Their primary duty was nothing other than to escort pedestrians safely across Broadway in Manhattan between Bowling Green and West 59th Street.

A new line in traffic control was added by the bicycle obsession of the 1890's. This was when many cyclists took over the streets of New York.

To control the speed-demon, "wheelmen", who exceeded the New York City speed limit of 8 miles per hour, approximately 13 kph, in December of 1895, Police Commissioner Theodore Roosevelt organized the police Department's old Bicycle Squad, which quickly acquired the nickname of the "scorcher" Squad. The Scorcher Squad soon found itself with the responsibility of enforcing the speed regulations not just for Bicycles, but for the newest toy of the wealthy: the automobile.

A Scorcher Squad officer stationed in a booth would record the speeds of passing vehicles. When excessive speed was observed, he would telephone ahead to the next booth, and a uniformed officer would be dispatched on a bicycle to stop the offender.

Traffic summonses did not exist during that time, therefore, the speeders caught by "Scorchers" were arrested on the spot and brought before the judge.

The difficulty that the public experienced attempting to negotiate the maze of people, horses, and bicycles on streets that were often unpaved, found some relief when the subway system began operating in October of 1904.

Yet, the great number of horses on the streets of that year was clear by that fact that the NYPD's Mounted Division alone had by that time reached its all-time high of 800 officers, with its primary unit being the "Traffic Squad".

Still, automobiles were becoming increasingly popular, and no longer just with the wealthy. With the great numbers of motor cars and trucks jamming the streets, it was not unusual to see traffic disputes settle by drivers "duking it out", and still further tying up traffic.

It soon became apparent that vehicular traffic regulations were necessary.

In December 1908, Police Commissioner Bingham was given the responsibility of creating the first traffic regulations after his authority had been specifically extended to encompass this area.

The original "rules of the road" that were adopted included keeping to the right so that slower-moving vehicles could be passed on the left and signaling one's intentions by extending or raising the hand or the whip before slowing, stopping, or turning.

Enforcing these regulations, however, was a little difficult at first as the state legislature did not give the Police Department the power to issue summonses for traffic infractions until 1910.

While it is not known how exactly many summonses were issued at that time, the number of motor vehicles in New York City had already mushroomed by 1912 to 38000.

Today there are over 2 million vehicles of all types registered in the city, in addition to the uncounted vehicles that commute from the suburbs every day.

Many of the traffic summonses issued today are for "running" the red lights, but no driver today would expect a summons for driving past a green light. However, this has not always been the case. The first traffic control devices at intersections in New York City were installed in 1915.

They were four-armed manually operated traffic lights with the words "STOP" and "GO" painted on their arms. A far grander device, however, made its appearance the following year.

In 1916, the first traffic tower was erected in the middle of the intersection of Fifth Avenue and 42nd Street. Standing inside a booth 16-inch, 40 centimeters, diameter electric lamps positioned on top of the booth. Three of these 500-watt lamps were red, amber, and green, and faced north, while three similarly colored lamps faced south.

However, at that time, a red light in New York City meant traffic in all directions had to stop. An amber light meant cross-town traffic would have to stop so that north and southbound traffic could pass. A green light would stop north and south bound lanes of traffic so that cross-town traffic could proceed.

The difficulty in understanding this confusing color sequence was compounded by neighboring towns using another system, the "railroad signal designation" sequence of red for stop, green for go, and yellow for slow. It came as no surprise that out-of-town drivers headed north on Madison Avenue were not thrilled to receive a summons for "passing a green light".

The confusion died down only after the city agreed in 1924 to utilize the railroad system that by then had been adopted by most towns in the United States.

Meanwhile, there were now 50 traffic towers throughout the city. Seven of these towers had been cast of bronze at the cost of $200,000 and were erected along 5th Avenue during the winter of 1922.

The Traffic Towers, like the semaphore system, cost a lot of money to operate. The towers required 100 officers working 16-hour per day. It costed the city an estimated of $ 250,000 a year in salaries, equipment, and maintenance.

In the case of traffic on Fifth Avenue, the towers took the two center lanes of the six-lane road which greatly constricted the flow of traffic. It was these reasons that the then NYC Department of Plant and Structures recommended a major change in 1924 that would revolutionize traffic forever. It was the electrically synchronized signal light.

By the following year, 75 experimental traffic lights atop pedestal posts had been installed at corners of various major Midtown intersections.

This system proved so successful that by 1934, the number of traffic lights in the city had grown to 7700. Although the art of timing the light sequence or "staggering" of the traffic devices took many years to refine, its was a success. It reduced the time needed to cross Manhattan by some eight minutes.

A fully automated traffic light system could not have come at a better time as the volume of traffic was about to increase dramatically.

In 1927, The Holland tunnel opened, thus increasing the number of cars driving into the city.

In 1931, the George Washington Bridge was placed into service.

By 1934, the volume of traffic in New York City had further exploded with the completion of the first four sections of the West Side Highway from Canal Street to West 48th Street. Construction of the Lincoln Tunnel also began in 1934 and was soon followed by Construction of the East River Drive in 1935.

In 1936 was the construction of both Queens-Midtown Tunnel and Tri-borough Bridge. It was obvious that with the new arrival of mobile commuters, an efficient system of expediting traffic had become essential for the city's survival. That's also why the need of Traffic Agents in the City is very important.

Traffic Enforcement Agents, TEA, had been employed by the City of New York as early as 1962 working alongside with Department of Transportation, D.O.T, to enforce the rules and regulations of New York City

.

Over the years, they have been referred to as brownies or meter maids; the proper civil service title is Traffic Enforcement Agent, code number 71651.

In 1996, Traffic Enforcement Agents merged with the New York Police Department, NYPD, to continue working and enforcing the rules and regulations of the City of New York.

Their position as Enforcement Agent was created because of the burden of traffic enforcement on police officers. The creation of TEAs freed up police officers to deal with harsher penal code violations, such as murders, rapes, robberies, etc.

An all-female work unit in its beginning, the agents were originally attached to the Department of Transportation working out of police precincts.

In 1966, men were offered the position. The uniform, which was originally blue, was changed to brown by then Transportation Commissioner Benjamin Ward.

In 1972, Commissioner Ward is also credited with instituting and promoting the level two position of traffic control.

In a major metropolis such as New York City, traffic flow is of the highest importance.

In our society, the transfer of goods and services is essential, enabling emergency response units to get their destinations in a timely fashion saving lives and property.

Just by simply enabling our everyday citizens to travel as swiftly and safely, it helps keep our city on an even tone.

Citizens get to work on time and get home on time, but it does not stop there. The Traffic Agents have pulled drivers to safety from burning vehicles. They have helped deliver babies and when necessary, they have captured or helped capture criminals.

During the 9/11 terrorist attacks, it was a Traffic Agent working at the Battery that first made the call about a low flying plane.

Agents Calvin Francis and Ismal Quinones also distinguished themselves on September 11, 2001, by putting other lives in front of their own. They help to pull victims from the rubble to safety.

In fact, on that day we had more heroes than we have space to mention. During the blackout and Hurricane Sandy, Traffic Agents worked around the clock to keep the city moving.

When an Amber Alert was activated, a Traffic Enforcement Agent was the one who was instrumental in observing motorists and restraining them while waiting for officers arrived.

Most recently, Traffic Enforcement Agents assisted in the Times Square terrorist attack on May 8, 2017, and the lower Manhattan bike path attack of October 31, 2017, not to mention the Con-Ed explosion in Chelsea on July 19, 2018. Traffic Enforcement Agents are as necessary as the air we breathe.

You may not like to get that ticket or being asked to make a turn you do not want to make, but New York City Traffic Enforcement Agents are necessary for the good of our city.

Their mission is to move traffic, save lives and reduce collisions. Traffic Enforcement Agents perform work of varying degrees of difficulty in traffic enforcement areas in New York City.

CHAPTER 17

NEW YORK CITY POLICE ACADEMY

The Police Academy opened in 1964. It was located at 235 East 20th Street in Manhattan, in the Gramercy Park area.

In 25 years, however, the facility was regarded as antiquated and obsolete. It no longer had capacity for larger classes of police trainees. Jeremy Travis, then the special counsel to the police commissioner, and years later the president of the John Jay College of Criminal Justice, urged construction of a new facility in 1985.

In 1989, Mayor Edward I. Koch promised a new facility to be in the South Bronx.

In 1992, during the mayoralty of David N. Dinkins, architects were chosen, and plans were released everything changed. Mayor Rudolph W. Giuliani canceled the plans for a new facility.

In 2007, plans for a new police training center were revived under Mayor Michael R. Bloomberg and Police Commissioner Raymond W. Kelly, with the new facility to be located on a 35-acre tract in College Point, Queens, that previously housed a police tow parking lot owned by the city.

The new facility is located at 130-30 28th Avenue, was constructed at a cost of $950 million, and has three buildings with a combined 730,000 square feet of space.

It is not easily accessible by public transit. The closest New York City Subway station, Flushing–Main Street, is more than one mile away.

Perkins & Will, Tactical Design, and Michael Fieldman were the project's architects, and Turner and STV were the construction managers.

The three buildings at the academy are a classroom and office building, eight stories, with an atrium, cafeteria, auditorium, and library. a "physical and tactical training" building, including a large gymnasium and swimming pool. There is also a central utilities plant.

The training facilities include simulated locations, such as a mock subway station, mock courthouses, and mock precinct houses. The main police academy site does not include a firing range, the NYPD range is located at Rodman's Neck in the Bronx, nor is the facility used for driving instruction NYPD officers train in driving at Floyd Bennett Field.

Seven other locations, including the vacant Flushing Airport, the Seaview Hospital and Farm Colony in Staten Island, and Floyd Bennett Field in Brooklyn, were considered before the College Point site was ultimately chosen.

Groundbreaking officially occurred in December 2009. Phase One opened in December 2015.

After the NYPD moved its academy to Queens, the fate of the old academy building was initially unclear.

In 2008 and 2013, residents and Manhattan Community Board 6 pushed to convert the eight-story building into a public school.

In October 2016, however, the NYPD opened its Candidate Assessment Center in the old building. The center recruits' applicants to join the police force.

CHAPTER 18

THE 1950 IMMENSE SCANDAL

This was the era of bookmakers and wire rooms. It was also the era of horse players with bankrolls and criminals in pin-striped suits. It was 1950, and a huge scandal. The police department was involved. The biggest scandal ever was about to break in the city that never sleeps....

At its center was a stocky, dazzlingly tailored, man with the fast accents of Flatbush. He had a nervous tic in his right eye. His name was Harry Gross. Even though he only 34 years old, he had been the superstar of gambling in the city for almost a decade.

Now, after years of insignificance, he found dead in California. It seems like an apparent suicide at the age of 69. He died in modest circumstances, facing the first drug charge of his life.

It was a world away from the elegant suite at the Towers Hotel in Brooklyn, where he reigned in the 1940's over a $20 million-a-year empire of 400 bookies, runners, accountants, and phone-handlers in 35 betting parlors in Manhattan, Brooklyn, the Bronx, Nassau County and northern New Jersey. Boasts of Payoffs

By today's standards, these establishments were hardly hidden. They lay wild and clanging, just beyond the unconvincing partitions of candy stores and soda fountains or little shops with dusty vacuum cleaners in their windows.

To keep the law at bay, Mr. Gross put hundreds of police officers from plainclothesmen to inspectors on his payroll. He bragged of having certain politicians in his pocket, as well.

Eventually, he said, his payoffs for protection totaled more than $1 million a year in cash and gifts that included cars, clothing, liquor, and other amenities.

A rackets-busting Brooklyn District Attorney, Miles F. McDonald, in a crackdown that made headlines for two years, arrested and squeezed testimony from a defiant Mr. Gross that led finally to the convictions of 22 policemen and the dismissal or resignation of 240 others.

The scandal, which encouraged sweeping police reforms, also saw the departure of Police Commissioner William P. O'Brien and other city officials and the resignation of Mayor William O'Dwyer, who was named Ambassador to Mexico by President Harry S. Truman during a cloud of accusations that were never fully answered.

Mr. Gross, who pleaded guilty to 66 charges, spent eight years in prison. In 1958, he moved to California. There, he was sent to jail for three years for manslaughter in the 1959 beating-death of his wife's grandfather.

He was later arrested several times for gambling, and last month was seized in a Los Angeles hotel on charges of trying to sell heroin to an undercover Federal agent.

Mr. Gross committed suicide by slashing his wrists at his modest home in Long Beach, California. He left a note saying he had decided to kill himself rather than go back to prison.

"He was a smooth, suave individual with gentlemanly manners," Mr. McDonald, now 81 years old. "He was smart as a whip. Without Harry, there was no fix." Mr. McDonald, who became a State Supreme Court Justice after rising to fame in the Gross case, expressed surprise that Mr. Gross had been arrested for selling drugs. "It would seem to me that Harry was too smart to be caught in a drug operation," he said.

Recalling the 1940's heyday of gambling in New York, Mr. McDonald said it was "just like the selling of liquor in Prohibition days - everybody ignored it, from the mob and police to the unions." The grafters found Mr. Gross central to its operation, he said.

"Once," he recalled, "when he went broke betting on basketball, he went to California and the police went and got him. They gambled him to $50,000 to run his operation again. They weren't making any money without him. With him, it was a fortune."

William J. Kelly, who was Mr. McDonald's administrative assistant during the long inquiry, recalled Mr. Gross as "a very neat dresser, very fancy and very confident of everything." He recalled extravagant hotel suites, wardrobes choked with suits and bars stocked with liquor.

"Of course, he had carte blanche with bookmaking activities at that time," Mr. Kelly said. "He had a setup that worked all right for him until the bubble burst. He knew his way around. You had to have an O.K. to operate, and it reached all the way to headquarters."

"Not everybody was on the take," Mr. Kelly said, but "it didn't stop at the precinct level or at the inspectors' level."

Son of Russian Immigrant Harold L. Fisher, a longtime Brooklyn attorney and former chairman of the Metropolitan Transportation Authority, recalled gambling and graft as systemic, with territories carved out by bookies and corrupt policemen.

"You almost had to get a license from the precinct to operate," Mr. Fisher noted.

Harry Gross was born in Brooklyn on Aug. 25, 1916, the third of four children of Bernard Gross, a Russian immigrant, and his wife, Rose Weintraub, who operated a small laundry in their flat and never stepped out of the poverty.

The boy quit school in the seventh grade to work. He swept floors, managed counters, and ran errands in dirty little stores that sold candy and comic books. In many of these places, small bets were taken as a sideline, and he learned how to make book.

By pocketing bets placed on losers, he began accumulating a small fortune as a teen-ager.

By 1940, at the age of 24, he had opened his own bookie joints. He quickly prospered. A thick heavily muscled young man with black brows and wavy hair, he became a flashy dresser, a man about town in his sporty convertible.

Mr. Gross once recalled how he began paying off the police. It was early in 1941. It was an episode that, by his own account, won him complete protection, from headquarters down to the officers on the beat.

"I was on the street taking business of a customer," he said, and a police officer "grabbed my hand where I was putting it in my pocket. He says, 'You're a sucker for working this way, cheating this way. You ought to get an O.K.'

"I asked him what he wanted, 50 or a hundred? He says, what won't hurt you? I gave him the 50 and asked him how I got an O.K. He says, "I'll let you know in a few days. "

He said he met the officer a few days later. "He says, 'I can get you an O.K. from the division, but you're a sucker if you don't go all the way. We won't bother you, but what about the men from the other commands?' I said I wanted to go all the way."

Business prospered until January 1942, when Mr. Gross was drafted into the Army. He lasted only four months and was discharged because a slight limp he had had since suffering a knee injury as a boy began suddenly to get worse. He was back in business by May.

In 1942, he also married a 22-year-old Brooklyn office worker, Lila Oransky. He bought a six-room brick-and-frame home in Atlantic Beach, L.I. When he was not attending to business in New York, he led a simple, middle-class, in the suburbs. The couple had two children.

"I knew he was a bookmaker," his wife recalled years later. "I wasn't ashamed of it. I had nothing to hide. There were lots of people who were bookmakers. It was a very common profession."

She said her husband gave her $60 to $65 a week to run the house. He never gave her no jewelry or other fancy presents.

Between 1942 and 1948, his bookmaking chain grew into an operation with horse parlors and wire rooms that reached across the city and into the suburbs.

The semimonthly payoffs to the police for protection were so large it took two men to carry the money. Morton Kapelsohn was one of Mr. Gross's top aides.

Mr. Kapelsohn said that he and Mr. Gross carried the cash to the Dugout, a Brooklyn restaurant, to make the protection payments.

"Gross gave me large packages of $50 and $100 bills," he testified later.

In the restaurant's kitchen, he said, Mr. Gross would pass the "ice" to representatives known as "cashiers," who would funnel it into channels of distribution.

Sometimes the fix-takers demanded double payments, "especially during Christmas month," he said.

On Sept. 15, 1950, in coordinated raids, investigators of the Kings County District Attorney's squad struck at all the betting parlors, and Mr. Gross himself was seized in his hotel suite.

After disobediently refusing to cooperate, Mr. Gross, facing a heavy prison sentence cracked and began naming names to a grand jury.

"Once he opened, the whole story was on the table," Mr. McDonald recalled. "His information flowed like water."

Largely based on his information, 21 police officers were indicted, and 56 others were named as conspirators in a sweeping indictment by a special rackets grand jury.

A year after his arrest, as the trial of the police officers began in 1951, a strange incident occurred. Mr. Gross, taken by two officers to visit his wife in Atlantic Beach. He escaped.

After a public uproar, he was found two days later at the $100 window of the Atlantic City Racetrack.

Mr. Gross explained that he "got fed up with hanging around all the time" and "wanted some action."

Officials said that he probably met someone and took a payoff to withdraw his cooperation from the case. Several days later, on the witness stand, he refused to testify. The case against all the indicted officers collapsed.

The court sentenced Mr. Gross, who had already pleaded guilty to the counts against him, to 12 years in prison, plus five years for contempt of court.

In 1952, he was again persuaded to testify against the officers, most of whom were convicted.

After being released in 1958, Mr. Gross moved to California. Trouble continued to bother him. He was charged with manslaughter in 1959 after his wife's 84-year-old grandfather was found dead of an apparent beating.

He was also charged with bookmaking violations in 1973. He was again convicted in a sweep of bookmaking operations in 11 California cities in 1975.

He started living a quietly alone in Long Beach. "As far as we were concerned, he was a low-profile criminal," George Fox, a homicide detective in Long Beach, stated.

Mr. Gross's body was found in a bathroom. His wrists were slashed, and pills were scattered around the room…

He killed himself, Mr. Fox said, "because he could not handle the idea of going back to jail and spending the rest of his life there."

John Gill, a police intelligence analyst, referring to Mr. Gross's drug arrest, said: "We were surprised that he would jeopardize himself this way. In narcotics, they play for keeps. Gambling was what he knew."

New York City has a long and rich history of scandal and corruption.

CHAPTER 19

THE HARLEM RIOT OF 1964

The Harlem riot of 1964 occurred between July 16 and 22, 1964. It began after James Powell, a 15-year-old African American, was shot and killed by police Lieutenant Thomas Gilligan in front of Powell's friends and about a dozen other witnesses.

Immediately after the shooting, about 300 students from Powell's school who were informed by the principal rallied. The shooting set off six consecutive nights of rioting that affected the New York City neighborhoods of Harlem and Bedford-Stuyvesant.

In total, 4,000 New Yorkers participated in the riots which led to attacks on the New York City Police Department, NYPD. Vandalism and looting in stores were all over the city. Several protesters were severely beaten by NYPD officers.

At the end of the conflict, reports counted one dead rioter, 118 injured, and 465 arrested.

The events of the Harlem riot of 1964 were recorded in the writings of two newspaper reporters, Fred C. Shapiro, and James W. Sullivan. They assembled testimonies from other reporters and from residents of each of the boroughs and gave testimony of their presence at the riots.

Consistently annoyed by the presence of young students on his stoops, Patrick Lynch, the superintendent of three apartment houses in Yorkville, at the time a predominantly working-class white area on the Upper East Side of Manhattan, hosed down the black students while insulting them according to them.

"Dirty niggers, I'll wash you clean"; this statement had been denied by Lynch. The angry wet black students started to pick up bottles and garbage-can lids and threw them at the superintendent. This immediately drew the attention of three Bronx boys, including James Powell.

Lynch then retreated to the inside of the building pursued by Powell, who according to a witness, "didn't stay two minutes."

As Powell exited the entrance, the off-duty police Lieutenant Thomas Gilligan, who witnessed the scene from a nearby shop, ran to the scene and shot at the 15-year-old James Powell three times.

The first round, said to be the warning shot, hit the apartment's window. The next shot hit Powell in the right forearm reaching the main artery just above the heart. The bullet lodged in his lungs.

Finally, the last one went through his abdomen and out his back. The autopsy concluded on the fatality of the chest wound in almost any circumstance. However, the pathologist said that Powell could have been saved suffering only the abdominal perforation with a fast response of the ambulance.

The sequence of events is still unclear on many aspects such as the spacing of the shots and, crucially, Powell's possession of a knife.

Lieutenant Gilligan's version of the actions

To the sound of broken glass, Gilligan ran to the apartment building holding his badge and gun. He first yelled, "I'm a police lieutenant. Come out and drop it."

He then fired the warning shot as he saw Powell raising the knife. With his gun, Gilligan blocked Powell's second attack deflecting the knife to his arm. The apparent attack led Gilligan to fire a third round that killed the young Powell.

In opposition, witnesses saw Powell ran into the building not carrying any knife. As he exited, some said he was laughing until the lieutenant shot him.

From the point of view of the French class which according to New York Times reporter, Theodore Jones, "have had the best view of the ensuing tragedy". When Gilligan pulled his gun, the young Powell threw up his right arm, not holding a knife but as a defensive gesture.

The most controversial episode remains the testimony of Cliff Harris, Powell's Bronx friend, interviewed the day following the death of James Powell.

On that morning, James Powell, Cliff Harris and Carl Dudley, left the Bronx around 7:30 A.M. Powell carried two knives on that day which he gave to each of his friends to be held for him.

On the scene, he asked for the knives back. Upon Dudley's refusal he asked Cliff who asked him why he wanted it back and then handed it over.

The knife, which was not seen on the crime scene now of the incident, was later found by a teacher, according to school principal France. The knife was situated in the gutter about eight feet from the body.

Lieutenant Thomas Gilligan served seventeen years in the Police Department and had a few notable entries to his record. Before the Powell incident, he had shot two other men. One of those men was trying to push him off a roof and the other much younger was looting cars in front of his apartment.

Let's talk about James Powell…

James Powell was a ninth grader in the Bronx attending summer school at the Robert F. Wagner, Sr., Junior High School on East 76th Street.

After his father's death, neighbors said the young boy had become "a little wild". He had four minor confrontations with the law. Twice he attempted to board a subway or bus without paying. He broke a car window and attempted robbery from which he was cleared.

CHAPTER 20

THE POLICE
BRUTALITY RIOTS

It all began on Thursday, July 16, 1964, day 1 of the riot had been surrounded by 75 police officers.

It happened right after the shooting of James Powell and the Police Department were securing the crime scene from approximately 300 people. The majority of were students. The confrontations between students and police officers predicted what was going to happen the next day.

Friday, July 17, 1964, 2nd day of the riot.

On that morning after the shooting, the Congress of Racial Equality, CORE, showed up at the school near the scene. They demanded a civilian review board to discipline the police officers. Instead, they were greeted by 50 police officers holding nightsticks.

Two hundreds pickets, mainly whites and Puerto Ricans, were situated in front of the school by noon, chanting "Stop killer cops!", "We want legal protection" and "End police brutality."

Saturday, July 18,1964 was the third day of the riots. On that July 18, the temperature went up to 92 °F, 33 °C, in Central Park and much higher on the pavement.

Two hundred and fifty people attended James Powell's funeral under strict supervision of barricaded police officers.

At the same time, another patrol was watching over a demonstration on the rising crime rate in Harlem. Both events ended peacefully with no incident. The CORE rally happened rather peacefully until most of the press corps had left.

Paul L. Montgomery stayed behind; except for a UPI summer intern on his first field assignment, Montgomery worked alone for most of the evening and became the source of information for what is to follow.

Reverend Nelson C. Dukes then called for action leading the march to the 28th precinct supported by Black Nationalist Edward Mills Davis and James Lawson.

After meeting with Inspector Prendergast, the committee addressed the crowd, but it was already too late. The crowd began to throw bottles and debris at the police line.

Soon the community took over rooftops and police shifted their goals to target those on the roofs. Easily accessible, rooftops were in bad shape and bricks, tiles and mortar were used as weapons. The policemen rapidly secured the rooftops arresting CORE members.

A group of rioters threw bottles and one hit Michael Doris in the face; the first police officer to be injured during the Harlem riot of 1964.

Subsequently, Inspector Pandergast instructed the force to clear the street after declaring that the crowd had become a disorderly gathering.

By 10 P.M., a thousand people had assembled at the intersection of the Seventh Avenue and 125th Street. "Go home, go home" shouted an officer in a way to disperse the crowd, but the crowd answered: "We are home, Baby."

The Tactical Patrol Force arrived on site and were attacked by bricks flying from rooftops. They started to break the crowd into smaller groups which created chaos. One group went down to 123rd Street and the aftermath could be seen the next morning by its destruction path.

Around 10:30 P.M. 22:30 ET, a group of rioters stopped in front of the Theresa hotel where a Molotov cocktail was thrown on a police car injuring one officer.

Police officers received permission to draw their firearms and fired into the air to occupy the Harlem area. Later TPF, Tactical Police Force, found one dead man due to the firing of a .38 caliber.

It was after the first round had been fired that reporter were sent back to Harlem. Shortly after the force started firing, an ordnance truck from the Bronx was loaded with ammunition to support the officers. Many Harlemites, exiting the subway and bars, got caught up in the riot and later realized that they were being pursued by the police.

The chaos finally ended at 8 o'clock ,08:00 ET, in the morning on Lenox Street, where what was left of the mobs had regrouped and then were dispersed by massive reinforcement.

According to Inspector Pendergast's announcement, one rioter died, 12 policemen and 19 civilians were injured, and 30 were arrested. Over 22 stores had been looted. The report of Pandergast was hotly contested by the hospital that counted 7 gunshot wounds and 110 persons who considered their injuries worth intensive care.

The fourth day, Sunday, July 19, through Monday, July 20, 1964

Commissioner Murphy distributed a statement to every church in Harlem after the incident of Saturday night. He stated: "In our estimation, this is a crime problem and not a social problem!"

Later that day, Malcolm X, Black Nationalist Leader answered, "There are probably more armed Negroes in Harlem than in any other spot-on earth" - "If the people who are armed get involved in this, you can bet they'll really have something on their hands." The hostility between the community and the New York Police_Department heightened as insulted policemen as well as firemen who would later use hoses on protestors in broad daylight throughout Sunday.

The NYPD conceded the ineffectiveness of tactical techniques, such as mounted police and tear gas, which were having no actual effect on the rooftop threat.

James Farmer, national director of CORE, who attended the riot, confirmed the assumption of police brutality, and testified to seeing bullet holes in windows and walls of the Theresa Hotel. He also claimed Inspector Pandergast was at the origin of the riot.

Meanwhile, a meeting of the Black Citizens Council had taken place at the Mount Morris Presbyterian Church. The overall voice was for "Guerilla warfare!" against an occupying NYPD, but the vast majority agreed on thoughtful action. "If we must die, we must die scientifically."

Bayard Rustin, engineer of the March on Washington and the New York's first school boycott, received cries of disapproval from the crowd and then decided to lead a crew of 75 volunteers to keep an outpost on the 125th Street and 8th Avenue, constituting an aide for teenagers and women in the closing riot.

Other speakers at the rally tried to reason with the crowd to join in a peaceful protest. An individual didn't want to be photographed and brought the crowd into a struggle, beating two reporters.

The police line on the sidewalk witnessed the scene but decided not to move or to intervene. The mob moved to the Delany Funeral Home where a service for Powell's death had been scheduled for 8 P.M.

At that point, someone threw a bottle at the police and the police threw it back at the crowd. The riot had started once again. Bricks and bottles were falling from rooftops like rain from clouds. Bayard Rustin and other speakers were trying to convince the rioters to save their souls, but they were booed, and the crowd shouted back at them: "Tom, Uncle Tom."

After a Molotov cocktail had been thrown, some police lowered their guns and wounded two young men as they charged. The riot was scattered by midnight and grew out of proportion once again after some disturbance.

Many Molotov Cocktails were used by protesters. Two more young men were wounded by bullets and one police officer had a heart attack. The violence ended around 1.30 A.M. and reports counted 27 policemen and 93 civilians injured, 108 arrested and 45 stores looted. Hospitals however counted more than 200 entries in their registries.

The 5th day of the riots, Monday, July 20,
through Tuesday Evening, July 21.

The situation was quieter in the street of Harlem on Monday. Paul R. Screvane confirmed that a New York County grand jury would investigate the murder of James Powell and at the same time, announced Mayor Wagner's hasty return.

The riot started after the UN demonstration to protest terrorism and genocide committed against Black Americans. The events that followed greatly resembled those of the Sunday riot, although at the end of the night, a reinforcement call was made for Bedford-Stuyvesant, foreshadowing the growing social issue that it became.

The conflict between African Americans and police at Fulton Street and Nostrand Avenue on July 21, in Brooklyn.

The Brooklyn CORE branch had prepared an all-day march for Monday in support of the rioters in Harlem. They protested the shooting of the young Powell and denounced police brutality against Harlemites.

After blocking four main intersections of Bedford-Stuyvesant, the CORE members and Brooklynites assembled at Nostrand and Fulton where they set up a rally.

As the speakers changed, the crowd became more emotional and was no longer paying attention to the rally. The police enforcement, which had kept a low profile in Bedford-Stuyvesant, suddenly called for reinforcements. CORE members tried to control the crowd and in a last attempt told them to go back home.

At that point, a thousand people were standing on the street corner, infuriated and ready for action. To the sound of sirens and tires, the reinforcements arrived at their destination and the police charged the mob, making no apparent distinction between innocents and enemies. The commotion stopped a little after 7 A.M. and CORE announced a new rally in not less than twelve hours.

The 6th day of the riots, Tuesday night, July 21, through Wednesday, July 22…

Tuesday in Brooklyn started by a meeting of all V.I.P. of Black organizations with Captain Edward Jenkins, commanding officer of the 79th precinct, at the Bedford YMCA.

Over the day, they looked at possible explanations of the riot's cause and at Lieutenant Gilligan's case.

That night, CORE's demonstration was replaced by Black Nationalist speakers who, every week, were present at this very same spot. The difference is that on a regular Tuesday there was no crowd to listen to them.

Tuesday, July 21, was certainly an opportunity out of the ordinary for the Black Nationalist Party to spread its ideas to the Black community.

After a 20-minute speech, the crowd started to be anxious even though the speaker, becoming worried about the situation, changed the tone of what he was saying and tried to convince the crowd to remain calm. The riot started again, and police charged the mob while angry rioter threw bottles and debris at them. Everything was under control by 2 A.M. on Wednesday

Meanwhile, The New York Times reported that a police investigation was underway into extremist agitators, specifically Black Nationalist and the Harlem Progressive Labor Club, the Harlem branch of the Progressive Labor Party.

According to the report, acting Mayor Paul R. Screvane consistently stood by this accusation and cause for the police investigation.

On Wednesday night, a troop of mounted police was set at the four corners of the intersection of Fulton and Nostrand. The buildings were lower and the street wider, reducing the risk of using horses for crowd control.

A sound truck with a NAACP logo had been driving down the streets of Bedford-Stuyvesant during the day and parked where the Black Nationalists had set a podium on the day before.

When the crowd that had formed in front of the truck was of a reasonable size, Fleary, one of the NAACP workers, addressed the crowd. He claimed that Bedford-Stuyvesant was a "community of law".

Furthermore, he insisted that riots weren't how they were going to get what they wanted. The mob seemed to generally agree with him until a group of men, among them four were wearing a green beret, appeared across the street and approached the sound truck.

They began to rock the truck while the mob got more and more agitated. Fleary will remain the only community leader affirming the presence of external agitators.

When Fleary lost the control of the microphone, the police charge to rescue the NAACP crew had the effect of starting another riot.

CHAPTER 21

THE RALLY

A scheduled rally organized by the Congress of Racial Equality, CORE, in the afternoon of Saturday, July 18 changed its focus upon the arrival of Louis Smith, a CORE field secretary.

The rally had for objective to clarify on the missing of three civil right workers in Mississippi, thus looked over the shooting of James Powell as well as pointed out police brutality as a constant threat upon the Black community.

The gathering seemed to end quietly leaving "the crowd excited, but not unruly."

After most of the reporters had left, Judith Howell, a young high-school student, and a member of the Bronx chapter of CORE climbed on a chair and said, "We got a civil rights bill and along with the bill we got Barry Goldwater and a dead black boy, this shooting of James Powell was murder!"

After her speech the cry was for action and was followed by Reverend Nelson C. Dukes from the Fountain Springs Baptist Church who, after his 20 minutes long speech, led the crowd to the 28th precinct supported by Black Nationalist Edward Mills Davis and James Lawson.

Upon arrival, the police department was in motion and Inspector Pandergast accommodated the committee formed by Dukes, Charles Russell, East River CORE, Charles Taylor and Newton Sewell, Black Nationalist. Their only demand was the suspension of Lieutenant Gilligan.

CHAPTER 22

THE JAMES MARCUS SCANDAL
1965-1968

James Marcus had few achievements in life. At age 35, his main path to development was his 1962 marriage to Lily Lodge. She was the daughter of John David Lodge, former governor of Connecticut and ambassador to Spain.

In 1965, Marcus connected himself to the mayoral campaign of John V. Lindsay.

In March 1966, Lindsay brought Marcus to City Hall and appointed him an assistant to the mayor charged with running the Department of Water Supply, Gas and Electricity.

Lindsay, confused by Marcus's pedigree by marriage, did not know Marcus was broke and in debt. Marcus's financial needs brought him under the influence of an experienced con man, Herbert Itkin.

Itkin earned his living brokering deals between corrupt labor union leaders who controlled union pension funds and marginal businessmen unable to get legitimate loans.

Itkin had also ingratiated himself with the CIA, had an informer's relationship with the FBI and, above all, was supremely street smart.

Itkin met Marcus during Lindsay's 1965 mayoral campaign and they became friends.

Under Itkin's tutelage, Marcus, as head of the Department of Water Supply, Gas and Electricity, demanded kickbacks from contractors repairing water main breaks. The small water main contracts yielded small money.

Marcus needed $100,000 to free himself from the loan sharks who had lent Marcus funds to meet his stock market debts. Marcus's opportunity came when his agency offered a million-dollar emergency contract to clean New York City's Jerome Park Reservoir in the Bronx.

There was mud lying on the bottom of the 96-acre reservoir had gotten into New York City's drinking water causing water in some areas of the city to appear dirty. The solution was to clean the mud from the reservoir.

Marcus's target was Henry Fried, the owner of S.T. Grand Co., a major contractor and probably the only local contractor capable of cleaning a reservoir as large as Jerome Park.

Marcus, under Itkin's guidance, extorted a $40,000 kickback from Henry Fried, which was never fully paid due to Marcus's ineptness and Fried's superior sophistication in such matters.

Marcus and Itkin in 1967 developed a more involved kickback system involving Consolidated Edison. The utility wanted to add additional power lines to towers built on the City's right-of-way for the aqueduct that carried water from upstate reservoirs to the city.

Consolidated Edison faced an urgent need to bring additional upstate electric power to New York City to prevent another City-wide blackout as had happened in November 1966.

Consolidated Edison needed a permit from Marcus's Department of Water Supply, Gas and Electricity.

Marcus and Itkin's plan was to squeeze Consolidated Edison by delaying the permit until Consolidated Edison agreed to award major construction contracts to S. T. Grand Co., the owner of which was Henry Fried, the same person who bribed Marcus for the Jerome Park Reservoir job. Henry Fried would then kickback a percentage of the Consolidated Edison revenue to Marcus and Itkin.

Marcus and Itkin's plan went nowhere until Carmine DeSapio joined the conspiracy and advised Marcus and Itkin how to properly manage the extortion conspiracy.

DeSapio, sophisticated in such matters, advised Marcus and Itkin to separate from the Mafia. They also would have to separate from union conspirators with whom they were working.

Fried and DeSapio were convicted after a trial in federal court in Manhattan. Both received jail sentences. Marcus pleaded guilty and served eleven months in prison.

Itkin, who became a cooperating witness, succeeded in entering the federal witness protection program. Consolidated Edison got its permit, but the Lindsay Administration, now alerted to the value of the aqueduct permit, raised the franchise fee considerably, so much so, that it would have been cheaper for Consolidated Edison's customers if Consolidated Edison had paid Marcus the bribe.

CHAPTER 23

WILLIAM M. TWEED

Unlike James Marcus, William M. Tweed successfully served as a municipal official with major accomplishments. He enjoyed unparalleled popularity as an elected official and political boss, became rich by trading on his public office in accordance with the mores of the day, and did not need an Itkin to show him how.

Between 1868 and 1870 Boss Tweed was at the height of his power. He had engineered the election of Tammany faithful Joseph Hoffman as governor of New York State; the election of A. Oakey Hall as Mayor of New York City; and the election of enough members of the New York State Assembly and Senate to constitute a majority.

Tweed then bribed the state legislature into enacting a new charter for the City of New York which restored to the city power over the city's finances and other activities.

Tweed's popularity reached a buildup as the public, including The New York Times, praised Tweed for ending State control of the City's government.

The new charter, however, placed near total control of City government in four officials known later as the Tweed Ring. Boss Tweed became the commissioner of public works, A. Oakey Hall as the elected mayor, Richard Connolly as the appointed comptroller, and Peter B. Sweeny as commissioner of parks.

In April 1870, also at Tweed's request, the State Legislature abolished the New York County Board of Supervisors which had been responsible for building a new county courthouse on Chambers Street.

The legislature created a new Board of Audit to replace the Board of Supervisors. The new Board of Audit consisted of three people. They were A. Oakey Hall as mayor, Richard Connolly as appointed comptroller, and Boss Tweed as president of the old Board of Supervisors.

The old Board of Supervisors had not paid many of the invoices for the work on the new county courthouse, invoices which totaled in the millions. These unpaid invoices were a huge opportunity for implantation for the new Board of Audit.

The Tweed Ring's scheme to profit was simple: pad the contractors' invoices by 50 percent or more. When the City paid the padded invoices, the contractors kicked back the money to the Ring.

The county courthouse, originally budgeted at $250,000, ultimately cost the city more than $6 million in padded invoices.

In 1871, when Tweed was still enjoying his celebrity as a result of the new charter, three important adversaries appeared. The New York Times started editorially attacking the Tweed Ring as corrupt; Harper's Weekly began printing cartoons drawn by Thomas Nast attacking Tweed. Tweed's Democratic Party adversary Samuel J. Tilden began a campaign against Tweed.

Harpers and the Times attacked Tweed openly, while Tilden waited for his moment. The attacks continued through the first six months of 1871 but lacked impact because neither the Times nor Harpers had facts to support their attacks. No one had proof of the kickbacks.

A major crack in the Tweed Ring's defenses occurred when a dissatisfied Tammany politician, unhappy with his share of the spoils and carrying a grudge against Tweed, delivered to The New York Times a package of secretly obtained handwritten copies of the padded payment records from the comptroller's office.

On July 22, 1871, the Times began publishing the amounts paid and to whom they were paid. The Times headline read:

"The Secret Accounts: Proofs of Undoubted Frauds Brought to Light." The surprisingly payments paid by the Board of Audit created a public sensation. The amount paid bore no relation to the work performed.

The Tweed Ring members panicked after the Times published "The Secret Accounts" and the reformers became encouraged to act.

The reformers went to court seeking to halt further payments and force a review of past payments. Judge George G. Barnard, a Tammany politician, found himself cornered and signed a court order on September 6, 1871, halting all payments by the city.

Under the order the city could not even pay salaries to city workers, who were soon protesting and demanding payment of their salaries.

A burglary greatly increased the drama. The New York Times possessed handwritten copies of the payment records, but the actual records remained locked in Comptroller Connelly's office in the new courthouse.

Sometime during the weekend of September 9-10, 1871, three burglars broke into the comptroller's office in the new courthouse and stole the account records from 1869 -70, and nothing else!

The burglars carried the paper records to the janitor's apartment in the courthouse and burned them. Two weeks later the three burglars were identified and caught, but they never disclosed who they were working for when they stole the crucial records.

The public was now fully stimulated, but no one had yet shown that any of the money from the padded payments had flowed to Tweed or a member of the Ring.

Known as Slippery Dick, Comptroller Connolly, to save himself, sided secretly with the reformers. Connolly met at night with Samuel J. Tilden. Tilden, an ambitious upper-class lawyer and leader of the wealthy, professional "Swallowtail" wing of the Democratic Party, was a personal and political enemy of Tweed.

Tilden had been waiting for an opportunity to overthrow Tweed. With Connelly now available, Tilden created of a complex strategy that would injure Tweed and put Tilden in control of the city.

Tilden demanded that Connolly appoint Tilden's former law partner and loyal reformer, Andrew Haswell Green, as deputy comptroller. Tilden did not want Connolly to resign because under the charter he could not be removed.

With Comptroller Connolly a figure head but still in office, authority over the City's money shifted to Tilden and to the newly appointed Deputy Comptroller Andrew Haswell Green.

Samuel J. Tilden then closed the circle on the padded invoices by recreating Tweed's banking transactions. Tilden obtained the personal banking records of the Tweed Ring from the Broadway Bank.

By analyzing Tweed's bank deposit slips and checks, Tilden traced the checks paid by the city as published by the New York Times to the contractor's bank accounts. Tweed's bank deposit was also analyzed. They were made into the accounts of the Ring members.

Tilden gave his brilliantly prepared charts to The New York Times. On October 26, 1871, they began publishing the damaging proof that Tweed and the Tweed Ring had been paid off.

Of the $5,710,913 paid by the city to the various contractors, Tilden showed that $932,858 ultimately ended up in Tweed's bank account.

With Tilden's evidence that the Tweed Ring had benefitted from the padded invoices, the Ring collapsed. Tweed was arrested on October 27, 1871, the day after the Times began publishing Tilden's charts.

In December 1873, a jury convicted Tweed of 204 counts of criminal misdemeanor. Tweed was sentenced to 12 years in prison. In December 1875 Tweed escaped to Cuba and then Spain.

Tweed was identified because of Nast's drawings. He was recaptured and brought back to New York City and was returned to jail.

Tweed, in hoping to be release, testified openly for eleven days in 1877 before a committee of the New York City board. He was not release. Tweed died in jail on April 12, 1878, at age 55.

Let me mention that Tweed was the only member of the Ring to go to prison. A. Oakey Hall was tried three times; two hung juries and an acquittal after the third trial.

Parks Commissioner Sweeny fled to Paris. He was not indicted and returned to New York City in 1886. Comptroller Connolly fled New York City and lived abroad until he died in 1899.

CHAPTER 24

HARRY GROSS AND WILLIAM O'DWYER 1940 – 1951

Crime reporters Norton Mockridge and Robert H. Prall, in The Big Fix. Implantation and corruption in the world's largest city, Henry Holt & Company, 1954, painted a full picture of the Harry Gross gambling empire.

The clash between Mayor William O'Dwyer and his successor as Brooklyn District Attorney, Miles McDonald, over McDonald's investigation into gambling.

At the end, hundreds of police officers were convicted, retired, demoted or resigned, and Mayor William O'Dwyer was forced to resign.

William O'Dwyer Brooklyn District Attorney
from 1939 to 1945

O'Dwyer was born in Ireland in 1890. He immigrated to the United States in 1910. O'Dwyer worked as a laborer, and then as a New York City police officer. He was studying while was police officer. He attended law classes at night at Fordham Law School.

O'Dwyer was elected Brooklyn District Attorney in 1939. As District Attorney he made his reputation prosecuting Murder, Inc., a vicious shakedown, protection, and murder-for-hire organization that terrorized Brooklyn shop owners.

District Attorney O'Dwyer's most prominent witness against Murder Inc. was Abe "Kid Twist" Reles, a Murder Inc. gangster who turned state's witness.

Reles was a marked man. District Attorney O'Dwyer placed Reles under custody at the Half Moon Hotel in Coney Island protected around the clock by a guard of six cops.

On the morning of November 12, 1941, with five of the six cops present at their stations, Reles went out of the sixth-floor window and fell to his death, taking with him any hope of convicting Murder Inc. members.

How Reles went through the window, jumped, thrown, or slipped was a mystery. That mystery was never settled. O'Dwyer claimed that Reles accidentally slipped to his death trying to escape, but Reles was in more danger free than protected.

Guess what? Reles had never tried to escape before. District Attorney O'Dwyer failed to investigate Reles' death. This failure fueled O'Dwyer's reputation as a reluctant prosecutor of major crime figures such as Joe Adonis, whose indictment O'Dwyer allowed to be dismissed.

Also, there was Albert Anastasia a vicious criminal who had been one of the founders of Murder Inc. Reles' death meant that O'Dwyer never had to go to trial against Anastasia.

In 1945 William O'Dwyer was elected Mayor of the City of New York and Miles McDonald was elected Brooklyn's District Attorney.

McDonald was born in 1905, grew up in Brooklyn and graduated from Holy Cross. After college he worked at a law firm while attending night classes at Fordham Law School.

He became an assistant D.A. in 1939 under Brooklyn District Attorney O'Dwyer. His work brought him to the attention of Brooklyn's political leaders. In 1945 he was elected District Attorney when O'Dwyer became mayor.

Gambling was a huge concern in the 1940s. Bookies operated openly out of storefronts, drug stores, delicatessens, and street corners.

Individual bookies were organized into groups and connected by telephones to central offices from which the boss managed the enterprise.

These illegal activities occurred more or less in the open and were the source of organized payoffs to police officers, including payoffs to officers of the highest ranks.

The conqueror of Brooklyn's gambling empire was Harry Gross. Gross was born in 1916, quit school in the seventh grade and worked in small stores where he noticed how bets were made and learned how to make book.

By 1940 he had opened his own bookie joints. Between 1942 and 1949 Gross had bookies operating out of 30 horse rooms and was the part owner of several night clubs and restaurants. He was paying $50,000 a month to police for protection.

Frequently, he gave gifts to as many as 200 police officers. Such gifts were suits, ties, hats, television sets and furs. Gross's gambling empire at its height annually grossed $20 million, of which $1 million was paid to police officers for protection.

O'Dwyer, as Brooklyn District Attorney, had ignored gambling and the police corruption that protected it. The new District Attorney Miles McDonald made gambling a major target, but quickly found that the police would not cooperate.

Mayor O'Dwyer was in control of the police department. When McDonald asked the police to check a bookie operation at a particular location, the police would investigate and report back that they could not find any gambling.

McDonald found a way to outmaneuver the police department. He got the department to assign 29 rookie police officers who had just graduated from the Police Academy as investigators for the Brooklyn District Attorney's office.

McDonald wanted cops assigned to the District Attorney's office who had not already been corrupted by the payoff system. With his rookies, McDonald made significant arrests of local bookies. McDonald's success brought him into conflict with Mayor O'Dwyer.

In the spring of 1950 McDonald raided a bookie establishment in Bay Ridge, Brooklyn. The bookies were outraged. They declared that they made regular payments to the police and were entitled to operate without being arrested.

The bookies were convicted but refused to identify the police officers they had paid. Captain John G. Flynn, the commander of the precinct in which the Bay Ridge bookies operated, was called to the grand jury and denied that he had received information that the bookie operation existed.

On July 16, 1950, Captain Flynn committed suicide. Mayor O'Dwyer seized upon the suicide to imply that Flynn had been pushed into taking his own life by McDonald's gambling investigation.

Mayor O'Dwyer attended Captain Flynn's funeral and ordered 6,000 uniformed police officers to stand in formation for two hours at the funeral. In the press after the funeral O'Dwyer was quoted calling McDonald's gambling investigations a "witch hunt."

Mayor O'Dwyer overplayed his hand. McDonald repeatedly made headlines on gambling and police corruption, and it was widely known that in 1941 O'Dwyer had had a meeting with Frank Costello, the crime boss.

O'Dwyer, in addition, had been unable to refute fully an accusation that in 1949 while mayor he had taken $10,000 in cash from the Uniformed Firemen's Association.

In the summer of 1950 Edward J. Flynn, the powerful Democratic Party boss of the Bronx, moved to overthrow Mayor O'Dwyer. Flynn knew that McDonald's gambling investigations would continue to reveal corruption in Mayor O'Dwyer's police department and that this would finish O'Dwyer as a political leader. Flynn feared that O'Dwyer's presence would hurt Senator Herbert Lehman who was up for reelection in 1950.

In July 1950, Flynn, who was also a national Democratic Committeeman, met with President Harry S. Truman. At the meeting President Truman agreed that if O'Dwyer resigned as mayor Truman would appoint O'Dwyer as ambassador to Mexico. Flynn met with O'Dwyer in a late-night meeting at Gracie Mansion. At the meeting O'Dwyer agreed to resign and accept the ambassadorship.

On August 14, 1950, the White House announced that New York City Mayor William O'Dwyer would resign as mayor and become ambassador to Mexico. The public was stunned. O'Dwyer explained to the surprised press that "my country's needs are first and foremost in my mind," and that "there was much critical work to be done," as ambassador to Mexico.

O'Dwyer left office two weeks later August 31, 1950, after serving only eight months into his second term. Vincent R. Impellitteri, City Council President, became Acting Mayor and was elected Mayor in November 1950.

On August 15, 1950, the day after the announcement of Mayor O'Dwyer's resignation, the Brooklyn grand jury investigating gambling filed a report. The grand jury demanded that O'Dwyer stop interfering with the gambling investigation, declared that O'Dwyer's witch hunt charge was unsupported, and proclaimed McDonald's investigation honest.

On September 15, 1950, two weeks after Mayor O'Dwyer left office, District Attorney McDonald's efforts finally paid off. McDonald arrested Harry Gross, head of Brooklyn's gambling syndicate. McDonald finally had a witness who could name top police officers on the take. Gross testified in the grand jury which then indicted high level police officers.

The trial of the first eighteen police officers indicted on Gross' testimony began on September 10, 1951. At the conclusion of the second day of jury selection Gross, guarded by police, asked to visit his wife.

During the home visit Gross slipped away and disappeared. Gross drove to New Jersey where, Mockridge and Prall report, Gross met with Meyer Lansky, the organized crime figure, and Willie Moretti, a New Jersey gangster. They gave Gross $60,000. Gross then droves to Atlantic City where he was recognized, captured, and returned to Brooklyn.

When Gross was taken back to the courtroom on September 18, 1951, he refused to testify. Gross shouted, "I won't answer any questions," and "I ain't coming back." Judge Samuel Leibowitz held Gross in contempt of court, but, without Gross' testimony, Judge Leibowitz was forced to dismiss the indictments against the eighteen police officers.

Judge Leibowitz, famed as the defender of the Scottsboro Boys, cited Gross for contempt 60 times and sentenced him to twelve years in prison. Gross never testified in a criminal trial but did later testify in police department civil disciplinary trials.

As a result of Gross' testimony and McDonald's investigation some fifty-two police officers were dismissed from the force and more than four hundred retired or resigned.

Gross was released from prison in 1958 and moved to California where he was put in jail on a manslaughter charge, released and then arrested again. He committed suicide in 1986.

Ambassador O'Dwyer testified before the Senate Crime Investigating Committee in March 1951, where he made a very poor witness, and before grand juries in Manhattan and Brooklyn.

On May 1, 1951, the Senate Crime Investigating Committee, in a 195-page report, charged O'Dwyer with accepting gambling, rackets, murders and police corruption. Manhattan District Attorney Frank Hogan asked O'Dwyer to return from Mexico and testify before a Manhattan grand jury.

O'Dwyer refused and never testified. O'Dwyer resigned as ambassador to Mexico in December 1952. He continued to live in Mexico until 1960 and died in New York City in 1964. Miles McDonald was reelected Brooklyn District Attorney and in 1952 was elected a State Supreme Justice.

In 1971, McDonald left the bench and became counsel to the law firm of Shea & Gould.

CHAPTER 25

CIVILIAN IN NYPD

Civilian members play critical roles in maintaining the NYPD's status as the nation's largest, best trained, most effective, and most technologically advanced law enforcement agency.

In association with uniformed members of the service, civilians work around the clock to keep New York City the safest big city in America.

In every area of the department, civilian members perform a wide variety of important duties.

At the present time, there are more than 17,000 civilian employees in the NYPD. They are a team of public servants dedicated to help the police officers and to help the city's many communities.

The history of civilian contributions to the NYPD and the city is rich and varied.

As you read you will understand the past and present of the work civilians did and are still doing in the New York City Police Department.

Let's look at the past....

In 1844, New York City, which then comprised only Manhattan and a small part of the Bronx, was a cosmopolitan community of 360,000 people in a state of dynamic growth.

From 1658 until then, public safety in New York City was maintained using a "watchman" system implemented by the Dutch.

This system was unable to control rising crime. The Municipal Police, the predecessor of our modern Police Department, was established.

The force consisted of 889 men, led by Chief of Police George Matsell. Those officers were sworn to protect life and property of those citizens back in 1658.

By 1898, there were 3.6 million people in the city, served by 7,457 police.

Civilians have been employed by the department for most of its history.

In 1898, civilians served primarily in clerical and custodial positions. Today, the population of New York exceeds 8 million and stretches over an area of more than 319 square miles.

The department, headquarter is at One Police Plaza. This building is in lower Manhattan. It performs a huge range of functions that affect many areas of city life. Uniformed members of all ranks now number more than 35,000.

In addition, the department employs about 15,300 full time and 2,300 part time civilians in over 200 titles, many of which require licensure and advanced, technical, graduate, and doctoral degrees.

Civilians come from more than a hundred countries. They speak many different languages. Most civilian employees reside in the five boroughs of New York. Several have dedicated more than 10 years of service to the department.

As far back as 1845, in the earliest days of the NYPD, there were civilian employees in the department.

Today, 175 years later, civilians are an essential part of the job. These workers were primarily utilized in clerical and custodial positions in the early years.

The civilians today serve with dedication and commitment in different job titles.

Civilian members of the department have played an important, and at times an unpredicted, role throughout the history of the greatest police department in the world.

In the early years, men predominated in the civilian ranks, but today, most of the civilian workforce in the NYPD are women.

In 1898, when the greater city of New York was merged and the modern police department emerged, most civilians were custodial workers and matrons. Those positions freed police officers to patrol the streets of the city.

One of the department's most notable civilian employees, Theodore Roosevelt, was sworn in 1895 to head the four-member Board of Police Commissioners.

Prior to 1901, a board of four to six commissioners jointly ran the department. Roosevelt had no prior law enforcement experience. He was appointed to a term of six years and earned an annual salary of $5,000.

Although Roosevelt only stayed with the NYPD for two years, he set the standard for fighting police corruption and establishing professional policing.

As one of his final acts as Governor of New York before becoming Vice President of the United States, Roosevelt signed legislation that replaced the police commission with a single commissioner. He was Michael Cotter.

Murphy became the first Police Commissioner in 1901…

In 1906, Police Commissioner Theodore A. Bingham introduced the concept of civilianization as we know it today. Commissioner Bingham's proposal called for the identification of police officers assigned to clerical positions. He pointed out who should be returned to patrol duties and replaced by non-uniformed civilians.

To address manpower shortages, Commissioner Bingham recommended that civilian employees fill the officers

previously performing clerical duties.

In the late 1930s and 1940s, Mayor Fiorello LaGuardia made intensive efforts to civilianize the police force. The number of civilians increased from 300 to 1,291 during this period.

Civilianization once again emerged in the 1950s with the introduction of the school crossing guard program. School crossing guard program remains in the NYPD.

School Crossing Guards is an important resource of the NYPD. At the time, the Police Benevolent Association opposed the idea of replacing police officers at school crossings.

In 1960, the cadet position was introduced, and followed by the Police Trainee Program in 1964. These initiatives had the dual benefit of providing a pool of civilian employees to perform non-enforcement duties, while at the same time maintaining a roster of candidates interested in pursuing a uniformed police career.

In 1968, a civilian position was created to increase job specifications and improve management's freedom in assigning duties and work hours. This was the first written test for the title of police administrative aide. It was given that year.

In the early 1970s, uniformed strength reached 31,859 with 2,159 civilians, 93.7% vs. 6.3%. A massive plan to hire 2,300 civilian employees began in 1972.

The department's civilian staff almost doubled in the first year, but the city experienced unrelated financial difficulties. There was a hiring freeze for both civilians and uniformed jobs. It took effect in 1974. Civilian hiring efforts only resumed in 1979.

Throughout the modern-day timeline of civilianization, many members have risen to the top of their fields. Their success is a testament to their determination and perseverance to excel under challenging circumstances.

The performance of certain duties by civilians has gained wide acceptance over time.

For example, today's residents and members of the department don't think twice about school crossing guards protecting children at school crossings.

Today, practically all the civilian job titles in the Police Department have promotional career ladders. It is the responsibility of all civilian employees to maintain a level of personal excellence and to take an active role in the advancement of their own careers.

During the mid-1960s the department was attempting to attract better educated professional civilian employees. Eligibility requirements for the department were stricter than for other city clerical positions.

The title included an age-range limit of 19 to 29 years of age. The first written test for the title of Police Administrative Aide was given in March 1968.

Forty men were hired from the first promotions list. The title of police administrative aide has become the predominant civilian title in the Police Department. The title was opened to women in 1970, and today it is primarily staffed by women.

In 1968, Chief of Personnel George McManus requested the establishment of the title of senior police administrative aide with the goal of developing a career path for the new cadre of civilian employees.

From all appearances, it seemed as though there was interest in cultivating a group of career civilian employees.

Yet, although the title of Senior Police Administrated Aide was established in 1969, it was not until 1972 that a test was given. No further promotional step was provided in the job specifications.

Unexpectedly, the hope for a career ladder turned into a simple step stool. It was not until 1978 that SPAAs were included in the direct line of promotion to Principal Administrative Associate, leading to eligibility to take the Administrative Manager examination.

Finally, an actual career path had been established. Today PAAs are essential to the NYPD, carrying out a variety of duties within precincts and administrative offices across the organization.

Many civilian titles offer the opportunity for advancement. Employees who have been appointed from a Civil Service exam list can advance through promotional exams.

The opportunity to advance to a higher position within the same job category is called a career ladder. Advancement through career ladders offers salary increases, new challenges, and greater responsibility.

The existence of a career ladder is important to both employee morale and to maintaining a capable workforce. The career ladders offer employees the chance to advance in satisfying careers and make sure that trained and talented employees have a future within the department.

Civilian members of the New York City Police Department have a unique opportunity to explore a wide variety of job titles and roles within the NYPD.

The highest-ranking civilian in the NYPD is, in fact, the Police Commissioner. The Police Commissioner, who serves at the request of the mayor, is appointed to a five-year term to manage the Department to meet the public's need for police services.

The Police Commissioner provides leadership, direction, and control of department governance, administration, and discipline.

The First Deputy Commissioner serves as the executive aide to the Police Commissioner and as Acting Police Commissioner in the Commissioner's absence.

The First Deputy Commissioner assists the Police Commissioner in the administration of the business affairs of the department. The First Deputy Commissioner also manages the department's training, support, and disciplinary function.

The NYPD is a massive organization which oversees more than 50,000 employees who work across New York City in various commands.

The department relies on its forward-thinking leadership

staff to motivate and inspire employees, create innovative plans and policies, and manage day-to-day operations.

Many of the department's leaders are civilians who oversee bureaus and implement essential policies. Civilian members in titles such as

deputy commissioner or director lead bureaus and offices which work to maintain and enhance our complex organization.

In 1918, Ellen O'Grady was the first woman to be appointed to deputy commissioner. Together, civilian, and uniformed leaders ensure that the NYPD is the most effective, best trained, most technologically advanced police department in the nation.

School crossing guards, SCGS, are trusted with the safety of New York City's school children on the city streets. They safeguard school children walking across busy intersections on their way to

and from school.

School crossing guards oversee and control traffic flow around schools in the morning, at lunch time, and at the end of the school day.

Traffic enforcement agents, TEA, are responsible for directing millions of vehicles daily to ensure the safe flow of traffic throughout New York City.

Prior to joining with the NYPD in 1996, traffic enforcement agent responsibilities were generally limited to summonsing cars parked at expired parking meters.

Currently, traffic enforcement agents are assigned to the NYPD Transportation Bureau's Traffic Enforcement District which enforces laws and regulations involving moving and parked vehicles, including expediting the movement of traffic.

TEAs perform work of adjusting degrees of difficulty in traffic enforcement areas including issuing summonses to illegally parked vehicles, directing traffic at intersections, testifying at administrative hearing offices and in court, and preparing required reports.

Administrative professionals work in partnership with sworn members of the department to ensure that members of the public and NYPD employees receive exceptional service and assistance. Employees in these titles may work at precincts, administrative commands or specialized units.

Their responsibilities may include the handling of confidential information and material, referring members of the public who ask for assistance to appropriate city agencies; and typing or maintaining records, reports, forms and schedules, as well as obtaining and transmitting information to the public or members of the police department.

Financial professionals manage the department's multi-billion-dollar budget to ensure funds are allocated appropriately.

As the largest municipal police force in the nation, the NYPD requires extensive funding to maintain operations and apply innovative initiatives.

Financial professionals are responsible for financial planning, payroll processing, purchasing, allocation of supplies and equipment, and implementation of contracts.

Employees who work in financial titles also play an instrumental role in securing funding for counterterrorism operations.

As a law enforcement organization, the NYPD relies on legal counsel to assist in interpreting and enforcing local, state, and federal laws.

The law professionals support the department by ensuring

that the rights of the public and all employees are protected. These members work in various bureaus including the Office of Equity and Inclusion, the Legal Bureau, the Risk Management Bureau, and the

Department Advocate's Office.

NYPD Management and Budget's Facilities Maintenance Division is responsible for the maintenance and improvement of all NYPD facilities. The division is continuously implementing projects to improve NYPD facilities and improve the quality of the workplace for employees.

Civilian members include experienced, licensed trades professionals who are responsible for upgrading, modernizing, repairing, sanitizing, and maintaining facilities to provide a safe, inviting, and professional appearance for employees and the public.

In the late 1880s, street cleaning was overseen by the Police Department and performed by civilian employees.

In 1898, custodial workers were called doormen, and that title was eventually rolled into the Patrolman title.

One civilian street cleaner was Joseph Petrosino, who would later rise to be the first Italian American Lieutenant. He is tragically remembered as the only member of the NYPD to be killed in the line of duty in a foreign country.

Working in partnership with the community is a top priority for the NYPD. Through Neighborhood Policing, our members collaborate with the public in meaningful ways to reduce crime, increase safety, and solve local problems.

Neighborhood Policing requires many resources and personnel, uniformed and civilian, to carry out its mission.

Civilians who work in titles that are responsible for engaging the community serve as liaisons between NYPD leadership and community members. They organize community meetings and events, provide victims with resources, and conduct program.

The department depends on their expert analysts and technicians using cutting edge technology to assist with criminal investigations as well as with economic and personnel research.

Employees in analyst or technician titles are critical members of various investigative and administrative bureaus such as the

Intelligence Bureau, the Detective Bureau, the Personnel Bureau, the Office of Crime Control Strategies, and the Office of Strategic Initiatives.

NYPD crime analysts strengthen the department's efforts to fight crime and terrorism…

The department also relies on analysts to perform administrative, operational, and fiscal research to manage its immense workforce and operating budget.

Technicians maintain and operate equipment necessary for investigations and forensic analysis of several kinds of physical evidence.

Civilians in these titles may be responsible for guaranteeing that the candidates for city employment or licenses are appropriately inspected, as well as preparing evidence for court.

The NYPD fleet is rated one of the top fifty managed government fleets in the country and is one of the greenest police fleets in the world.

Employees assigned to Fleet Services are responsible for keeping every police vehicle in exceptional working condition and for modifying vehicles as necessary for specialty functions.

Civilian employees who maintain and enhance the vehicles are highly skilled and trained trade workers who ensure the fleet is operational and sustainable.

NYPD employees are the department's most valuable resource, and the wellbeing of the workforce has direct implications for how members fulfill their duties and responsibilities.

Civilian employees work in numerous titles that help support the physical, mental, emotional, and spiritual wellness of all employees.

These members ensure that employees are in the best position to provide exceptional service to the public.

The NYPD's Medical Division dates to the beginning of the organization and its responsibilities have grown as the department developed.

The division consists of medical professionals from various specialties, including orthopedics, cardiology, pulmonology, dentistry, and obstetrics who ensure that our employees maintain optimal health.

Working in law enforcement can be dangerous and demanding. Police Officers are at continual risk, and in the event of an incident involving the hospitalization of an officer, police surgeons are dispatched to provide each member with the best care.

The department psychologists play a critical role in evaluating candidates for suitability for employment and fitness for duty, as well as providing counseling, trauma responses, grief management, and addiction services.

The Patrol Services Bureau is the largest and most visible bureau in the NYPD. The bureau relies on civilian members to assist with protecting New York City's residents, workers, and visitors.

Auxiliary police officers and police cadets help patrol officers ensure the safety of the city's neighborhoods.

The NYPD's auxiliary police program is the largest auxiliary police program in the United States, with thousands of volunteer officers contributing more than one million hours of public service each year.

Auxiliary officers are trained to observe and report conditions requiring the attention of the officers on patrol and are known as the "eyes and ears" of a community.

The current Cadet Corps is an internship program within the New York City Police Department, started by Mayor Ed Koch in 1985.

The Cadet program offers college students tuition assistance and other benefits as they explore interest in starting a career as a police officer. It provides a unique opportunity to experience working with police officers while testing one's ability and commitment to improving the quality of life for the people of New York City.

While they are considered civilians, cadets do wear uniforms and must attend regular trainings, which will make for an easier transition into a uniformed police role once they take and pass the promotional or open competitive police officer exam.

In 2009, civilian employees came together to find the Advancement of Civilian Employees Society, ACES. The organization was established to advocate for more career and education opportunities in the department, as well as to increase friendship and networking among civilians.

The founding members were civilians from various titles, ranks, and commands who sought to create an organization that focused specifically on the concerns of NYPD civilian employees.

In 2011, the NYPD formally recognized ACES as an employee organization which allowed the group to work with the department to address the needs of its membership. ACES members participate in various department initiatives to improve the civilian workplace experience and create opportunities for advancement.

ACES also offers educational scholarships for members and their children pursuing higher education.

In addition to professional support, ACES provides a social outlet where members can interact as equals without regard for rank title, seniority, or union affiliation.

The organization hosts annual social and volunteer events where members can network and experience a fellowship with coworkers and give back to their communities.

ACES often partners with other organizations to organize toy drives, coat drives, and food donations.

ACES strives to build a spirit of cooperation between civilians and uniformed members.

The ACES logo features an image of a person holding up a shield to illustrate how civilian members support uniformed members. The organization attends annual memorials and police events in solidarity with uniformed members.

Uniformed members are welcome to join ACES as associate members.

The Managerial Employees Association, MEA, is a professional membership association dedicated to protecting and improving the civil service and other rights of public employees who are not eligible for collective bargaining under state and/or local law.

Membership extends to every city agency within the five boroughs of New York City and includes many NYPD civilian executives.

MEA was founded in the summer of 1968 in reaction to the passage of New York State's Taylor Law and the implementation of the city's Management Pay Plan, both of which troubled managers' power to bargain with the city for compensation and benefits.

Since its founding, the primary purpose has been to provide superior advocacy services and support to all members.

Throughout the history of the NYPD, civilian employees have been an important part of its work, helping to achieve New York City's status as the safest big city in the country.

A wide range of civilian professionals have dedicated themselves to law enforcement. The future success of the department relies on its investment in, and commitment to, all employees, including the continued expansion of civilian roles and titles.

The combined efforts of the Office of Equity and Inclusion, the Human Resources Division, and the Office of Professional Development will help to ensure the continued advancement of civilian employees.

As the city and its communities continue to change, the department workforce must stand ready to meet the public's needs.

CHAPTER 26

UNTIL THE COPS SHOWED UP

The Summer of Love was a social phenomenon that occurred during the summer of 1967, when as many as 100,000 people, mostly young people sporting hippie fashions of dress and behavior, met in San Francisco's neighborhood of Haight-Ashbury.

More broadly, the Summer of Love included the hippie music, hallucinogenic drugs, anti-war, and free-love scene throughout the West Coast of the United States, and as far away as New York City.

Hippies, sometimes called flower children, were a diverse group. Many were suspicious of the government, rejected commercial values, and generally opposed the Vietnam War.

A few were interested in politics; others were concerned more with art, music, painting, poetry, or spiritual and meditative practices.

In Manhattan, near the Greenwich Village neighborhood, during a concert in Tompkins Square Park on Memorial Day of 1967, some police officers asked for the music's volume to be reduced.

In response, some people in the crowd threw various objects, and 38 arrests ensued. A debate about the "threat of the hippie" ensued between Mayor John Lindsay and Police Commissioner Howard Leary.

After this event, Allan Katzman, the editor of the East Village Other, predicted that 50,000 hippies would enter the area for the summer.

After losing his position as an instructor on the Psychology faculty at Harvard University, Timothy Leary became a major advocate for the recreational use of psychedelic drugs.

After taking psilocybin, a psychoactive chemical produced by certain mushrooms that causes effects like those of LSD, Leary endorsed the use of all psychedelics for personal development.

He often invited friends as well as an occasional graduate student to consume such drugs along with him and colleague Richard Alpert.

On the West Coast, author Ken Kesey, a prior volunteer for a CIA-sponsored LSD experiment, also advocated the use of the drug. Soon after participating, he was inspired to write the bestselling novel One Flew Over the Cuckoo's Nest.

Subsequently, after buying an old school bus, painting it with psychedelic graffiti and attracting a group of similarly minded individuals he dubbed the Merry Pranksters, Kesey and his group traveled across the country, often hosting "acid tests" where they would fill a large container with a diluted low dose form of the drug and give out diplomas to those who passed their test.

Along with LSD, cannabis was also much used during this period. However, as a result, crime increased among users because new laws were subsequently enacted to control the use of both drugs. The users thereof often had sessions to oppose the laws, including The Human Be-In referenced above as well as various "smoke-ins" during July and August; however, their efforts at repeal were unsuccessful.

At the end of summer, many participants had left the scene to join the back-to-the-land movement of the late 1960s, to resume school studies, or simply to "get a job".

Those remaining in the Haight wanted to commemorate the conclusion of the event. A mock funeral entitled <u>"The Death of the</u>

Hippie" ceremony was staged on October 6, 1967, and organizer Mary Kasper explained the intended message:

We wanted to signal that this was the end of it, to stay where you are, bring the revolution to where you live and don't come here because it's over and done with.

In New York, the rock musical drama Hair, which told the story of the hippie counterculture and sexual revolution of the 1960s, began Off-Broadway on October 17, 1967.

Fifty years later, that utopian vision of the Summer of Love prevails. But underground papers like those in Reveal Digital's Independent Voices Collection testify to the dark underbelly of that fateful season.

The June 23 edition of the Berkeley Barb, for instance, includes an advertisement for the Berkeley PROVOS, a group of people who intended to help deal with the influx of people into the area.

Although embracing the spirit of the Summer of Love, the article amounts to a plea for help. It reads, "We still need food, clothes, places to stay, beds, sheets, soap, blankets, coat hangers and HELP."

In fact, the hippie demonstrations and the publicization of hippie culture that united in the Summer of Love were met with controversy rather than acceptance.

Even the participants varied in what they understood the meaning of the event to be. They knew something was happening, but it was hardly the simple introduction of peace and love to American culture.

CHAPTER 27

THE CHIEF CLERK'S OFFICE

Let me begin this chapter with one of the greatest human beings I have ever met. His name was Louis Stutman…

Louis Stutman was a World War II Veteran and former 1st Commander of the Milton L. Finel Post of the Jewish War Veterans. He was also former 1st Commander of the Milton L. Finel Post of the Jewish War Veterans.

He began his New York City Police Department career in the Legal Bureau. Later, he was Executive Secretary to Police Commissioner Kennedy.

Stutman had several positions throughout the department including Chief Clerk, Deputy Police Commissioner of Licenses and Deputy Commissioner of Trials.

He was the first Chairman of the Civilian Complaint Review Board, counsel to the PBA and a proud member of the Shomrim Society.

In August 1968, I was assigned to work in the Chief Clerk's office. That was when Louis Stutman was the Chief Clerk.

During that time, police headquarter was located at 240 Centre St. NY 10031…

Let me inform you that the Chief Clerk's Office did numerous jobs. We were located on the third floor, room 307.

As you entered the office, one can see the busy bees. We never stopped. The work was endless. We prepared the PA 15 for future police officers.

Let's look at the office setting.

There was a division between the civilian personnel records and the police officers. There were no walls. It was just a lot of black cabinets dividing us.

The civilian section had a hand full of civilians that worked very hard. Their supervisor was Mary Butler.

No one really knew they were back there...

I supervised the Police Trainees Program. It was easy getting the records from the civilian section. Their transfer from civilian to police officer was done in no time.

At our side of the office, everyone had to stop whatever they were doing to do the proper paperwork on those new police officers.

There was a change in their tax number. The Tax number is the pension number police officer or civilian is assigned. It was imperative to change it the minute the police trainee became an officer.

The force card had to be done to be place it in the famous wheel....

The wheel had all the information of a police officer.

For example: Name, date of birth, appointment date, rank,

Shield number and Assigned command

There had to be roster made for the new members. This roster indicated their precincts or command.

This was done not only to police trainees to officers, but also new police officers that passed the police exam. Those names came from a civil service list.

It was hard work, however, the great team of workers in that tiny office did miracles.

Mr. Louis Stutman, the Chief Clerk, made the difference because he was always with a big smile thanking us for a job well done. It was our job, however, he made sure that we were happy specially on hot summer days with just one tiny fan.

Let me tell you something that happened on June 10, 1975.

It was a very hot summer day. Mr. Stutman got a call for us to stay in the office and work late.

We never said no to the Chief....

We had to get some records and place photo on everyone. We started to work fast because it was very warm in that office. I remember getting the photos. My partner got their folders, and the rest of the workers got the necessary information.

It took us about one hour and half to get everything together. I informed the Chief that the work was completed.

I decided to take all those folders and lock them up in the shield room. My supervisor told me that it was great idea.

We all finished and left for the day. The time 6:30 pm....

This is what happened a few minutes after we left: A tremendous explosion rocked Police Headquarters at 240 Centre Street, heavily damaging offices on the second story of the five-story building.

Police officials said that a bomb with the force of 10 to 15 sticks of dynamite exploded at 6:57 P.M. on the second-floor men's washroom.

Glass, bricks, mortar, and other trash were blown across Centre Street in front of the building and into Centre Market Place, a small street behind headquarters.

This was all over the news. ....

That bomb was placed on the second floor. We were right above on the third floor. We were blessed because we left just in time.

CHAPTER 28

OLD NYPD HEADQUARTERS
240 CENTRE STREET

For more than 60 years, police officers called the old headquarters, the big white castle, the nerve center of the nation's largest and most sophisticated police department.

Over the years, the New York City Police Department's Centre Street headquarters would combat mobsters, bootleggers, jewel thieves and serial killers...

The old NYPD headquarters was built between 1905 and 1909 on a wedge-shaped parcel of land bounded by Grand, Centre and Broome Streets where the old Centre Market had stood since 1817.

A new Headquarters was needed following the consolidation of the five boroughs in 1898, when the police force quadrupled in size.

On November 29, 1909, Police Commissioner William F. Baker inaugurated New York's era of scientific policing when telephone switchboards at the old police headquarters at 300 Mulberry was shut down and transferred to the new Central Office.

On the first floor of 240 Centre Street, visitors would find an elaborated reception room. To the left of reception, guests could find the Chief Inspector's office, the Bureau of Information, and the Boiler

Squad. A NYPD unit was responsible for testing steam heaters in buildings throughout the city.

To the right of the reception room, the chief detective's office could be found next to the lineup room for criminal suspects, the homicide room, and Lt. Giuseppe "Joseph" Petrosino's famed Italian Squad.

Formed to investigate the growing threat of a criminal organization known as the Black Hand, Lt. Petrosino and his Italian speaking squad uncovered the existence of a secret criminal society known as the Mafia waiting in the shadows of New York's Little Italy.

Lt. Petrosino was assassinated while investigating the Mafia in Sicily. He never had the chance to see the new Police Headquarters.

After the assassination of Joseph Petrosino, Michael Fiaschetti took command of the Italian Squad at 240 Centre Street.

For over sixty years, police officers called it <u>the big white castle</u>, the nerve center of the nation's largest and most sophisticated police department.

Built by the architectural firm: Hoppin, Koen, and Huntington for approximately $750,000, Old Police Headquarters, or the Central Office as it was once called, represents one of the most beautiful Beaux-Arts masterpieces Manhattan has to offer

The building was not intended to look like a police station; however, it was inspired by the dignity of City Hall. The finest building on Manhattan Island was designed to impress both officers and prisoners.

Another flight up was the Chief Clerk's office and a police science library. This was stocked with the most up to date texts on investigation, forensics, and criminal identification.

On the fourth floor was the Police Academy. The City's Police Academy operated at 240 Centre Street until it moved to 400 Broome Street in 1928. The facilities included a gym, a drill room, heavy bags, and a running track.

The fifth floor was the Police Department's nerve center. It had a sophisticated switchboard and dispatch system for the entire city. According to the New York Evening Post.

Nearby in the Bertillon room, officers photographed and exactly measured and recorded different parts and components of known criminals' bodies.

Their findings were then printed on 5"X 3" index cards, an early system of criminal identification, and sent to the Old Police Headquarters' Rouges Gallery. Fingerprinting eventually replaced the Bertillon system.

The cellar had a pistol shooting range, the property clerk, 72 cells for high profile Detective Bureau prisoners, and most notably a secret tunnel.

During prohibition, officers went to great lengths to get their drinks. They were digging a tunnel under Centre Street to O'Neill's tavern so that the police officers could drink in uniform.

Almost overnight, gunsmiths and gun dealers grew behind headquarters on Centre Market Place where officers could buy guns, billy clubs and uniforms.

Famous gun dealers such as John Jovino and Frank Lava operated there for many years...

The Police Department officially closed 240 Centre Street in 1973, moving headquarters to 1 Police Plaza.

Rather than relocating the historic records into a library, the department abruptly dumped a half-century worth of police records into the East River.

Headquarters was later converted into a luxury apartment building named the Old Police Building.

CHAPTER 29

LIEUTENANT JOE PETROSINO

Lieutenant Joe Petrosino the most fearless cops in NYPD History...

During his career, Petrosino would go from street sweeper to NYPD Lieutenant only to be cut down by assassin's bullets on the streets of Palermo.

Born Giuseppe Petrosino in 1860, the detective got his start with the New York Police Department in an unusual way, sweeping streets...

In those days, street cleaners or whitewings, as they were known, fell under the command of the New York's Metropolitan Police Department.

Petrosino scrubbed the streets of the district. This was a rowdy neighborhood populated by brothels and casinos. The noisy quarter was commanded by police inspector Alexander "Clubber" Williams, a famous brawler who earned his nickname as a beat cop in the force.

Sensing Petrosino's linguistic skills, Williams put the Italian street sweeper to work as a special assistant in leftover cases involving Italians.

At age of 23, the 5'7" Petrosino became the shortest patrolman on the force. This was a favor that came as courtesy from Williams, who forced the Police Board to wave the height regulations.

By 1890, Petrosino moved up to the investigation section, policing the crime wave sweeping little Italy. Called the Black Hand or La Mana Nero by the newspapers because of the distinct extortion letters signed with a black handprint. The Black Hand gangsters specialized in kidnapping, extortion, and bombings.

The newspapers failed to realize that the Black Hand was a myth dreamed up by a New York Tribune reporter. The newspapers could not have imagined that the real reason behind these crimes was a secret criminal society known as the Mafia, a term unknown at the time.

Led by a ruthless villain with a deformed hand, Giuseppe "Peter" Morello ruled New York's first crime family. This organization was heading to be absorbed by Lucky Luciano and Vito Genovese.

Morello made his bones in the old country as an assassin, counterfeiter, and kidnapper before escaping to America to avoid murder charges.

While Morello sailed across the Atlantic, Petrosino made a name for himself in the NYPD.

By 1890, he moved up to the investigation section. A master of disguise, the young detective possessed a collection of costumes.

Petrosino's tricks amused Police Commissioner Theodore Roosevelt and the pair became instant friends.

A clever politician, Roosevelt realized that the arrival of Italians would further his political base if he had his own inside man.

This was the main reason, Teddy promoted Petrosino to Sergeant Detective, the first Italian American to achieve that rank.

By 1903, there were more Italians in New York than there were in Rome. Together the Italian population was 1/4 of the entire city, however, only eleven police officers spoke Italian.

After a rash of tenement bombings, the NYPD formed the Italian Squad. The five-man band included Maurise Bonil, Peter Dondero, George Silva, John Lagomarsini, and Ugo Cassidi.

The great grandfather of the NYPD Bomb Squad, the Italian Squad specialized in bomb disposal.

Meanwhile, it seemed that every Italian gangster with a scrap of paper and a pen was turning to Black Hand extortion while true Mafioso, like Giuseppe Morello, worked to freeze their criminal empires.

Upon arriving in America, Morello enlisted the help of a savage enforcer, Ignacio Lupo "the Wolf", and Don Vito Cascioferro, an unusual Mafioso by all accounts.

Ferro started life as an anarchist who took part in uprisings, protests, and political assassinations in Sicily. Later he served as president of the Fasci of Bisaquino.

Petrosino quickly became the curse of the Morello Crime Family. After Cracking the Barrel Murder, Pertrosino issued an arrest warrant for Cascioferro, who fled to Sicily.

In 1909, Lt. Petrosino traveled over 4,000 miles to Palermo to uncover the secrets of the Mafia. It would be the detective's undoing. Cascioferro's assassins caught up with Petrosino murdering him on the Piazza Marina.

CHAPTER 30

HISPANIC IN NYPD

A long-anticipated trial over discrimination at the New York City Police Department was prevented when the Latino Officers Association, the City of New York and the department reached a settlement shortly before the trial was scheduled to begin.

The lawsuit, commenced in 1999 by 22 individuals and the association, was certified as a class action three years later by Judge Lewis A. Kaplan of the United States District Court for the Southern District of New York.

The class includes all African American and Hispanic police officers and certain civilian employees of the New York Police Department since 1995.

There were charges that the police department violated their city, state and federal civil rights. The plaintiffs claimed a hostile work environment where they were subjected to insulting remarks, racist graffiti on lockers and similar conduct which was often accepted by superiors.

One of the worst problems was revenge against officers who complained, according to the plaintiff's lead counsel, Richard Levy. Levy stated that the officers became "outcasts in many precincts."

The claimants also claimed unequal and discriminatory application of disciplinary rules and procedures. The lawsuit maintained that disciplinary charges were brought against blacks and Hispanics more often than against white officers.

More convictions were returned, and more serious penalties were imposed for departmental convictions resulting in transfers, denials of benefits, suspensions, and terminations. The charges against the officers ranged from rudeness to murder.

A lot of the cases fell into a generic category of conduct prejudicial to the NYPD...

Statistics trusted on by plaintiffs indicate that when civilian charges against police officers originated at the Civilian Complaint Review Board, an independent non-mayoral agency cited for comparison purposes, disparities based on race or ethnicity were minor or nonexistent.

The complaints filed by the public; blacks were charged at the same rate as whites. The figures for Hispanics were slightly more. However, when charges originated internally at the New York Police Department, overall differences increased enormously with blacks and Hispanics much more likely to be charged than their white counterparts.

Likewise, when departmental trials were held, blacks were much less likely to be acquitted and have their charges dismissed, than whites.

In fact, if the case, Latino Officers Association against City of New York, and NYPD, had gone forward, the plaintiffs expected to prove that blacks were 60 percent more likely and Hispanics 30 percent more likely to be found guilty at departmental trial than whites.

In terms of overall dispositions, charges against whites were more often dismissed, or resulted in findings of not guilty, while African Americans and Hispanics were far more often found guilty.

In addition, when findings of guilt were handed down, blacks and Hispanics were terminated from the police force with greater frequency than white officers, who received lesser penalties.

If the settlement is approved by the court as expected, the class, which includes approximately 12,000 members, and their lawyers, will share a monetary settlement of $26.8 million of which 20 million is dedicated to claims and two million to administration.

A panel is to be created to decide how many of the Hispanic and African American members of the police force who served since 1995 may be eligible to share in the settlement and to what extent.

It is not known how many claims will be submitted, or how many members will "opt out" and settle, litigate, or withdraw their own cases. Claims may also be filed for lost benefits, but there are no provisions for reinstatement of individuals whose employment was terminated. The awards can range from $3,500 to $400,000.

In addition to the monetary provisions, the settlement includes an injunction against discrimination by the police department.

While the defendants do not admit any wrongdoing, they accept that the police department is enjoined from discriminating based on race, color, national origin, or ethnicity in the future.

The settlement also requires the establishment of a review unit to analyze the NYPD's disciplinary process regarding discrimination and retaliation and whether African American and Hispanic members of police service are being investigated, charged, or penalized in a discriminatory manner.

The proposed order which is being submitted to Judge Kaplan for his approval and signature details the steps the police department will take to establish procedures to prevent discrimination.

All members of the certified class can apply for awards from the fund which is to be held by the New York City Comptroller. The payment is to be administered by the Special Masters Kenneth Feinberg and Peter Woodin.

Mr. Feinberg is also head of the federal program of compensation to families of victims of the September 11th attacks...

According to plaintiffs' attorney Richard Levy, the case would not have settled without the Special Masters. Feinberg had immediate access to Mayor Bloomberg, Police Commissioner Kelly, and Mike Cardozo Corporation Counsel. No one had met with the attorney at this level before.

CHAPTER 31

NYPD HISPANIC SOCIETY

On July 29th, 1957, the New York City Police Department Hispanic Society was founded, with the approval of Police Commissioner Stephen F. Kennedy.

The organizations founding fathers were William Rodriguez, Peter Rodriguez, Isabel Barber, Eric Seise, Ivan Marfisi, Eugene Calderon, Victor J. Ortiz, Alex Cuesta, and Thomas Martino.

They always indicated that the formation of the organization was "to promote and develop a friendly and fraternal spirit among all members of Spanish descent in the police force of the City of New York. It was also to create a more harmonious relationship within the police department and the City of New York.

Shortly before its beginning, there were approximately 40 officers of Hispanic origin. These officers were told by Police Officer Victor J. Ortiz of the need to form a fraternal organization that would address and voice the concerns of Hispanic officers.

From its very beginnings, the Hispanic Society has been involved in enhancing the opportunities for appointments and promotions of its members.

Hispanic Society members were not only concerned with the dilemma of the officers it represented, but they also set forth on an immediate recruitment drive to increase the number of Hispanic candidates taking the police entrance examinations.

At that time, Hispanics did not join the Police Department for various reasons...

In 1954, there were only 20-30 Hispanics in a police force of 20,000. In their recruitment effort, the Hispanic Society members appealed to the Commonwealth of Puerto Rico to assist them in their recruitment attempt.

To improve the prospective candidates' chances of selection, tutorial sessions were held.

As a result of these attempts, the number of Hispanics joining the Police Department increased dramatically.

Throughout the years, the Hispanic Society has been involved in challenging entrance and promotional examinations and assessing the status of Hispanic officers in the department.

In the early 1970's, because of the recruitment drives, Society members discovered that many Hispanics were unable to realize their dream of becoming police officers because they did not meet the departments height requirement. The Hispanic Society addressed the problem locally by attempting to have the Police Department change these criteria. This was an unsuccessful venture, but in 1972, congress amended the Civil Rights Act of 1964, prohibiting the height requirement as it was ruled discriminatory.

This resulted in a change in personnel selection practices in the law enforcement field. The removal of this barrier substantially increases the number of women and Hispanics in the Police Department.

In 1972, the Hispanic Society joined the Guardians in contesting the entry-level examinations administered in 1968 and 1972.

An injunction prohibited the selection of candidates from those lists. Later, that lawsuit had an impact on those Hispanic and African

American officers who were hired off that list. Those affected received retroactive monies due to their newly designated appointment dates.

On October 5, 1979, the Guardians Association and the Hispanic Society settled a lawsuit, which challenged the June 1979, police examination as not being job-related and its format unlike that of previous examinations.

Federal Judge Carter ruled on December 17, 1978, that New York City could not use its latest Civil Service Exam to select new police recruits until he decided on a plan to assist African American and Hispanic applicants to the Police Department. This lawsuit resulted in a hiring quota of 1/3 of the recruits selected being of Hispanic and African American descent.

In 1981, yet another challenge, the Hispanic Society mandated that the promotion of new police sergeants should be consistent with the number of police candidates competing for that position.

Not only is the Hispanic Society actively involved with issues relevant to its members, but it also engages in matters directly affecting the community.

An example would be the significant role played immediately after the island of Puerto Rico's devastation by Hurricane Hugo in September 1989.

The New York City Police Department gathered personnel as well as heavy equipment from its exclusive Emergency Services Unit to assist the Puerto Rican government and the Red Cross in their post-hurricane assistance.

To further these efforts, the Hispanic Society appealed to its members to volunteer their time and travel to Puerto Rico to help the many affected families. The officers that unselfishly left their families behind for three weeks provided diverse aid. Some those officers were translators for those Puerto Ricans who could not describe to Red Cross personnel the hardship suffered.

Others accompanied Red Cross staff to remote areas of the island that had not yet been assessed as to the damage incurred.

Others distributed food and emergency supplies to non-for-profit organizations that's would in turn distribute supplies to the community. The Hispanic Society also raised funds and provided aid for Hurricane George in 1998.

The Hispanic Society has helped during other catastrophic events, such as the tragedy of American Airlines Flight# 587 bound for the Dominican Republic, which crashed in Belle Harbor, Queens on November 12th, 2001.

They raised funds, served as translators, and helped the families in the recovery effort. The Hispanic Society also participated in fundraisers for the victims of Hurricane Katrina in August 2005.

The Society also held a fundraiser for the victims in the Dominican Republic of Hurricane Noel in October 2007 and for the victims of the floods in Mexico in October & November 2007.

On the local level the Society has been involved in the restoration of a church in the Lower East Side in Manhattan. The Annual Christmas Party is dedicated to raising funds for sick or injured children who are spending the holiday in local hospitals.

The Hispanic Society has hosted and participated in vest drives, for law enforcement in Puerto Rico and the Dominican Republic.

CHAPTER 32

FALLEN HISPANIC POLICE OFFICERS

New York Police Officer Jason Rivera was no stranger to the tensions between police and some communities.

Growing up in a Dominican neighborhood in Manhattan, he saw it up close. His brother got pulled from a taxi and frisked for no reason at all.

Wilbert Mora, too, knew it from his youth in East Harlem. He spent his college years thinking about ways to bridge the division with police officer and the community.

Both officers wanted to be the compounds of changes when they became police officers. Neither got the chance they deserved. Both were fatally wounded by a gunman who ambushed them while they responded to a call about a family dispute at a Harlem apartment.

Rivera's casket, draped in a green, white, and blue NYPD flag, was carried into St. Patrick's Cathedral. Cardinal Timothy Dolan supervise over his funeral Mass.

A line of hundreds of mourners, many wearing uniforms and badges, wound through rows of barricades outside, waited in sub-freezing temperatures to pay their respects. Two officials from the

Dominican consulate open their country's flag, in homage to the officers' heritage.

JoAnn Pappert traveled an hour from Queens. Though she never met Rivera, she said she was compelled to be there by what she'd heard about his approach to policing.

"What he had in mind was beautiful. It was something peaceful. He wanted to unite the community with the police department that, you know, has been struggling," Pappert said. "I was really deeply touched by his vision."

Rivera, 22, had been a police officer for barely a year. Mora, 27, was in his fourth year on the job. His wake and funeral Mass were planned for next week, also at the Roman Catholic cathedral.

Friends remembered the officers as caring and dedicated. Mora, a gentle giant with a strong body and a warm heart. Rivera was a loving newlywed who would FaceTime his wife from his locker.

Marisa Caraballo, a former neighbor of the Rivera family in Manhattan's heavily Dominican Inwood neighborhood, said his mother objected when he told her he wanted to become a police officer. She said it was dangerous, but Rivera insisted, and his mom surrendered.

"She said, 'OK. I support you,'" Caraballo said.

Stephanie McGraw, founder of anti-domestic violence group We All Really Matter, said she got to know Mora during frequent visits to the police station where he worked.

"He was from the hood," McGraw said. "He understood the importance of getting into this very crucial and important role as a police officer, to not only make a difference but to bring some more men and women of color into the NYPD."

Hundreds of officers and plenty of residents attended a vigil for the slain officers.

"Officer Rivera and Officer Mora made a decision that they wanted to be part of the solution," the Rev. Ronald Sullivan said.

"We're not believing the narrative that the community and the police are on different teams."

In an essay describing why he became a police officer; Rivera recalled the injustice of being pulled over in a taxi and seeing officers frisk his brother.

"My perspective on police and the way they police really bothered me," Rivera wrote. But he said he got interested in becoming a cop himself because he saw the department "pushing hard" to improve community relations.

Rivera and Mora were part of the newest generation of NYPD officers, one increasingly thoughtful of the city's diversity.

As youths, they saw the end of "broken windows" policing that treated low-level offenses as a gateway to bigger crimes. They saw the court-ordered reduction in officers' use of a tactic of routinely stopping young men and searching them for weapons.

Today's NYPD is 45% white, 30% Hispanic and nearly 10% Asian. Black New Yorkers, who account for nearly a quarter of the city's population, make up just 15% of its police force. The city's newly appointed police commissioner, Keechant Sewell, is the first woman and third Black person to lead the department.

Rivera's wife, Dominique Rivera, posted on Instagram that she and her husband were friends since childhood. She shared a message he wrote her in their school days saying he loved her and wanted to marry her.

After their wedding last October, Dominique wrote that Rivera was her "soulmate, best friend and lover from now until the end of time."

"But now your soul will spend the rest of my days with me, through me, right beside me," Dominique wrote over a picture of her husband's police locker. "I love you till the end of time."

Before joining the department, Mora studied at John Jay College of Criminal Justice, where he impressed Professor Irina Zakirova with sharp questions and a keen interest in striving for ways to build bridges between police and the neighborhoods they serve.

CHAPTER 33

EDWIN RAYMOND

<u>As a Sergeant</u>

Sergeant Edwin Raymond is accusing the NYPD of failing to promote him based on his outspoken support for Colin Kaepernick.

According to the Daily News, Raymond scored No. 26 out of 1,325 sergeants on the lieutenants' test. His promotion was halted due to accusations filed by cops in his command regarding his handling of two domestic violence complaints. However, Raymond believes these allegations are just an excuse not to fix the underlying issue of racism in the department.

"It is unfortunate. I did a press conference in support of Colin Kaepernick, using his status to put a spotlight on issues in policing that need to be fixed," the 33-year-old explains. "Because of the controversy a lot of cops criticized him. Me being aligned with him was seen as standing with the enemy."

Raymond's version of the events says that the man was sitting in his vehicle with his current girlfriend when his ex-walked by, taking a bat to his car mirror. He fled from the car and called 911.

When Raymond got to the scene, the man asked that the cops not arrest her as she is the mother of three of his children, according to the Daily News.

She's the mother of my kids," the man said. "The damage to my car won't cost anything."

The ex, however, had an order of protection against the man and wanted him arrested. Based on the circumstances, Raymond made a judgement call to let him go.

"These cops went thinking the numbers would give their claims more plausibility, and unfortunately the department is choosing to entertain this and use it as a dagger to end my promotion," Raymond said. "They are not happy with me. I don't enjoy having to speak out, but it's historically what makes the department budge."

Raymond is now suing the NYPD over these "illegal quotas," CBS News reports.

Decisions are made on the sly, and there are people who have pending charges and still get promoted, and others whose promotions are held back for reasons that are never explained," Ed Mullins, the president of the Sergeants Benevolent Association, said. "If this doesn't appear to be retaliation, then I don't know what is."

<u>As a Lieutenant</u>

A NYPD lieutenant who blew the whistle on police corruption is now running for city council. Lt. Raymond is the first active-duty cop in recent history to vie for the elected position.

Lt. Edwin Raymond, 34, of Brooklyn North told The Post he hopes he can use his 12 years on the force to help the bridge the gap between lawmakers and cops when it comes to reform.

"I understand the mentality and the psyche of police officers enough to tailor the message in a way that they'll be receptive," Raymond said.

"Many cops are unable to separate themselves as individuals from the department as an entity. So when you criticize the department, they just feel personally attacked and they shut down, and they get defensive."

Raymond, who is running to replace term-limited Councilman Mathieu Eugene in Brooklyn's 40th district and aims to make the changes to the force that he couldn't as a cop.

As a black Brooklyn native who has worked on the force, Raymond says he's had a "front-row seat to all of the detriments."

The lieutenant and 11 other black and Hispanic cops took the department to federal court in 2015, claiming in a lawsuit that supervisors in the Transit Bureau pushed quotas targeting minorities and told officers to look the other way when it came to white or Asian offenders, court records show.

The class-action suit, which is still pending in the Southern District of New York, made headlines again late last year with explosive allegations against Deputy Inspector Constantin Tsachas through new affidavits.

Raymond said his legal action led to retaliation from inside the department for blowing the whistle on the policing practice something he wants to change not only within the NYPD but citywide.

"I want to create a true safe haven for whistleblowers," he said. "Internal affair is just not equipped to deal with systemic corruption. You're literally asking the department to investigate itself."

Raymond also said he'd like to tackle the NYPD's bias training and police transparency if he's elected.

Bronx historian Lloyd Ultan said he can't recall any active cop recently running to be a city lawmaker.

James Davis won Brooklyn's 35th City Council seat in 2001 while he worked as an instructor at the NYPD's academy. Davis, a former corrections officer, and cop was assassinated during a council meeting inside City Hall in 2003.

In 2021, Edwin Raymond, thirty-five, fit, not tall, long dreadlocks, walked into Kaché, a Haitian restaurant in the Marine Park section of Brooklyn, ready, as always, to tell his story.

All political candidates are serial self-narrators, but Raymond, who is running for a seat on the City Council, has an unusual biography.

At a moment of plain opposition between police officers and radical critics of policing, he is both…

He made his way from table to table, providing familial greetings a hand on the shoulder, a pleasantry in English or Haitian Creole to those he knew, and a grip-and-grin to those he didn't.

A loudspeaker played Sinatra "New York, New York," "My Way."

Celeste Saint-Jean, eating alone but not guarding her solitude, struck up a conversation about the mayoral race. "I like the guy with the business approach," she said. "Wang?"

"Yang," Raymond corrected her.

"I like Eric Adams, too, because he was a cop," she continued.

"I'm a police lieutenant, actually, and I fought against corruption in the department," Raymond said, handing her a campaign flyer. "I'm also a candidate."

Saint-Jean's eyes widened. "Well, excusez-moi," she said.

Outside, it was a bright spring afternoon. Inside, the lights were dimmed for a film screening. Off went the Sinatra; up came a title card in English, "Crime and Punishment" and Creole "Krim Ak Pinisyon".

The documentary, released in 2018, follows a dozen N.Y.P.D. officers, including Raymond, who became whistle-blowers, secretly recording their bosses with concealed microphones and camera pens.

The officers, known as the N.Y.P.D. 12, sued the department in federal court, alleging that supervisors instituted monthly arrest and summons quotas and encouraged officers to meet those quotas by targeting people of color.

"The reality is, law enforcement uses Black bodies to generate revenue," Raymond says in the film. Such quotas are illegal, and the N.Y.P.D. denies that they exist. This denial is harder to believe when one hears the undercover recordings.

Raymond, after allegedly being hit back against for making too few arrests…

"What's the issue with me? Just activity? Just the quota?" Supervisor: "That's what it is."

Raymond is running to represent District 40, which has one of the country's highest concentrations of Haitian Americans.

"When I meet people on the street who want to know, 'Are your pro-cop or anti-cop?' I go, 'You kind of have to watch the documentary to understand,'" he said. But many of these voters do not speak English as a first language.

So, this past winter, Raymond dubbed the movie into Creole. First, he carefully transcribed it.

"When I told the director, he went, 'We already had a transcript, you just had to ask for it,'" he said. "I went, 'I really wish you hadn't told me that."

Raymond sent his transcript to a cousin in Puerto Rico, who translated it into Creole; then Raymond assembled a group of friends, many of them community activists or Instagram influencers with some fluency in Creole, and they spent several nights at a music studio in Queens, recording a dubbed version.

"It took way longer than I anticipated," Raymond said. He played a couple of minor characters, and himself.

A few months before, Raymond took a leave of absence from the N.Y.P.D. to focus on his campaign. "I wake up happier every morning," he said. "I didn't realize the toll it was taking, constantly putting on that mental armor."

He was referring not to his normal police duties. "Breaking up fights, robberies. I have no fear about those situations" but to working alongside his fellow-cops, many of whom, since the film and the lawsuit, have called him a snitch, a rat, or worse.

After he voiced public support for Colin Kaepernick, Raymond received anonymous death threats and racist messages. "The department offered me security, but I didn't trust it," he said.

The N.Y.P.D. did not respond to a request for comment. "I'm good in Brooklyn people know me, I've lived here all my life. But I've been told, 'If you go to Long Island, or upstate, you'd better bring your gun.'"

The N.Y.P.D. 12 lawsuit remains unresolved, and Mayor Bill de Blasio has not taken up their cause...

"If you're supposed to be progressive, and you have whistle-blowers risking their lives to expose wrongdoing, how do you not support us?" Raymond said. "If we don't make some real changes, fast, then all the increased tensions we've seen since George Floyd. Cops getting ambushed, vans being set on fire, it's only going to keep getting worse."

Most people stayed after the film ended, and Raymond worked the crowd, chatting with a rapper, a TikTok comedian, and a former Miss Teen Haiti.

The only person who got a mixed welcome was a reporter from the Haitian Times. The paper had just released its endorsements, and Raymond had ranked fourth out of four. The article referred to his relative lack of political experience.

"Man, we need people in politics who aren't caught up in that system," Raymond told the reporter. "I've put my life on the line for my people. That's on another level."

CHAPTER 34

GREEN LANTERNS OUTSIDE POLICE PRECINCTS

Here are some stories or tales about the green lantern outside the police precincts....

On this day, Aug. 12, in 1658, a so-called "rattle watch" was formed in the Dutch colony known as New Amsterdam, becoming one of the first public police forces in America.

The rattle watchmen patrolled what is now New York City, using wooden rattles to warn people of threats or fires.

The watchmen carried green lanterns at night from sunset until dawn.

When the lawmen returned, they hung their lanterns on a hook by the front door of the watch house to show they were on the job.

Today, green lights are still placed outside the entrances of police stations as a symbol that the "watch" is present and vigilant.

Police lights, whether the precinct house is old or new, all New York police stations should have two green lights at the side of their entrance.

There is a story explaining why, and it has to do with the first men who patrolled New Amsterdam in the 1650s.

Peter Stuyvesant established an eight-member "rattle watch" who were "paid a small sum to keep an eye on the growing, bustling town," and look out for pirates, beggars, and robbers, according to one source.

The rattle watchmen carried green lanterns over their shoulders on a pole, like a hobo stick, so residents could identify them in the dark, unlit streets.

When the watchmen returned to the watch house after patrol, they hung their lantern on a hook by the front door to show people seeking the watchman that he was in the watch house.

Watchmen were organized groups of men, usually authorized by a state, government, city, or society, to deter criminal activity and provide law enforcement as well as traditionally perform the services of public safety, fire watch, crime prevention, crime detection, recovery of stolen goods.

Watchmen have existed since earliest recorded times in various appearances throughout the world and were generally succeeded by the emergence of formally organized professional policing.

Watchmen in the United States of America

The first form of societal protection in the United States was based on practices developed in England. The City of Boston was the first settlement in the 13 colonies to establish a night watch in 1631.

It is believed that the Rattle Watchmen, who patrolled then "New Amsterdam" in the 1650's, carried lanterns at night with green glass sides in them, as a means of identification.

When they returned to the watch house after patrol, they hung their lantern on a hook just to show the people le that the watchman was on duty.

Today, green lights are hung outside the entrances of police precincts as a symbol that the 'watch' is present and on the alert.

The loveliest old police lantern I have ever seen must be the one outside the 108th Precinct in Hunters Point, Queens.

The front wall of the station house is currently undergoing construction. The cast-iron, crica-1903 lantern does not do it justice; therefore, brand new lights were placed. It is a beauty!

The NYPD is replacing some of the old green lanterns in front of police stations throughout the city. They are being replaced with modern energy efficient L.E.D. lanterns.

Today, green lights are hung outside the entrances of police precincts as a symbol that today's modern 'Watch'. The men and women of the NYPD are always present and ready to protect the people of New York City.

CHAPTER 35

HOW IT ALL BEGAN

Before I go on with the past, let us look at how the United States got its first police force....

It would be easy to think that a police officer is a figure who has existed since the beginning of civilization. That is the idea on display in the proclamation from President John F. Kennedy on the dedication of the week of May 15 as "National Police Week," in which he noted that law-enforcement officers had been protecting Americans since the nation's birth.

In fact, the United State, police force is a relatively modern invention. It sparked by changing notions of public order, driven in turn by economics and politics, according to Gary Potter, a crime historian at Eastern Kentucky University.

Policing in Colonial America had been very informal, based on a for-profit, privately funded system that employed people part-time.

Towns also commonly relied on a "night watch" in which volunteers signed up for a certain day and time, mostly to look out for fellow colonists engaging in prostitution or gambling. Boston started one in 1636, New York followed in 1658 and Philadelphia created one in 1700.

This system was not very efficient because the watchmen often slept and drank while on duty, and they were put on watch duty as a form of punishment.

Night-watch officers were supervised by officers, but that was not exactly a highly sought-after job, either. Early policemen "didn't want to wear badges because these guys had bad reputations to begin with, and they didn't want to be identified as people that others didn't like.

When localities tried compulsory service, "if you were rich enough, you paid someone to do it for you. Ironically, a criminal or a community gangster."

As the nation grew, however, different regions made use of different policing systems.

During the 19th century, cities were increasing drastically. Urbanization provided the night-watch system completely useless the communities got too big.

The first publicly funded, organized police force with officers on duty full-time was created in Boston in 1838.

Boston was a large shipping commercial center, and businesses had been hiring people to protect their property and safeguard the transport of goods from the port of Boston to other places. The merchants came up with a way to save money by transferring to the cost of maintaining a police force to citizens by arguing that it was for the "collective good."

In the South, however, the economics that drove the creation of police forces were centered not on the protection of shipping interests, but on the preservation of the slavery system.

Some of the primary policing institutions there were the slave. There were huge patrols tasked that would chase down runaways and preventing slave revolts.

The first formal slave patrol had been created in the Carolina colonies in 1704…

During the Civil War, the military became the primary form of law enforcement in the South, but during Reconstruction, many local sheriffs functioned in a way like the earlier slave patrols, enforcing segregation and the disqualification of freed slaves.

In general, throughout the 19th century and beyond, the definition of public order that which the police officer was charged with maintaining peace, depended on who was asked.

For example, businessmen in the late 19th century had both connections to politicians and an image of the kind of people who most likely to go on strike and disrupt their workforce.

Therefore, it is no coincidence that by the late 1880s, all major U.S. cities had police forces. They mostly feared the labor union organizers.

To begin with, there was a large wave of Catholic, Irish, Italian, German, and even Eastern European immigrants, who looked and acted differently from the people who had dominated cities.

Those so call businessmen were just afraid that their profit will go elsewhere. It drove the call for the preservation of law and order, or at least the version of it promoted by dominant interests.

For example, people who drank at taverns rather than at home, were "dangerous" by some people. They also pointed out other factors such as how living in a smaller home makes drinking in a tavern more appealing.

The irony of this logic was that the businessmen who maintained this belief were often the ones who profited off the commercial sale of alcohol in public places.

Also, the late 19th century was the era of political machines, so police captains and sergeants for each precinct were often picked by the local political party ward leader, who often owned taverns or ran street gangs that intimidated voters. They did so they were able to use police to harass opponents of that political party or provide payoffs for officers to turn a blind eye. This also allowed illegal drinking, gambling and prostitution.

This situation was worsened during Prohibition, leading President Hoover to appoint the Wickersham Commission in 1929 to investigate the ineffectiveness of law enforcement nationwide.

It was decided by the businessmen that to make police independent from political party ward leaders, the image of police precincts was changed so that they would not correspond in any political districts.

The drive to professionalize the police followed. This means that the concept of a career cop, as we recognize it today, is less than a century old.

Further campaigns for police professionalism were promoted as the 20th century progressed, but crime historian Samuel Walker's The Police in America: An Introduction argues that the move toward professionalism was not all good: that movement, he argues, promoted the creation of police departments that were "inward-looking" and "isolated from the public."

Crime-control tactics ended up worsening tensions between police and the communities they watch over.

So, more than a half-century after Kennedy's 1963 proclamation, the improvement and modernization of America's surprisingly young police force continues to this day.

CHAPTER 36

NEW YORK CITY
POLICE DEPARTMENT

<u>Let us go back to the famous WATCH SYSTEM</u>

The watch system was composed of community volunteers whose primary duty was to warn of impending danger.

In New York was implemented in 1658.

I am mentioning this again.... Why the night watch was not an effective crime control device. The Watchmen often slept or drank on duty they were mostly "volunteers". They were simply attempting to evade military service, who were forced into service by their town.

Some were performing watch duties as a form of punishment. New York instituted a day watch in 1844 as a supplement to its new municipal police force.

The New York City Police Department had its origins in the city government of New York trying to find a better way to control the rising crime rate in early mid-19th century.

Keep in mind that some of the crimes were brought on by the massive population growth, caused primarily by poor Irish immigrants from Ireland beginning in the 1820s.

The city implemented the London, England policing model of a full-time professional police force in 1845, with the establishment of the Municipal Police, replacing the inadequate, out of date night watch system. This system was founded by the Dutch colonial city of New Amsterdam.

In 1857, the Municipal Police were excitedly replaced by a Metropolitan Police, which consolidated other local police departments.

During the 19th and early 20th century, there was a fashion of professionalization. They were struggling against corruption.

Prior to the establishment of the NYPD, New York City's population of about 320,000 was served by a force consisting of one-night watch, one hundred city marshals, thirty-one constables, and 51 municipal police officers.

On May 7, 1844, the New York State passed the Municipal Police Act, a law which authorized creation of a police force and abolished the night watch system, however, because of a lengthy dispute between the Common Council and the Mayor of New York City regarding who would appoint the officers, the law was not put into effect until the following year.

Under Mayor William Havemeyer, the city finally repealed their watch system and adopted the Municipal Police Act as an ordinance on May 23, 1845. This created the New York Police Department.

For the purposes of policing, the city was divided into three districts, with courts, magistrates, and clerks, and station houses. The NYPD was closely modeled after the Metropolitan Police Service in London, England which used a military-like organizational structure, with rank and order.

A navy-blue uniform was introduced after long debate in 1853.

In 1857, Republican reformers in the state capital, Albany, created a new Metropolitan police force and abolished the Municipal police, as part of their effort to rein in the Democratically controlled New York City government. The Metropolitan police bill consolidated the police in New York, Brooklyn, Staten Island, and Westchester County, which then included the Bronx, under a governor-appointed board of commissioners.

Unwilling to be abolished, Mayor Fernando Wood and the Municipals resisted for several months, during which time the city effectively had two police forces. The State-controlled Metropolitans and the Municipals. The Metropolitans included three police officers and seven captains who left the Municipal police but was primarily made up of raw recruits with little or no training.

The Municipals were controlled directly by Wood and including eight hundred police officers and fifteen captains who stayed.

By this time, the division between the forces was culturally determined, with immigrants largely staying with the Municipals, and those of Anglo-Dutch heritage going to the Metropolitans.

Chaos followed.... Criminals had a high old time.

This era was bad because criminals were arrested by one force, however, they were rescued by the other....

Rival cops fought over possession of station houses. There were so many bad situations without control...

In mid-June, in 1857, a Metropolitan police captain attempted to deliver a warrant for the mayor's arrest. He was thrown out by a group of Municipals. They were armed and had with them a second warrant, which was more powerful. This powerful group was made up of Metropolitans police officers who marched against City Hall.

Both groups began to fight....

The mayor's supporters began clubbing and punching the outnumbered Metropolitans away from the seat of government. The Metropolitans gained the day after the State-controlled. The Seventh Regiment came to its rescue, and the warrant was served on Wood.

This setback for the mayor was followed by another: on July 2, 1857, the Court of Appeals ruled in favor of the state law. Wood disbanded the Municipals late in the afternoon of July 3, 1857, leaving the Metropolitans in possession of the field.

Unfortunately, the untested Metropolitans failed to prevent rioting in the city the next day, Independence Day, July 4, 1857. They had to be rescued by the nativist Bowery Boys gang. This was when the Irish-immigrant gang, the Dead Rabbits attacked the "Mets".

Barricades were built and the battle went on for hours. This was the worst riot in the city since 1849…

The following Sunday, peace was maintained by the State Militia, but a week later, on July 12, 1857, the German-immigrants in Little Germany, rioted when the Metropolitans attempted to enforce the new reform liquor laws. This was to close saloons.

A blacksmith was killed in the battle, and the next day, ten thousand marched up Broadway with a banner proclaiming Opfer der Metropolitan-Polizei "Victim of the Metropolitan Police".

Throughout the years, the New York Police Department has been involved with several riots in New York City.

In July 1863, the New York State Militias were aiding Union troops in Pennsylvania, when the 1863 Draft Riots broke out. Their absence left it to the police who were then outnumbered to disperse the riots.

The Tompkins Square Riot occurred on January 13, 1874. This was when police defeated a demonstration involving thousands of unemployed in Tompkins Square Park.

Newspapers, including The New York Times, covered numerous cases of police brutality during the latter part of the 19th century.

Many cases often involved officers using clubs to beat suspects and people who were drunk or rowdy.

Some wanted to challenge the officers' authority or refused to move along down the street. In most cases of police brutality, they occurred in poor immigrant neighborhoods. This included Five Points, the Lower East Side, and Tenderloin.

At beginning of the 1870s, politics and corruption of Tammany Hall, a political machine supported by Irish immigrants infiltrated the NYPD. This was used as political tool, with positions awarded by politicians to loyalists.

It is so sad to say that many officers and leaders in the police department took bribes from local businesses, overlooking things like illegal liquor sales.

The Police also served political purposes such as manning polling places, where they would turn a blind eye to ballot box stuffing and many acts of fraud.

The Lexow Committee was established in 1894 to investigate corruption in the police department. The committee was made up of reform recommendations, including the suggestion that the police department adopt a civil service system.

Corruption investigations have been a regular feature of the NYPD, including the Knapp Commission of the 1970s, and the Mollen Commission of the 1990s.

In 1895, Theodore Roosevelt became President of the NYPD Police Commission. Under his leadership many reforms were instituted in the NYPD.

On January 1, 1898, the city expanded to include Brooklyn. The department absorbed eighteen existing police departments, requiring more modern organization and communication as it is now protecting 320 square miles and over three million residences.

About the turn of the century, the New York Police Department began to professionalize under leadership of then President of the Police Commission, Theodore Roosevelt.

With the many innovations in science and technology, the police force was able to establish new units, such as the Bomb Squad in 1905, Motorcycle Squad in 1911, Automobile Squad in 1919, Emergency Service Unit in 1926, Aviation Unit in 1929 as well as the Radio Motor Patrol, RMP, in 1932.

The department was also among the earliest to implement fingerprinting techniques and mug shots.

In 1919, the department adopted its own flag...

In 1911, the department hired Samuel, Jesse, Battle as its first black officer. He went on to become the first black sergeant and lieutenant and retired after a thirty-year career.

In 1896 Commissioner Roosevelt authorized the purchase of a standard issued revolver for the NYPD. It was the Colt New Police Revolver in .32 Long Colt caliber. He also instituted required firearms training including pistol practice and qualification for officers.

In 1907, the Colt Police Positive revolver in .38 caliber, was adopted by the department.

In May 1926, the NYPD adopted the .38 Special cartridge as the standard issue ammunition for the department and started issuing its officers the Smith & Wesson Model 10 revolver and the Colt Official Police revolver.

In 1994 the NYPD replaced the revolver as its main service weapon and adopted the 9mmsemiautomatic pistol as its standard issued sidearm, replacing the .38 Special revolver.

NYPD officers who were "on the job" on or prior to 1994 could continue to carry their revolvers if they wished. The .38 Special can still be found as a backup or off duty weapon, particularly with long serving personnel.

The economic downturn of the 1970s led to some extremely difficult times for the city. The Bronx was plagued by arson, and an atmosphere of lawlessness permeated the city.

Frank Serpico wrote about corruption. He encountered in his time as a police officer in this era in a book, which was later turned into a movie and television series.

In addition, the city's financial crisis led to a hiring freeze on all city departments, including the NYPD, from 1976 to 1980.

This was followed by the crack cocaine epidemic of the late 1980s and early 1990s, which was one factor in the city's homicide rate soaring to an all-time high.

By 1990, New York, a city with 7.3 million people at the time, set a record of 2,262 murders, a record that has yet to be broken by any U.S. city. Petty thefts associated with drug addiction were also increasingly common.

In 1993, Mayor David Dinkins appointed the Mollen Commission, chaired by Milton Mollen, to investigate corruption in the department.

The Lebow Committee was established in 1894 to investigate corruption in the police department. The committee made reform recommendations, including the suggestion that the_police department adopt a civil service system.

Corruption investigations have been a regular feature of the NYPD, including the Knapp Commission of the 1970s, and the Mollen Commission of the 1990s.

In addition, the city's financial crisis led to a hiring freeze on all city departments, including the NYPD, from 1976 to 1980.

In the mid-1990s, under Mayor Rudy Giuliani, the NYPD oversaw a large reduction in crime across the city, which has been attributed to the NYPD's implementation of the CompStat program under Police Commissioner Bill Bratton, broken windows policing, as well as general demographic changes and subsiding of the crack cocaine epidemic.

CompStat was a concept that is generally attributed to Deputy Police Commissioner Jack Maple.

He was a police lieutenant serving in the New York City Transit Police. This is when it came to the attention of then NYC Transit Authority Police Chief Bratton. in fact, it was first implemented by Captain Mario Selvagi in Far Rockaway's 101 precinct.

Since Selvagi was unable to secure the cooperation of the department's MIS department, he used pin maps. Selvagi went on to become a "super chief" but was forced out by Bill Bratton.

In 1995, Bratton as the former NYC Transit Police Chief, is now Police Commissioner of the NYPD. The New York City Transit Police and the New York City Housing Authority Police Department are merged in with the NYPD.

The enforcement and traffic control elements of the City's Department of Transportation were merged into the NYPD in 1996.

The enforcement and traffic control elements of the City's Department of Transportation were merged into the NYPD in 1996.

In 1998 the NYC Board of Education's school safety agents were merged into the newly formed New York City Police Department School Safety Division, to improve safety in NYC public schools.

On September 11, 2001, 23 NYPD officers were killed when the World Trade Center collapsed due to terrorist attacks. More lives were lost that year than in any other year in the department's history.

The NYPD Counter-Terrorism Bureau was founded in 2002 because of the tragedy and the threats to attack the city that followed.

In the last two weeks of 2005, two officers were shot to death by criminals using illegal weapons.

In 2014, two highly publicized attacks were committed against the NYPD.

On October 23, 2014, two NYPD officers were injured, one critically, in a hatchet attack, but both officers survived their injuries.

In December, two NYPD officers, <u>Wenjian Liu and Rafael Ramos</u>, were shot to death in an ambush in Brooklyn.

In both cases, the perpetrators later died. In the hatchet attack, the suspect was killed by police, while in the gunfire attack. The suspect killed himself after being confronted by police.

In 2015 the Strategic Response Group was formed.

On June 20, 2016, three officers were arrested as part of a federal corruption investigation.

CHAPTER 37

WOMEN IN THE NEW YORK CITY POLICE DEPARTMENT

In 1845, the New York City Police Department hired its first female jail matrons. Legislation was enacted to appoint female police matrons in 1888.

The first four were hired in 1891 and 1895.

The first woman to work at Police Headquarters, Minnie Gertrude Kelly, was appointed Secretary to the Police Board.

In 1912, Isabella Goodwin was appointed as the first female, first grade detective. In 1917, two unknown women were assigned special patrolwomen's badges.

I put together a timeline so you can appreciate the assignments and appointments of these brave women…

In 1918, the first female Deputy Commissioner, Ellen O'Grady, was appointed.

In August 1918, the first group of policewomen in the NYPD were appointed, there were six altogether.

In 1919, the title "policewoman" was changed to "patrolwoman".

In 1921, the Women's Police Precinct was formed with 20 patrolwomen assigned; Mary Hamilton was assigned as director.

November 13, 1923, Governor Walker appointed Sylvia Daly Connell, a widow with two children, the first woman Deputy Sheriff in New York State. She was assigned to Richmond County.

In 1924, the New York Police Department's Women Bureau was created.

In 1934, female officers began to have pistol practice with male officers.

In 1938, the first civil service exam for the title "Policewoman". About 5,000 women took the exam, with 300 passing it.

In 1942, there began a requirement of a college degree for female officers.

In 1958, women and men began to train together at the Police Academy.

In 1961, Felicia Schpritzer of the NYPD sued to allow women the right to take the sergeant's exam. As a result of this lawsuit, 126 policewomen took the sergeant's exam for the first time in 1964.

Schpritzer and another policewoman, Gertrude Schimmel, became the first female sergeants and after suing again, the_duo became the first female lieutenants in 1967. Schimmel went on to become the first female police Captain in 1971 and the first female Deputy Inspector in 1972.

In 1970, the first woman could take the test for Police Administrative Aides, and the first women were hired from the Police Administrative List.

Also in 1970, Police Commissioner Murphy assigned the first group of women to patrol.

In 1973, the Bureau of Policewomen was abolished, and the first gender-neutral civil service exam for police officers was held.

It wasn't until 1970, that the term "Policewomen" and "Patrolmen" were officially renamed "Police Officers".

In 1974, Gertrude Schimmel was appointed as the first female Inspector.

In 1976, <u>Captain Vittoria Renault</u> was appointed as the first precinct Commander.

In 1977, the first group of women were assigned to the Homicide Unit. There were nine of them altogether.

In 1978, <u>Gertrude Schimmel</u> was appointed as the first female Deputy Chief. Also, that year, the Department entered into an agreement to increase the Number of female detectives.

In 1981, Suzanne Medici's became the first woman to receive the Combat Cross, and Sharon Fields and Tanya Braithwaite became the first women to receive the NYPD's Medal of Honor.

In 1984, <u>Irma Lozada </u>became the first female police officer killed in the line of duty.

In 1984, <u>Mary Bembry</u> became the first woman shot in the line of duty.

In 1985, the first Women in Policing Conference was held.

In 1987, <u>Paula Berlinerman</u> and Joan Clark were appointed as the first civilian women Civil Service Managers.

In 1988, <u>Mary Lowery</u> became the first female police officer assigned to the Aviation Unit.

In 1991, for the first time, most of the deputy commissioners were female.

In 1992, <u>Deputy Inspector Kathy Ryan</u> was appointed as the first female Commanding Officer of the Mounted Unit.

In 1994, <u>Joyce A. Stephen</u> became the first African American female captain, and an Action Plan on Women's Concerns was prepared and submitted to the Police Commissioner.

In 1995, <u>Gertrude Lafora</u> was appointed as the first female Assistant Chief Borough Commander.

It has been a slow process in allowing females in the department, however, it is happening....

CHAPTER 38

THE PRIMARY LAW ENFORCEMENT AGENCY

The City of New York Police Department, more commonly known as the New York Police Department and its initials NYPD, is the primary law enforcement and investigation agency within the United States.

Established on May 23, 1845, the NYPD is one of the oldest police departments in the United States and is the largest police force in the United States.

The NYPD headquarters is at 1 Police Plaza, located on Park Row in Lower Manhattan across the street from City Hall.

The department's mission is to "enforce the laws, preserve peace, reduce fear, and provide safe environment." The NYPD's regulations are compiled in title 38 of the New York City Rules. The New York City Transit Police and New York City Housing Authority Police Department were fully integrated into the NYPD in 1995 by New York City Mayor Rudolph W. Giuliani.

In June 2004, there were about 45,000 sworn officers plus several thousand civilian employees; in June 2005, the number of officers dropped to 35,000. As of December 2011, that figure increased slightly to over 36,600, helped by the graduation of a class of 1,500 from the New York City Police Academy. As of Fiscal Year, 2018, the NYPD's current authorized uniformed strength is 38,422.

There are also approximately 4,500 Auxiliary Police Officers, 5,000 School Safety Agents, 2,300 Traffic Enforcement Agents, and 370 Traffic Enforcement Supervisors currently employed by the department.

The Police Benevolent Association of the City of New York, NYC PBA, the largest municipal police union in the United States, represents over 50,000 active and retired NYC police officers.

The NYPD has a broad range of specialized services, including the Emergency Service Unit, K9, harbor patrol, air support, bomb squad, counterterrorism, criminal intelligence, anti-gang, anti-organized crime, narcotics, public transportation, and public housing. The NYPD Intelligence Division & Counter-Terrorism Bureau has officers stationed in 11 cities internationally.

In the 1990s, the department developed a CompStat system of management which has also since been established in other cities.

The NYPD has extensive crime scene investigation and laboratory resources, as well as units which assist with computer crime investigations. The NYPD runs a "Real Time Crime Center", essentially a large search engine and data warehouse operated by detectives to assist officers in the field with their investigations.

A Domain Awareness System, a joint project of Microsoft and the NYPD, links 6,000 closed-circuit television cameras, license plate readers, and other surveillance devices into an integrated system.

Due to its high-profile location in the largest city and media center in the United States, fictionalized versions of the NYPD and its officers have frequently been portrayed in novels, radio, television, motion pictures, and video games.

The Municipal Police were established in 1845, replacing an old night watch system. Mayor William Havemeyer shepherded the NYPD together, originating the phrase "New York's Finest."

In 1857, it was tumultuously replaced by a Metropolitan force, which abolished the Municipal police. Twentieth-century trends included professionalization and struggles against corruption.

CHAPTER 39

THE CHAOTIC BIRTH
OF THE NYPD

People got mugged a lot of times growing up in Brooklyn and other boros. It was rough in the early days, but some didn't have it nearly as bad as the German immigrant who, on a wintry night in the 1840s, took a walk-through Battery Park.

The immigrant was killed by robbers who then searched his pockets and got angry when they found only 12 cents. They tossed his body into the harbor. And guess what? It did not sink — it landed on the ice, where it remained in the morning, glowering at those who came to look.

Tough town is how New York was called. The main reason was the lack of a police force. Instead, a loosely organized group of "constables" was responsible for public safety. They often got paid by the job and were regularly mocked, harassed, and beaten by the many criminals who hang around in the alleys and packed the taverns and brothels of the roiling young city.

The Chaotic Birth of the NYPD was the beginning of what is today the largest municipal police force in the United States.

There are so many stories that expresses the story of New York in those murderous decades through the prism of how it policed itself, or at least tried.

Anyone would like to relish New York's history will enjoy this highlight reel. All the big stories, places and characters of those days are here. To mention a few, James Gordon Bennett and the penny press, the Five Points, Walt Whitman, Horace Greeley, the Astor Place riot, Boss Tweed, the Helen Jewett murder, the death of the beautiful cigar girl.

New Yorkers at first did not even want a police force. One reason was high taxes, but the other was set deep in their collective panics. The city had been occupied by the British during the Revolutionary War: Many believed the police would just be a standing army in different colored uniforms. '

In the meantime, the disorder continued. Riot after riot bloodied the streets. Then editors like Bennett discovered that crime sold newspapers. So did outrage about crime. There are many stories about what a bunch of idiots the constables were.

The newspapers and a band of reformers demanded the creation of a real police force, and in 1845 it came to be.

The city traded one set of problems for another...

To avoid the fates of their unfortunate predecessors, the new police officers were overly fond of their billy clubs. The real police brutality arrived with the real police. Then, feeling overwhelmed, the new officers drew closer together in a tight-knit camaraderie with its own codes and culture. This was the origin of today's blue wall of silence.

Nothing ever gets better. The city's municipal police department is quickly replaced by a state-managed metropolitan police force after the two groups battle in the streets, but "the new police did not do much more than the old municipal force."

Finally, in the 1870s, Civil Service arrives, and a truly professional force takes charge, but that is just a few sentences the speech.

The word "cop" was born later when police officers got copper badges. This refers to that scandalous penny press papers as "tabloids," even though they were printed on broadsheets.

Today's New York City Police Department is, indeed, a standing army of about 36,000 officers. Roughly 500 of them are armed with assault rifles to confront terrorist attacks. Others are posted to foreign capitals. Still others zoom across the skyline in state-of-the-art helicopters, scan crowds from horseback and zip around the harbor in speedboats.

The department has made some monstrous missteps in recent years. It engaged in the widespread surveillance of tens of thousands of innocents and mostly minority New Yorkers by frisking them without legal justification.

Individual officers caused immeasurable suffering to men like Eric Garner, Amadou Diallo, and Abner Louima, among others, and to their families.

Overall, it is a remarkable organization, policing a sprawling metropolis that often doesn't want to be policed. Doing so with a level of professionalism that is, for the most part, impressive. If the terrorists come, I have no doubt that those officers will go straight at them.

CHAPTER 40

RANKS WITHIN THE NYPD

Officers begin service with the rank of "probationary police officer," also referred to as "recruit officer".

After successful completion of five and a half to six months, sometimes longer of Police Academy training in various academic, physical, and tactical training, officers graduate from the Police Academy. While officially retaining the title of "probationary police officer,"" graduates are referred to as a "police officer," or informally as a "rookie", until they have completed an additional 18-month probationary period.

There are three career "tracks" in the NYPD: supervisory, investigative, and specialist.

The supervisory track consists of nine sworn titles, referred to as ranks. Promotion to the ranks of sergeant, lieutenant, and captain are made via competitive civil service examinations.

After reaching the civil service rank of captain, promotion to the ranks of deputy inspector, inspector, deputy chief, assistant chief, bureau, chief and chief of department is made at the discretion of the police commissioner.

Promotion from the rank of police officer to detective is discretionary by the police commissioner or required by law when the officer has performed eighteen months or more of investigative duty.

The entry level appointment to detective is third grade or specialist. The commissioner may grant discretionary grades of second and finally first.

These grades offer compensation roughly equivalent to that of supervisors. Specifically, a second-grade detective's pay roughly corresponds to a sergeant's and a first-grade detective's pay roughly corresponds to a lieutenant. Detectives are police officers who usually perform investigatory duties but have no official supervisory authority.

A "detective first grade" still falls under the command of a sergeant or above. Just like detectives, sergeants and lieutenants can receive pay grade increases within their respective ranks.

<u>Uniform rank that has no police powers</u>
<u>Officers from the Emergency Service Unit</u>

<u>Police boat patrolling the East River</u>

There are two basic types of detectives in the NYPD: "detective-investigators" and "detective-specialists".

Detective-investigators are the type most people associate with the term "detective" and are the ones most frequently portrayed on television and in the movies.

Most police officers gain their detective title by working in the Narcotics Division of the Detective Bureau. Detectives assigned to squads are co-located within each precinct and are responsible for investigating murders, rapes, robberies, burglaries, and other crimes within that precinct's boundaries.

Other detective-investigators are assigned to specialized units at either the major command or citywide level, investigating terrorist groups, organized crime, narcotics dealing, extortion, bias crimes, political corruption, kidnappings, major frauds, or thefts committed against banks or museums, police corruption, contractor fraud and other complex, politically sensitive, or high-profile cases. A squad of detective-investigators is also assigned to each of the city's five district attorneys' offices.

Promotion from "police officer" to "detective-investigator" is based on investigative experience. Typically, a police officer who is assigned to investigative work for 18 months will be designated "detective-investigator" and receive the gold shield and pay increase commensurate with that designation.

In the recent past, however, there has been controversy over the budget-conscious department compelling police officers to work past the 18 months without receiving the new title.

Newly appointed detectives start at "detective third grade," which has a pay rate roughly between that of "police officer" and "sergeant".

As they gain seniority and experience, they can be "promoted" to "detective second-grade," which has a pay grade slightly less than sergeants.

"Detective first-grade" is an elite designation for the department's most senior and experienced investigators and carries a pay grade slightly less than lieutenants.

All these promotions are flexible on the part of the commissioner and can be revoked if warranted. While senior detectives can give directions to junior detectives in their own squads, not even the most senior detective can lawfully issue orders to even a junior patrol officer.

All detective grades still fall under the "chain of command" of the supervisory ranks beginning with "sergeant" through "chief of department".

Detectives, like police officers, are eligible to take the promotional civil service exams for entry into the supervisory ranks.

While carrying with them increased pay and prestige, none of these detective grades confer on the holder any supervisory authority.

Contrary to some media portrayals, there is no specific rank of "detective sergeant" or "detective lieutenant".

Lieutenants and Sergeants are assigned to oversee detective squads as supervisors and are responsible for all investigations. There is a small percentage of lieutenants and sergeants who work as investigative supervisors and are granted the prestigious pay grade designations of "Sergeant—Supervisor Detective Squad" (SDS), or Lieutenant—Commander Detective Squad (CDS) therefore assuming full investigative command responsibility as opposed to operational supervision. Their pay grade rises to an approximate midpoint between their normal rank and the next highest rank's pay grade, and like a detective's "grade", is also a discretionary promotion.

This pay grade designation is achieved by assignment to investigative units, i.e. Detective Bureau, Internal Affairs Bureau, Counter-Terrorism Bureau, and the Intelligence Bureau. Lieutenants and sergeants in non-investigatory assignments can be designated lieutenant-special assignment or sergeant-special assignment, pay equivalent to their investigative counterparts. "Detective-specialists" are a relatively new designation and one unique to the NYPD. In the 1980s, many detectives resented that some officers were being granted the rank of detective to give them increased pay and status but were not being assigned to investigative duties. Examples included officers assigned as bodyguards and drivers to the mayor, police commissioner and other senior officials.

To remedy this situation, the rank of detective-specialist was created. These officers are typically found in specialized units because they possess a unique or esoteric skill the department needs, e.g., crime-scene tech, sharpshooter, bomb technician, scuba instructor, helicopter instructor, sketch artist, etc. Like detective-investigators, detective-specialists start at third grade and can be promoted to second- or first-grade status.

Motorcycle police officer speaks with a passerby

The Department is administered and governed by the Police Commissioner, who is appointed by the mayor. Technically, the commissioner serves a five-year term; as a practical matter, the commissioner serves at the mayor's pleasure. The commissioner in turn appoints numerous deputy commissioners. The commissioner and his subordinate deputies are civilians under an oath of office and are not uniformed members of the force who are sworn officers of the law.

Police commissioner who comes up from the uniformed ranks retains that status while serving as police commissioner. This has ramifications for their police pensions and the fact that any police commissioner who is considered sworn does not need a pistol permit to carry a firearm and retains the statutory powers of a police officer. Some police commissioners carry a personal firearm, but they also have a full-time security detail from the police commissioner's squad. A first deputy police commissioner may have a security detail when they act as commissioner or under other circumstances as approved by the police commissioner.

These individuals are administrators who supersede the chief of department, and they usually specialize in areas of great importance to the Department, such as counterterrorism, support services, public information, legal matters, intelligence, and information technology. Despite their role, as civilian administrators of the department, deputy commissioners are prohibited from taking operational control of a police situation the Commissioner and the first deputy commissioner may take control of these situations, however.

Within the rank structure, there are also designations, known as "grades", that connote differences in duties, experience, and pay. However, supervisory functions are generally reserved for the rank of sergeant and above.

Badges in the New York City Police Department are referred to as "shields", the traditional term, though not all badge designs are strictly shield-shaped. Every rank has a different badge design except for "police officer" and "probationary police officer", and upon change in rank officers receive a new badge. Lower-ranked police officers are identified by their shield numbers, and tax registry number. Lieutenants and above do not have shield numbers and are identified by tax registry number. All sworn members of the NYPD have their ID card photos taken against a red background. Civilian employees of the NYPD have their ID card photos taken against a blue background, signifying that they are not commissioned to carry a firearm. All ID cards have an expiration date.

Police Academy

The police academy is a training school for new police recruits, also known as a law enforcement academy. Some are known as colleges or universities. They all have various background checks, examination, physical requirements, medical requirements, legal training, driving skills, equipment training and firearm training for new police recruits. The academy prepares the recruits for the police force they will be assigned to when they graduate.

The Police Academy is the NYPD's state-of-the-art training facility that provides academic and physical preparation to uniformed and civilian members of the NYPD. Members of the department undergo extensive, rigorous preparation, befitting the most highly trained and effective law enforcement professionals in the country.

The Police Academy provides them with the latest technology, education, and tactical knowledge to enhance their ability to protect the lives, rights, property, and dignity of all New Yorkers and visitors.

Recruit and in-service training focus on effective community policing, de-escalation, communication skills, safe tactics, and the privilege of serving the nation's most diverse population. With the increased threat of terrorism, the Police Academy also provides new recruits and in-service personnel with the latest counterterror methodologies. These include highly specialized curricula, such as intelligence gathering, active-shooter training, and counter surveillance. Additional areas of instruction include training for the department's Highway, Traffic Enforcement, and School Safety personnel.

The 32-acre campus, located in College Point, Queens, and operated by the NYPD Training Bureau, opened its doors in 2014, consolidating the old Police Academy in Manhattan and existing training facilities throughout the city into one central location.

The 750,000-square-foot facility has nearly three times the amount of useable space as the old academy and features modern classrooms, a gymnasium and indoor track, and a tactical village that emphasizes hands-on scenario-based training. Mock-environment training rooms include a precinct station house, multi-family residence, grocery store, restaurant, park, court room, bank, and a subway car and platform.

Passive visual warnings

Passive visual warnings are the markings on the vehicle. Police vehicle markings usually make use of bright colors or strong contrast with the base color of the vehicle. Modern police vehicles in some countries have retroreflective markings which reflect light for better visibility at night. Other police vehicles may only have painted on or non-reflective markings. Most marked police vehicles in the United Kingdom and Sweden have reflective Battenburg markings on the sides, which are large blue and yellow rectangles.

These markings are designed to have high contrast and be highly visible on the road, to deter crime and improve safety. Another passive visual warning of police vehicles is simply the interceptor's silhouette. This is easily observed in the United States and Canada, where the ubiquitous nature of the Ford Crown Victoria in police fleets has made the model synonymous with police vehicles.

Police vehicle marking schemes usually include the word Police or similar phrase, such as State Trooper, Highway Patrol, or the force's crest.

Some police forces use unmarked vehicles, which do not have any passive visual warnings at all, and others, called secrecy cars, have markings that are visible only at certain angles, such as from the rear or sides, making these cars appear unmarked when viewed from the front.

Organization of the New York City Police Department
One Police Plaza, NYPD HQ
Office of the Chief of Department

The Chief of Department serves as the senior sworn member of the NYPD. Terence Monahan is the 40th individual to hold the post, which prior to 1987 was known as the chief of operations and before that as chief inspector.

The Department is divided into twenty bureaus, which are typically commanded by a uniformed bureau chief, such as the chief of patrol and the chief of housing or a civilian deputy commissioner and as the Deputy Commissioner of Information Technology.

The bureaus fit under four umbrellas: Patrol, Transit & Housing, Investigative, and Administrative. Bureaus are often subdivided into smaller divisions and units.

Demographics

As of the end of 2010, 53% of the entire 34,526-member police forces were white and 47% were members of minority groups.

Of 22,199 officers on patrol, 53%, 11,717, were black, Latino of any race or Asian or Asian-American, and 47%, 10,482, were non-Hispanic white.

Of 5,177 detectives, 57%, 2,953, were white and 43%, 2,225, were people of color.

Of 4,639 sergeants, 61%, 2,841, were white and 39%, 1,798, were minorities. Of 1,742 lieutenants, 76%, 1,323, were white and 24%, 419 were people of color.

Of 432 captains, 82%, 356, were white and 18%, 76, were minorities.

Of 10 chiefs, 7 were white and 3 were people of color.

In 2002, whites accounted for 60% of members in the rank of police officer. Between 2002 and 2010, the number of minorities in top-tier positions in the force increased by about 4.5%.

CHAPTER 41

DOMAIN AWARENESS SYSTEM

In August 2008, the Lower Manhattan Security Initiative in a partnership between the New York City Police Department and Microsoft began the Domain Awareness System to monitor New York City.

The program allowed the department to track surveillance targets and gain detailed information about them. The system is connected to 6,000 video cameras around New York City as well as check radiological and nuclear detectors onboard helicopters, trucks, and boats as well as detectors on police officers' gun belts that were so sensitive that people who have had medical procedures may trigger them.

Lower Manhattan now includes thousands of surveillance cameras that can identify shapes and sizes of unidentified "suspicious" packages and can track people within seconds using descriptions such as "someone wearing a red shirt".

In 2009, an extension into Midtown Manhattan was announced and by 2012 the program was fully implemented.

The system was also licensed out to other cities with New York City getting 30% of the profits. The system's development costs were estimated at US$40 million.

CHAPTER 42

THE CIVILIAN COMPLAINT REVIEW BOARD

The first steps towards creating what is now the Civilian Complaint Review Board were taken in 1950.

This went into effect when a coalition of 18 organizations formed the Permanent Coordination Committee on Police and Minority Groups to lobby the city to deal with police misconduct in general. Also, with police misconduct in their relations with the community specially with Hispanics and Afro Americans.

In response to their demands, the New York City Police Department established the Civilian Complaint Review Board in 1953 as a committee of three deputy police commissioners to investigate civilian complaints.

While the board was granted wider authority under Mayor Robert Wagner in 1955, it remained an organization within the police department.

The police officers conducted the investigations and the decision on whether to recommend discipline was made by the deputy commissioners.

Lindsay's Plan

After his election in 1965, Mayor John Lindsay appointed former federal judge Lawrence E. Walsh to investigate the operation of the police department and make suggestions for improvement.

While most of the Walsh's report focused on modernization, the report also argued that the Board itself should have civilian representation, to inspire public confidence that the investigations of civilian complaints would be handled fairly.

Lindsay formed a search committee, chaired by former Attorney General Herbert Brownell, to find civilians to serve on the board. John Cassese, the president of the Patrolman's Benevolent Association, PBA, rigorously opposed a civilian presence on the board, stating, "I'm sick and tired of giving in to minority groups with their impulses, their complaints and shouting."

The mayor's search committee found four candidates, whom the mayor appointed, and for the first time in the city's history, people outside the department oversaw the investigations of complaints against police officers.

Lindsay's board did not last long. Cassese and the PBA collected signatures to force a ballot measure to bar civilians from having any oversight of police complaints.

The resulting campaign was bitter on all sides; the PBA made appeals to safety and fear, stating that with civilian oversight, the police would not be able to do their job properly, and the forces in favor of civilian participation painted their opponents as racists. The ballot measure won tremendously, and the board returned to its previous all-police makeup.

In 1987, in accordance with legislation passed in 1986 by the city council, the board was restructured as one where private citizen served alongside non-uniformed police officers; the mayor, with the advice and consent of city council, appointed six members and the police commissioner appointed six.

At this time, the Civilian Complaint Investigations Bureau began to hire civilians to investigate complaints, though these civilians served alongside police department investigators and were supervised by department employees.

In 1988, an event helped influence public opinion in favor of more civilian control over the investigation of complaints made against NYPD officers.

In response to complaints of drug trafficking and disorderly groups in Tompkins Square Park, the department chose to enforce an existing 1:00 a.m. curfew that had previously not been enforced. A rally protesting the curfew on July 31 turned into a confrontation with police in which four people were arrested and four officers were injured.

On August 6, demonstrators were forced from the park in a series of violent incidents between the police, demonstrators, and bystanders. Video footage showed police officers striking people with nightsticks, kicking people who were on the ground, and covering their shields to hide their identity.

The CCRB commissioned a special report on the incident, concluding that "there is no evidence that any effort was made to limit the use of force ... Force was used for its own sake." Even though the report was extremely critical of the NYPD, the event itself galvanized support for an all-civilian review board.

In 1993, after extensive debate and public comment, Mayor David Dinkins and the New York City Council created the Civilian Complaint Review Board in its current, all-civilian form.

The agency was granted subpoena power, one issue cited in the Tompkins Square Park report by the police department's CCRB was that without subpoena power, it could not obtain filmed footage from local media outlets, and authority to recommend discipline in cases that the board substantiated. However, the agency was underfunded at its inception, leaving it unable to cope with the large number of complaints it received.

After the Abner Louima incident in 1997, the CCRB's budget was steadily increased, allowing the agency to hire dozens more investigators and experienced managers who oversee investigations. This has led to dramatic improvement in the agency performance.

Now the largest civilian oversight agency in the country, the CCRB has investigated tens of thousands of complaints, leading to discipline for thousands of police officers.

The Civilian Complaint Review Board is an all-civilian, 13-member panel tasked with investigating misconduct or lesser abuse accusations against NYPD officers, including use of excessive force, abuse of authority, discourtesy, and offensive language.

Complaints against officers may be filed online, by mail, by phone or in person at any NYPD station.

CHAPTER 43

AFFILIATIONS

The NYPD is affiliated with the New York City Police Foundation and the New York City Police Museum. It also runs a Youth Police academy to provide positive interaction with police officers and to educate young people about the challenges and responsibility of police work.

The department also provides a citizen Police Academy which educates the public on basic law and policing procedures.

Police vehicles in New York City

The current colors of NYPD vehicles are an all-white body with two blue stripes along each side. The word "POLICE" is printed in small text above the front wheel wells, and as "NYPD Police" above the front grille.

The NYPD patch is embroidered on both sides, either on or just forward of the front doors. The letters "NYPD" are printed in blue Rockwell Extra Bold font on the front doors, and the NYPD motto "Courtesy, Professionalism, Respect" is printed on the rear ones.

The unit's shop number is printed on the rear decklid. The shop number is also printed on the rear side panels above the gas intake, along with the number of the unit's assigned precinct.

A modified paint scheme, with dark blue or black, for some Auxiliary units, body and white stripes on the sides was used for some divisions. The text was also white. This was phased out in favor of a modified version of the regular scheme, with the words "AUXILIARY", "SCHOOL SAFETY" or "TRAFFIC" on the rear quarter panels and trunk.

New York Police Department Vehicles and Its Usgage

The first police car was a wagon run by electricity fielded on the streets of Akron, Ohio, in 1899. The first operator of the police patrol wagon was Akron Police officer Louis Mueller, Sr. It could reach 16 mph, 26 km/h, and travel 30 mi, 48 km, before its battery needed to be recharged.

The car was built by city mechanical engineer Frank Loomis. The US$2,400 vehicle was equipped with electric lights, gongs, and a stretcher. The car's first assignment was to pick up a drunken man at the junction of Main and Exchange streets.

Ford introduced the Ford flathead V-8 in its Model B, as the first mass-marketed V8 car in 1932. In the 1940s, major American car makers began to manufacture specialized police cars.

A police car, also called a police cruiser, patrol car, cop car, prowler, squad car, radio car, or radio motor patrol, RMP, is a ground vehicle used by police for transportation during patrols and to enable them to respond to incidents and chases.

Typical uses of a police car include transporting officers so they can reach the scene of an incident quickly, transporting and temporarily detaining suspects in the back seats, as a location to use their police radio or laptop or to patrol an area, all while providing a visible warning to crime.

Some police cars are specially adapted for certain locations, e.g., traffic duty on busy roads or for certain operations, e.g., to transport police dogs or bomb squads.

Police cars typically have rooftop flashing lights, a siren, and emblems or markings indicating that the vehicle is a police car. Some police cars may have reinforced bumpers and alley lights, for illuminating darkened alleys.

Terms for police cars include area car and patrol car. In some places, a police car may also be informally known as a cop car, a black and white, a cherry top, a gumball machine, a jam sandwich, or panda car. Depending on the configuration of the emergency lights and livery, a police car may be considered a marked or unmarked unit.

In some areas of the world, the police car has become more widely used than police officers "walking the beat". Placing officers in vehicles also allows them to carry more equipment, such as automated external defibrillators for people in cardiac arrest or road cones for traffic obstructions and allows for more immediate transport of suspects to holding facilities.

Vehicles also allow for the transport of larger numbers of personnel, such as a SWAT team.

Decommissioned police cars are often sold to the public, either through a police auction or a private seller, after about 3–5 years of use. Such cars are usually sold relatively cheaply due to the extremely high mileage on such cars, in some cases exceeding the 300,000-mile, 480,000 km, mark.

In some cases, the cars are re-purposed as a taxicab as an inexpensive way for cab companies to buy cars instead of fleet vehicle services.

In all cases, the cars are stripped of their police markings as well as most internal equipment; however, the engines are usually left intact, and are often larger engines than their civilian counterparts.

Patrol car

The patrol car replaces walking the 'beat' of a police officer. Their primary function is to deliver communications between police officers.

Patrol cars are also able to respond to emergencies, and as such are normally fitted with visual and audible warnings.

A Response car or Pursuit car

A response car is like a patrol car, but is likely to be of a higher specification, capable of higher speeds, and will certainly be fitted with audible and visual warnings. These cars are usually only used to respond to emergency incidents, so are designed to travel fast, and may carry specialist equipment, such as assault rifles, or shotguns.

In the UK, each station usually only has one, which is called an area car.

The Traffic car

Traffic police cars, known in the UK as Road Policing Units, are cars designed for the job of enforcing traffic laws, and as such usually have the highest performance of any of the police vehicles, as they must be capable of catching most other vehicles on the road. They may be fitted with special bumpers designed to force vehicles off the road, and may have visual and audible warnings, with special audible warnings which can be heard from a greater distance.

In some police forces, the term traffic car may refer to cars specifically equipped for traffic control in addition to enforcing traffic laws. These cars may differ only slightly from a patrol car, including having radar and laser speed detection equipment, traffic cones, flares, and traffic control signs.

Multi-purpose car

Some police forces do not distinguish between patrol, response, and traffic cars. They may use one vehicle to fulfill some or all roles even though in some cases this may not be appropriate.

For example, a police city vehicle in a motorway high speed pursuit chase, the vehicle must be driven very fast. These cars are usually a negotiate between the different functions with elements added or removed.

Sport utility vehicles (SUV) and pickup trucks

SUVs and Pickups are used for a variety of reasons; off-road needs, applications where a lot of equipment must be carried, K-9 units, etc.

Community liaison car

This is a standard production car, visibly marked, but without audible and visual warning devices. It is used by community police officers to show a presence, transport them between jobs and make appearances at community events. These cars do not respond to emergencies.

Unmarked car
German unmarked Mercedes-Benz E-Class

Many forces also operate unmarked cars, in any of the roles, but most frequently for the use of traffic enforcement or detectives.

They have the advantage of not being immediately recognizable and are a valuable tool in catching criminals while the crime is still taking place.

In the United States, unmarked cars are also used by federal law enforcement agencies such as the FBI and the Secret Service. They can be recognized by their U.S. government plates.

There have been cases where criminals have pulled over motorists while pretending to be driving unmarked police cars, a form of police impersonation.

Some U.S. police officers advise motorists that they do not have to pull over in a secluded location and instead can wait until they reach somewhere safer.

In the UK, officers must be wearing uniform to make traffic stops. Motorists can also ask for a police badge.

Motorists often have the option to call a non-emergency number or if the country does not have one, the emergency number. This telephone call can then be used verify that the police car and officer is genuine.

Dog unit vehicle

An Australian Federal Police dog unit van is based on the pickup chassis, in Canberra.

This type of car is used to transport police dogs. In some jurisdictions, this will be a station wagon or car-based van, due to the installation of cages to carry the dogs. These units may also be known as K9 units a homophone of canine, also used to refer to the animals themselves. These cars are typically marked to warn people that there is a police dog on board.

Surveillance car

Forces may operate surveillance cars. These cars can be marked or unmarked and are there to gather evidence of any criminal offence. Overt marked cars may have CCTV cameras mounted on the roof to discourage wrongdoing, whereas unmarked cars would have them hidden inside. This type of vehicle is particularly common in the United Kingdom. In the United States, some police departments' vice, narcotics, and gang suppression units utilize vehicles that contain no identifiable police equipment, such as lights, sirens, or radios to conduct covert surveillance.

Some police vehicles equipped with surveillance are Bait cars which are deployed in high volume car theft areas.

Visibility Decoy Car

Some police forces use vehicles or sometimes fake "cut outs" of vehicles to deter crime. They may be old vehicles retired from use, stock models restyled as police cars, or a metal sign made to look like a police car. They are placed in areas thought to be susceptible to crime to provide a high visibility presence without committing an officer.

Examples of these can be seen on many main roads, freeways, and motorways.

In Chicago, Illinois a small fleet of highly visible vans are parked alongside major state and federal routes with automated speed detection and camera equipment, monitoring both for speeders and other offenders by license plate. Tickets are then mailed to the offenders or, in case of other crimes related to the licensed owner, may be served by a manned vehicle further down the road.

Rescue unit

In some jurisdictions, the police may operate a rescue service, and special units will be required for this.

Explosive ordnance disposal

In jurisdictions where the police are responsible for, or participate in, explosive ordnance disposal squads, bomb squads, dedicated vehicles transport the squads' crews and equipment.

An Abu Dhabi Police Chevrolet Camaro in the United Arab Emirates used for publicity.

Cars which are not for active duty, but simply for display. These are often high performance or modified cars, sometimes seized from criminals, used to try to get across specific messages such as with the D.A.R.E. program, or to help break down barriers with certain groups such as using a car with modified 'jumping' suspension as a talking point with young people.

To show the police what is new, a marked police car with the manufacturer's name, Ford, General Motors, and Chrysler can be displayed with the words "Not in Service" to show what is new with that model of car and get feedback from police departments.

Companies like Whelan, Federal Signal and Code 3 also have demo cars with their names on the side and showing the police what is new in the field of emergency vehicle equipment.

Riot control vehicles

These vehicles could be divided into three sub-categories. Modified trucks equipped with water cannons, modified stock cars and modified APCs, Armored Personnel Carriers.

Their function is to help control riots. Modified stock cars will have caged windows for protection against objects thrown at them and could include minibuses, 4x4s or prisoner transport vans. APCs usually will not require any added protection, but their modifications might include some sort of tear gas ejecting method or shields that unfold to create barriers.

The water cannon vehicles are used either to break up riots or extinguish fires set by the rioters. Although plain water is usually used some variations might include tear gas or special dye (to mark the people that are present for later apprehension). Previously[when?] fire trucks were used as anti-riot vehicles of this type. As a non-lethal, and effective method of clearing out protesters or rioters, the Long-Range Acoustic Device, LRAD, can be used. The LRAD is a device that can send announcements, warnings, and harmful pain-inducing tones.

Equipment

Main article: Emergency vehicle equipment

The police car on the left is fitted with a lightbar, making it instantly recognizable as a police vehicle. The one on the right, commonly known as a 'slicktop' in the US and Canada does not have a lightbar, making it less obvious, particularly when seen from the front, e.g., in a driver's rear-view mirror.

A Beijing Municipal Public Security Bureau car at Tiananmen Square.

Police cars are usually passenger car models which are upgraded to the specifications required by the purchasing force. Several vehicle manufacturers, such as Ford, General Motors, and Dodge, provide a "police package" option, which is built to police specifications in the factory. Police forces may add to these modifications by adding their own equipment and making their own modifications after purchasing a vehicle.

The active visual warnings are usually in the form of flashing-colored lights, also known as 'beacons' or 'lightbars'. These flash to attract the attention of other road users as the police car approaches, or to provide warning to motorists approaching a stopped vehicle in a dangerous position on the road. Common colors for police warning beacons are blue and red, however this often varies by force.

Several types of flashing lights are used, such as rotating beacons, halogen lights, or light emitting diode strobes. Some police forces also use arrow sticks to direct traffic, or message display boards to provide short messages or instructions to motorists. The headlights of some vehicles can be made to flash, or small strobe lights can be fitted in the headlight, taillight, and indicator lights of the vehicle.

Mechanical modifications

Modifications a police car might undergo include adjustments for higher durability, speed, high-mileage driving, and long periods of idling at a higher temperature. This is usually accomplished by heavy duty suspension, brakes, calibrated speedometer, tires, alternator, transmission, and cooling systems, and sometimes includes slight modifications to the car's stock engine or the installation of a more powerful engine than would be standard in that model. It is also usual to upgrade the capacity of the electrical system of the car to accommodate the use of additional electronic equipment.

Safety equipment

Police vehicles are often outfitted with AEDs (Automated external defibrillator), first aid kits, fire extinguishers, flares, life buoys, barrier tapes, etc.

Audible and visual warnings

Police vehicles are often fitted with audible and visual warning systems to alert other motorists of their approach or position on the road. In many countries, use of the audible and visual warnings affords the officer a degree of exemption from road traffic laws (such as the right to exceed speed limits, or to treat red stop lights as a yield sign) and may also suggest a duty on other motorists to move out of the direction of passage of the police car or face possible prosecution.

Visual warnings on a police car can be of two types: either passive or active

Passive Visual Warnings

Passive visual warnings are the markings on the vehicle. Police vehicle markings usually make use of bright colors or strong contrast with the base color of the vehicle.

Modern police vehicles in some countries have retroreflective markings which reflect light for better visibility at night. Other police vehicles may only have painted on or non-reflective markings.

Most marked police vehicles in the United Kingdom and Sweden have reflective Battenburg markings on the sides, which are large blue and yellow rectangles.

These markings are designed to have high contrast and be highly visible on the road, to deter crime and improve safety. Another passive visual warning of police vehicles is simply the interceptor's silhouette. This is easily observed in the United States and Canada, where the ubiquitous nature of the Ford Crown Victoria in police fleets has made the model synonymous with police vehicles.

Police vehicle marking schemes usually include the word Police or similar phrase, such as State Trooper or Highway Patrol, or the force's crest. Some police forces use unmarked vehicles, which do not have any passive visual warnings at all, and others, called stealth cars, have markings that are visible only at certain angles, such as from the rear or sides, making these cars appear unmarked when viewed from the front.

Active Visual Warnings

Ford Crown Victoria Police Interceptor with emergency lights system, ELS, activated.

The active visual warnings are usually in the form of flashing-colored lights, also known as 'beacons' or 'lightbars'. These flash to attract the attention of other road users as the police car approaches, or to provide warning to motorists approaching a stopped vehicle in a dangerous position on the road.

Common colors for police warning beacons are blue and red, however this often varies by force. Several types of flashing lights are used, such as rotating beacons, halogen lights, or light emitting diode strobes. Some police forces also use arrow sticks to direct traffic, or message display boards to provide short messages or instructions to motorists. The headlights of some vehicles can be made to flash, or small strobe lights can be fitted in the headlight, taillight, and indicator lights of the vehicle.

Equipment Consoles

These are used to house two-way radios, light switches, and siren switches. Some may be equipped with locking compartments for safe storage of firearms or file compartments.

Suspect transport enclosures

These are steel and plastic barriers which ensure that a suspect—who has been frisked, disarmed, handcuffed and seat belted, is unable to attack the driver or passenger and unable to tamper with equipment in the front seat. These may be simple bars or grilles, although they can include highly impact resistant but not bullet resistant glass. Many uses expanded steel instead of plastic glazing for the upper half of the partition.

Firearm lockers

In certain countries, including the United States, some police vehicles are equipped with lockers or locking racks in which to store firearms. These are usually tactical firearms such as shotguns or rifles, which would not normally be carried on the person of the officer.

Mobile Data Terminal

Many police cars are fitted with mobile data terminals, or MDTs, which are connected via wireless methods to the police central computer and enable the officer to call up information such as vehicle license details, offender records, and incident logs.

Vehicle Tracking System

Some police vehicles, especially traffic units, may be fitted with equipment which will alert the officers to the presence nearby of a stolen vehicle fitted with a special transponder, and guide them towards it, using GPS or simpler radio triangulation.

Evidence Gathering CCTV

Police vehicles can be fitted with video cameras used to record activity either inside or outside the car. They may also be fitted with sound recording facilities. This can then later be used in a court to prove or disprove witness statements, or act as evidence, such as evidence of a traffic violation.

Automatic Number Plate Recognition, ANPR

This computerized system uses cameras to observe the number plates of all vehicles passing or being passed by the police car and alerts the driver or user to any cars which are on a 'watch list' as being stolen, used in crime, or having not paid vehicle duty.

Speed Recognition Device

Some police cars are fitted with devices to measure the speed of vehicles being followed, such as ProViDa, usually through a system of following the vehicle between two points a set distance apart. This is separate to any radar gun device which is likely to be handheld, and not attached to the vehicle.

Remote Rear Door Locking

This enables officers in the front to remotely control the rear locks—usually used in conjunction with a transport enclosure.
Damage from a PIT maneuver on a Crown Victoria

PIT bumper

The Pursuit Intervention Technique, PIT, bumper attaches to the front frame of a patrol car. It is designed to end vehicle pursuits by spinning the fleeing vehicle with a nudge to the rear quarter panel. Cars not fitted with a PIT Bumper can still attempt a PIT Maneuver at risk of increased front-end damage and possible disablement if the maneuver fails and the pursuit continues.

Push bumper (aka nudge bars)

Fitted to the chassis of the car and located to augment the front bumper, to allow the car to be used as a battering ram for simple structures or fences, or to push disabled vehicles off the road.

Run lock

This allows the vehicle's engine to be left running without the keys being in the ignition. This enables adequate power, without battery drain, to be supplied to the vehicle's equipment at the scene of an incident. The vehicle can only be driven off after re-inserting the keys. If the keys are not re-inserted, the engine will switch off if the handbrake is disengaged or the footbrake is activated.

The installation of this equipment in a car partially transforms it into a desk. Police officers use their car to fill out different forms, print documents, type on a computer or a console, consult and read different screens, etc.

Ergonomics in layout and installation of these items in the police car plays an important role in the comfort and safety of the police officers at work and preventing injuries such as back pain and musculoskeletal disorders.

Ballistic protection

Some police cars can be optionally upgraded with bullet resistant armor in the car doors.[26] The armor is typically made from ceramic ballistic plates and aramid baffles. A 2016 news report said that Ford sells 5 to 10 percent of their US police vehicles with ballistic protection in the doors.

In 2017 Bill de Blasio, the mayor of New York City, announced that all NYPD patrol cars would be installed with bullet-resistant door panels and bullet-resistant window inserts.

Police Cars in Popular Culture

Police chases have been dramatized in television programs and movies, and occasionally feature in television news coverage of unusual circumstances, showing footage from an airborne camera.

In crime drama, such as Police procedural stories, police cars are often portrayed as containing a team of at least two police officers so that they may converse and interact with each other while on patrol. Depending on local policy, real patrols, especially rural and low population areas, may have only one officer per vehicle, although at night this may increase to two.

CHAPTER 44

FIREARMS ON DUTY

New NYPD officers can choose from one of three 9mm service pistols: the SIG Sauer P226 DAO, Glock 17 Gen4, and Glock 19 Gen3. All duty handguns are modified to a 12-pound, 53 N, NY-2 trigger pull.

The Smith & Wesson 5946 was initially issued to new recruits; however, the manufacturer stopped producing the weapon. It is no longer an option for new hires, though officers who currently utilize the weapon are grandfathered in and may continue to use it.

After the switch in 1994 to semiautomatic pistols, officers who privately purchased revolvers before January 1, 1994, could use them for duty use until August 31, 2018. They were then grandfathered in as approved off-duty guns.

Shotgun-certified officers were authorized to carry Ithaca 37 shotguns, which are being phased out in favor of the newer Mossberg 590. Officers and detectives belonging to the NYPD's Emergency Service Unit, Counter-terrorism Bureau and Strategic Response Group are armed with a range of select-fire weapons and long guns, such as the Colt M4A1 carbine and similar-pattern Colt AR-15 rifles, Heckler & Koch MP5 submachine gun, and the Remington Model 700 bolt-action rifle.

Off duty

The firearms approved by the NYPD for off duty carry are the Glock 26, Smith & Wesson 3914 DAO, Smith & Wesson 3953TSW, Smith & Wesson Model 640, .38 revolver, SIG Sauer P239 DAO, Springfield XDS, Smith & Wesson M&P Shield and the Beretta 8000D Mini Cougar.

Discontinued From Service

From 1926 until 1986 the standard weapons of the department were the Smith & Wesson Model 10 and the Colt Official Police .38 Special revolvers with four-inch barrels.

Female officers had the option to choose to carry a three-inch barrel revolver instead of the normal four-inch model due to its lighter weight. Prior to 1994 the standard weapon of the NYPD was the Smith & Wesson Model 64 DAO, Double Action Only, .38 Special revolver with a three- or four-inch barrel. This type of revolver was called the Model NY-1 by the department.

Prior to the issuing of the 9mm semi-automatic pistol NYPD detectives and plainclothes officers often carried the Colt Detective Special and/or the Smith & Wesson Model 36 "Chief's Special" .38 Special caliber snub-nosed, 2-inch, barrel revolvers for their ease of concealment while dressed in civilian clothes.

The Kahr K9 9 mm pistol was an approved off-duty/backup weapon from 1998 to 2011. It was pulled from service because it could not be modified to a 12-pound trigger pull.

CHAPTER 45

LIEUTENANT
CHARLES BECKER

Charles Becker was born on July 26, 1870, and died on July 30, 1915, at the age of 45. He was a lieutenant in the New York City Police Department between the 1890s and 1910s. He is best known for being tried, convicted, and executed for the murder of a Manhattan gambler, Herman Rosenthal.

After the trial, Charles Becker became the first American police officer to receive the death penalty for murder. The scandal that surrounded his arrest, conviction, and execution was one of the most important in progressive era in New York City.

Let me tell you a little bit about Charles Becker....

Charles Becker was born to a German American family from Bavaria in the village of Callicoon Center, Sullivan County, New York. He arrived in New York City in 1890 and went to work as a bouncer in a German beer hall just off the Bowery before joining the New York City Police Department in November 1893.

Becker received national attention in the fall of 1896 when he arrested a known prostitute named Ruby Young, alias Dora Clark, on Broadway. The disgrace of the case was due to one of Young's companions, the writer Stephen Crane, the author of The Red Badge of Courage.

The next day, at Ruby Young's hearing, Stephen Crane stepped forward and defended Ruby Young. The word of the then highly popular Stephen Crane weighed heavily on the sentencing of Young, resulting in the Magistrate Robert C. Cornell dismissing the case.

Afterwards, Stephen Crane told reporters, "If the girl will have the officer prosecuted for perjury, I will gladly support her."

Three weeks following the trial Ruby pressed formal charges against Becker. Becker knew he was in a dangerous situation and started preparing himself. He gathered evidence, hired an experienced lawyer, Louis Grant. He also got the support of his colleagues.

By doing this, Becker was allowing himself to make a powerful entrance to his trial.

On October 15, 1896, Becker was ready. He entered the court room surrounded by a group of police officers...

Commissioner Frederick Grant, son of Ulysses S. Grant, headed the proceeding and after almost five hours of examination Becker was acquitted. The trial taught Becker the power of the badge and how he could call on his colleagues for help....

In 1902 and 1903 Becker was one of the leaders of a patrolman's reform movement. This movement was disturbing because he really wasn't trying to work with the introduction of the Three Platoon System. This system was to reduce the number of hours the beat police officer was expected to work.

In 1906 he was assigned to a special unit. He started working out of police headquarters to inquire about the unproven corruption of Police Inspector Max F. Schmittberger, who had been widely hated within the NYPD since giving detailed testimony to the 1894.

The Lexow Committee investigated the case for police corruption in New York...

As the result of Becker's work, Schmittberger subsequently stood trial, and Deputy Police Commissioner Rhinelander Waldo was therefore satisfied with his work,

When Waldo became New York City Police Commissioner in 1911, he had Becker, promoted to lieutenant. He appointed him as head of one of the city's three anti-vice squads.

Becker apparently used his position to get substantial amount of money. It was later shown a total of over $100,000, from Manhattan illegal gambling casinos in exchange for immunity from police interference.

Percentages of the take were regularly delivered to politicians and other police officers...

In July 1912, Becker was mentioned in New York, as one of three senior police officials involved in the case of Herman Rosenthal. Rosenthal was a small-time bookmaker who had complained to the press that his illegal casinos had been badly damaged by the greed of Becker and his associates.

Two days after the story appeared, Rosenthal walked out of the Hotel Metropole at 147 West 43rd Street, just off Times Square and was gunned down by a crew of Jewish gangsters from the Lower East Side, Manhattan.

In the aftermath, Manhattan District Attorney Charles S. Whitman, who had made an appointment with Rosenthal before his death, made no secret of his belief that the gangsters had committed the murder at Becker's request.

In a major public uproar, Becker was transferred to the Bronx and assigned to desk duty...

On July 29, 1912, Becker was approached at the precinct's closing hour by special detectives from the District Attorney's Office. Becker was placed under arrest. He was tried and convicted of first-degree murder of Rosenthal that fall.

The verdict was overturned on appeal on the grounds that the presiding judge, John Goff, had been prejudiced against the defendant. Still, a retrial in 1914 affirmed Becker conviction.

Although contemporary newspapers were unanimous in asserting his guilt, Becker went to the electric chair in Sing Sing on July 30, 1915, admitting his innocence. Becker was buried at Woodlawn Cemetery, in the Bronx, on August 2, 1915.

The day before Becker died on July 30, 1915, he told the warden that he wanted them to put Rosenthal out of the way. He also said that he didn't mean wanted him kill.

Becker just wanted them to get him out of town so he wouldn't tell. Killing him was Rose's idea and the others. They wanted to save their own skins.

Jack Rose was one of the prosecution witnesses along with Harry Vallon, Sam Schepps and Bridgey Webber. They were underworld figures who were involved in the crime. They were promised immunity if they would testify against Becker.

Becker's electrocution took nine minutes. This caused him intense agony. This killing was described for years afterward as "the clumsiest execution in the history of Sing Sing."

Becker had only one son. His name was Howard P. Becker who later became a Professor of Sociology at the University of Madison Wisconsin. He also had a daughter, Charlotte Becker, who was conceived shortly before his arrest. She died less than a day after her birth in 1913 and is buried alongside her father at Woodlawn Cemetery.

CHAPTER 46

INSPECTOR
THOMAS F. BYRNES

Thomas F. Byrnes was born on June 15, 1842 and died May 7, 1910. He was an Irish-born American police officer. Byrne served as head of the New York City Police Department detective department from 1880 until 1895, who promoted the term rogue's gallery.

<u>Who was Thomas F. Byrnes?</u>

Thomas F. Byrnes was born in Dublin, Ireland. His parents were James and Rose Byrnes. The Burnes family immigrated to New York when Thomas was a child. He worked as a skilled gasfitter until the Civil War began.

Byrnes enlisted with Elmer E. Ellsworth's "Zouaves" in 1861. He served two years with that unit. After his service, Byrnes became a firefighter, joining Hose Company No. 21 in New York City. He remained as a firefighter until December 10, 1863, when he was appointed as a police officer.

Byrnes began his career in the police department as a police officer. He then got promoted to sergeant in 1869.

Finally, in 1870, he became a captain. He gained fame through solving the Manhattan Savings Bank robbery of 1878. He became Detective Bureau chief in 1880.

As inspector, Byrnes quickly won national distinction. He increased the detective force from 28 to 40 men. In four years, they made 3,300 arrests.

In 1882, Byrnes obtained legislative approval of changes in the department which gave him immense power.

In 1886, Byrnes instituted the "Mulberry Street Morning Parade" of arrested suspects before the assembled detectives in the hope they would recognize suspects and link them to more crimes.

Also, that same year, his book Professional Criminals of America was published. He built up a book of photographs of criminals, which he called the "Rogues Gallery". Those outlaws were photographed very relaxed in the alley of Mulberry Street by photographer by Jacob Riis in 1888.

Byrnes was one of the people who popularized the third degree due to his brutal questioning of suspected criminals. From the descriptions, the third degree as practiced by Byrnes was a combination of physical and psychological torture.

Jacob A. Riis, who was a police reporter for the New York Sun knew Byrnes well, declared that he was "a great actor", and later a great detective. Riis called him a dishonest "big policeman" and a genuine giant in his time.

In 1891, three years after publicly criticizing London police officials on the way they handled the Jack the Ripper investigations, Byrnes was faced with a similar crime in New York.

In massive publicity, Byrnes accused an Algerian, Ameer Ben Ali, nicknamed Frenchy, of the crime. He was convicted despite the evidence against him being doubtful but pardoned eleven years later.

Byrnes also successfully obtained a confession from gang leader Mike McGloin, who was convicted and executed for the murder of a tavern-owner during a robbery.

In 1895, the new president of the New York City Police Commission, future <u>President of the United States Theodore Roosevelt</u>, forced him to resign as part of Roosevelt's drive to rid the force of corruption.

Byrne died on May 7, 1910, at 9 o'clock at his home, 318 West Seventy-seventh Street of stomach cancer. He was survived by his wife Ophelia and five daughters. His funeral was at the Church of the Blessed Sacrament at Broadway and Seventy-first Street in Manhattan, New York City.

CHAPTER 47

SERGEANT CHARLES HENRY "CHARLIE" COCHRANE, JR.

Charles Henry "Charlie" Cochrane, Jr. was born August 5, 1943, and died on May 5, 2008. He was an American law enforcement officer and sergeant with the New York City Police Department.

Following his delivery of public testimony on anti-discrimination legislation pending before the New York City Council, Cochrane became the first openly gay officer of the NYPD. He later helped to form the Gay Officers Action League, GOAL.

In 1963, Cochrane enlisted in the United States Army, and joined the New York City Police Department in 1967.

For the first 10 years of his time on the force, Cochrane kept his homosexuality a secret. It was known only to a limited circle of friends. He first came out to his patrol partner in 1977, gradually becoming less fearful over time, until by the early 1980s.

He believed that "hundreds of guys and women in the department" were aware of his sexual orientation.

Cochrane became a member of the NYPD's Manhattan South Task Force, rising to the rank of sergeant.

In 1981, the New York City Council announced plans to conduct hearings leading towards a ban on discrimination against gay citizens in the city.

Cochrane believed it is important for gay residents from a wide range of occupations to participate in the process and in the first week of November met with a group of nine friends and acquaintances who knew of his sexuality to discuss possible effects that he might suffer if he himself gave public testimony on the matter.

Deciding to move forward with the procedure, Cochrane met with his parents and came out as gay for the first time.

Cochrane wrote a letter to NYPD Police Commissioner Robert J. McGuire on November 15, 1981. He informed him of his intent to testify before the City Council on the matter. He did it at the witness table in front of the council five days later.

In reading his prepared statement before the council, Cochrane thereby became the first New York City Police Department member to publicly announce his homosexuality.

Cochrane followed Pat Burns, first vice president of the Patrolmen's Benevolent Association to the witness stand. Having heard Burns declare that he knew of no gay New York City police officers, and that he was opposed to the NYPD hiring homosexuals to the force.

Cochrane dramatically contradicted Burns' statement, stating that he was "very proud of being a New York City policeman" and "equally proud of being gay."

Cochrane further testified that gays were not "cruel, wicked, cursed, sick, or possessed by demons. "I've always been gay", Cochrane declared to a slightly shocked council chamber. They exploded after a short pause into a loud standing cheer from Cochrane's assembled supporters.

A news story that quoted journalist Andy Humm reported:

""He gets up and says, 'I'm proud to be a New York City police officer,'" Humm said. "And then he says, 'I'm equally proud to be gay.' And the City Hall chamber, Council chamber almost fell out."

Despite Cochrane's testimony, the New York City Council defeated this 1981 anti-discrimination proposal, leaving Cochrane largely unprotected by law to deal with any discriminatory consequences of his action.

He found the reaction surprisingly positive, noting in an interview by The New York Times that he had received about 15 letters from other NYPD officers in the two weeks after his testimony. All were positive, and had a positive discussion with a fellow officer who was black about stereotypes and prejudice.

Cochrane remarked at that time:

Everyone I talked to within the department felt I probably would meet a lot of negative response, but I could not believe the support. Even the biggest clowns had nothing to say. Now maybe some of those cops who are already suspect and are teased a bit may finally say, "Hey, knock it off, I am gay."

The most hurtful reaction to Cochrane was a breaking of personal relations by the officer who had originally persuaded Cochrane to join the police force following the public revelation of his sexuality.

The terrible warnings of other officers who had offered Cochrane advice before his testimony. They told him that by doing so he would be committing career suicide.

After giving testimony before the City Council, Cochrane was instrumental in establishing the Gay Officers Action League, GOAL, a support organization advocating on behalf of gay and lesbian officers in the New York City Police Department.

Cochrane died of cancer on May 5, 2008, in Pompano Beach, Florida He was 64 years old at the time of his death.

On June 17, 2016, Cochrane's courageous 1981 testimony was honored with New York City Street signs marking "Charles H. Cochrane Way", with the new signs unveiled at Washington Place and Sixth Avenue.

At the unveiling ceremony, NYPD Chief of Department James O'Neill paid tribute to Cochrane's fortitude, noting "Charlie had come out as a gay cop during a time when gay cops were afraid of losing their jobs and of being physically harmed." He added that "through the efforts of Charlie, this is now a very different New York City than it was 35 years ago and it's a very different NYPD."

CHAPTER 48

THE KNAPP COMMISSION

The Commission to Investigate Alleged Police Corruption, known informally as the Knapp Commission. It was named after its chairman Whitman Knapp. This commission was a five-member panel initially formed in April 1970 by Mayor John V. Lindsay to investigate corruption within the New York City Police Department.

The creation of the commission was largely a result of the publicity generated by the public revelations of police corruption made by Patrolman Frank Serpico and Sergeant David Durk. The commission concluded that the NYPD had systematic corruption problems, confirming the existence of widespread corruption and made several recommendations.

Its members

In 1970, Mayor Lindsay appointed five members to serve on the Knapp Commission:

Whitman Knapp, chairman
Arnold Bauman later replaced by John E. Sprizzo
Joseph Monserrat

Franklin A. Thomas

Cyrus Vance

At an investigation and public hearings

While the Knapp Commission began its investigation of corruption in the police department in June 1970, public hearings did not start until October 18, 1971.

In addition to the testimony of "lamplighters", whistleblowers, Serpico and Durk, testimony from dozens of other witnesses, including former Police Commissioner Howard R. Leary, corrupt patrolmen, and the victims of police shakedowns, was heard.

From 1970 to 1972, Michael F. Armstrong was chief counsel to the Knapp Commission. Nicholas Scoppetta served as associate counsel.

As an immediate result of the testimony of the witnesses, criminal indictments against corrupt police officials were handed down.

Commissioner Patrick V. Murphy was appointed by Mayor Lindsay shortly after the commission was formed to clean up the department. They implemented proactive integrity checks, transfer senior personnel on a huge scale. There was also a rotation of critical jobs. They ensure sufficient funds to pay informants and crack down on citizen attempts at bribery.

On June 15, 1972, Whitman Knapp, Chairman of the Knapp Commission, was nominated as a federal judge for the Southern District of New York by President Richard M. Nixon.

"Grass Eaters" and "Meat Eaters"

The Knapp Commission Report on Police Corruption identified two classes of corrupt police officer, which it called "Grass Eaters" and "Meat Eaters".

This classification refers to petty corruption under peer pressure, "eating grass" and aggressive deliberate major corruption, "eating meat".

The term "Grass Eaters" is used to describe police officers who "accept gratuities and solicit five, ten, twenty-dollar payments from contractors, tow-truck operators, gamblers. They do not pursue corruption payments".

"Grass eating" is something that a significant number of officers are guilty. They learned to do things from other cops or from imitating the troublemakers they watch and investigate every day.

The commission even concluded that "grass eating" was used by police officers in New York City to prove their loyalty to the brotherhood. They came from incentives like side jobs.

One method of preventing cops from becoming corrupt is to eliminate this step by removing veteran cops who do this; without any veteran cops to learn this from, new officers might decide to never "eat grass".

"Meat Eaters" are officers who "spend a good deal of time aggressively looking for situations they can exploit for financial gain".

An example of this is shaking down pimps and illicit drug dealers for money. This is not only for the material profit to the officers, but for the relief from guilt that the officers derive by convincing themselves that their victims deserve such treatment.

They justify taking advantage of these kinds of criminals because they are considered the wastes of society.

CHAPTER 49

THE MOLLEN COMMISSION

The Mollen Commission is formally known as The City of New York Commission to Investigate Allegations of Police Corruption and the Anti-Corruption Procedures of the Police Department.

The former judge Milton Mollen was appointed in June 1992 by then New York City mayor David N. Dinkins to investigate corruption in the New York City Police Department.

Mollen's mandate was to examine and investigate "the nature and extent of corruption in the Department. This commission was assigned to evaluate the department's procedures for preventing and detecting that corruption. They would recommend changes and improvements to those procedures".

In June 1992, Mayor Dinkins appointed five members to serve on the Mollen Commission:

Milton Mollen, Chairman
Harold R. Tyler, Jr., Commissioner
Harold Baer, Jr., Commissioner
Herbert Evans, Commissioner
Betsy Barros, Commissioner

In December 1993, The New York Times reported that the "special mayoral panel asserted that the New York City Police Department had failed at every level to uproot corruption and had instead tolerated a culture that fostered misconduct and concealed lawlessness by police officers."

The conclusion that Mollen issued on a report in July 1994.

Today's corruption is not the corruption of Knapp Commission days. Corruption then was largely a corruption of accommodation, of criminals and police officers giving and taking bribes, buying, and selling protection. Corruption was, in its essence, consensual.

Today's corruption is characterized by brutality, theft, abuse of authority, and active police criminality.

The Mollen Commission transcripts and videotapes are housed in the Special Collections of the Lloyd Sealy Library, John Jay College of Criminal Justice.

CHAPTER 50

POLICE CORRUPTION

Police corruption is a form of police misconduct in which law enforcement officers end up breaking their political contract and abuse their power for personal gain.

This type of corruption may involve one or a group of officers. Internal police corruption is a challenge to public trust, cohesion of departmental policies, human rights and legal violations involving serious consequences. Police corruption can take many forms, such as bribery.

There are many types of corruption. I will explain some in the following:

Soliciting, accepting bribes in exchange for not reporting organized drug, prostitution rings or other illegal activities. Violations of any law, county, city ordinances, state, and federal laws.

Bribes may also include leasing unlawful access to proprietary law enforcement databases and systems. Disobeying the police code of conduct to secure convictions of civilians and suspects.

By using falsified evidence, law enforcement officers may deliberately and systematically participate in organized crime themselves.

In most major cities, there are internal affairs sections to investigate suspected police corruption or misconduct, including selective enforcement.

There are situations where Internal Affairs also hides departmental and individual corruption, fraud, abuse and waste by individual officers, groups of officers or even unwritten departmental policies.

There are also Police Commissions who are complicit in the same cover-ups, often to hide internal and departmental problems, both from public view, and from inter-departmental reviews and investigations.

Certain officers can be fired, then rehired by petition after they accrue enough signatures, often from the very criminals and violators from whom corrupt officers have garnered previous favors in exchange for officers "turning a blind eye", resulting in selective enforcement of violations being deterred, but promoted.

Police officers have several opportunities to gain personally from their status and authority as law enforcement officers. The Knapp Commission, which investigated corruption in the New York City Police Department in the early 1970s, divided corrupt officers into two types.

The meat-eaters, who "aggressively misuse their police powers for personal gain", and grass-eaters, who "simply accept the payoffs that the chances of police work throw their way."

There are multiple typologies of police corruption that have been asserted by academics. However, common corrupt acts that have been committed by police officers can be classified as follows:

Corruption of authority is when police officers receive free drinks, meals, and other gratuities, because they are police officers, whether intentionally or unintentionally, they convey an image of corruption.

Extortion/bribery is when demanding or receiving payment for criminal offenses, to overlook a crime or a possible future crime. Types of bribery are protection for illegal activities, ticket fixing, altering testimony, destroying evidence, and selling criminal information. Bribery is one of the most common acts of corruption.

Theft and burglary are when an officer or department steals from a suspect, victim, or corpse.

Examples are taking drugs for personal use in a drug bust and taking personal objects from a corpse at the scene of a crime. A theft can also occur within a department.

An officer can steal property from the department's evidence room or property room for personal use.

Shakedowns is when a police officer is aware of a crime and the violator but accepts a bribe for not arresting the violator.

"Fixing" is undermining criminal prosecutions by withholding evidence or failing to appear at judicial hearings, for bribery or as a personal favor.

Perjury is lying to protect other officers or oneself in a court of law or a department investigation.

Internal payoffs are prerogatives and prerequisites of law enforcement organizations, such as shifts and holidays, being bought and sold.

The "frameup" this is planting or adding to evidence, especially in drug cases.

Ticket fixing is when Police officers canceled traffic tickets as a favor to the friends and family of other police officers.

Corrupted behavior can be caused by the behavioral change of the officer within the department's "subculture".

A subculture is a group of individuals within a culture that share the same attitudes and beliefs. Police officers within the department share the same norms and that new behavioral development can be attributed through psychological, sociological, and anthropological paradigms.

Psychological paradigm- The psychological paradigm suggests that behavior is based and structured through an individual's early stages of life. Those attracted to the police occupation tend to be more "authoritarian". The authoritarian personality is characterized by conservative, aggressive, cynical, and rigid behaviors.

Corruption may involve profit, or another type of material benefit gained illegally because of the officer's authority. Psychological corruption can be a part of a department's culture or from the certain individual.

Sociological paradigm- The sociological paradigm focuses on individual exposure to a police training academy, regular in-service training, and field experience all shape occupational character. Police learn how to behave, discretion, morals and what to think from their shared experiences with other police officers.

New recruits develop definitions with their peers either positive or negative. These definitions are then reinforced, positively or negatively, by the rewards or punishments that follow their behavior.

For example, a recruit may be given an order by his peer to arrest an individual sitting in the passenger seat for a DUI. This action can end up negatively or positively for the officer depending on how the situation is perceived by the court later.

Anthropological paradigm- When an individual's social character is changed when an officer becomes part of the occupational culture. The term culture is often used to describe differences among large social groups where they share unique beliefs, morals, customs, and other characteristics that set them apart from other groups.

Within the police culture, officers learn to be suspicious of the public. Police culture can also be quite racist and shot through with assumptions about the criminal tendencies of certain minority groups, such as African Americans, or the competency of fellow officers from minority backgrounds, which can lead officers to make corrupted choices for personal benefits or gains.

CHAPTER 51

DETECTIVE FRANK SERPICO

Francesco Vincent Serpico was born on April 14, 1936. He was a former police officer in the New York City Police Department.

Serpico holds both American and Italian citizenship. He is known for whistleblowing on police corruption in the late 1960s and early 1970s. This was an act that encouraged Mayor John V. Lindsay to appoint the landmark Knapp Commission to investigate the NYPD.

Much of Serpico's fame came after the release of the 1973 film Serpico, which was based on the book by Peter Maas, and which starred Al Pacino in the title role, for which Pacino received an Oscar nomination.

Serpico was born in Brooklyn, New York, the youngest child of Vincenzo and Maria Giovanna Serpico, Italian immigrants from Marigliano.

At the age of 17, he enlisted in the United States Army and was stationed for two years in South Korea as an infantryman. He then worked as a part-time private investigator and a youth counselor while attending Brooklyn College.

On September 11, 1959, Serpico joined the New York City Police Department. He was assigned to the 81st precinct. He then worked for the Bureau of Criminal Identification for two years.

Serpico was finally assigned to work in plainclothes, where he uncovered widespread corruption. He was assigned to work in Brooklyn, the Bronx and Manhattan.

As soon as he got to those areas, he started to expose corruption in the department.

In 1967, he reported credible evidence of widespread organized police corruption. Nothing was happening until he met another police officer, <u>David Durk,</u> who helped him. Serpico believed his partner knew about his secret meetings with police investigators.

Finally, he contributed to an April 25, 1970, New York Times front-page story on widespread corruption in the NYPD. This story drew national attention to the problem.

Mayor John V. Lindsay right away appointed a five-member panel to investigate accusations of police corruption. The panel became the Knapp Commission, named after its chairman, Whitman Knapp.

Serpico was shot during a drug arrest attempt on February 3, 1971, at 778 Driggs Avenue, in Williamsburg, Brooklyn. Four officers from the Brooklyn North police precinct received a tip that a drug deal was about to take place. Two police officers, Gary Roteman and Arthur Cesare, stayed outside, while the third, Paul Halley, stood in front of the apartment building.

Serpico climbed up the fire escape, entered by the fire escape door. He went downstairs and listened for the password. After that, Serpico followed two suspects outside.

The police arrested the young suspects, and found one had two bags of heroin. Halley stayed with the suspects, and Roteman told Serpico, who spoke Spanish, to make a fake purchase attempt to get the drug dealers to open the door.

The police officer went to the third-floor landing. Serpico knocked on the door, keeping his hand on his revolver. The door opened a few inches, just far enough to slice his body in. Serpico called for help, but his fellow officers ignored him.

Serpico was then shot on the face by a suspect with a .22 LR pistol. The bullet struck just below the eye, lodging at the top of his jaw. He fired back and fell to the floor. He then began to bleed freely. His police colleagues refused to make a "10-13" dispatch to police headquarters. The 10-13 call will indicate that an officer had been shot or that an officer is in danger.

An elderly man who lived in the next apartment called the emergency services. He was the one that reported that a man had been shot. He and stayed with Serpico.

When a police car arrived and aware that Serpico was a fellow officer, they transported him to Greenpoint Hospital in Brooklyn.

The bullet had separated an auditory nerve, leaving Serpico deaf in one ear...

Ever since that incident, Serpico has been suffering from chronic headaches due to bullet fragments stuck in his brain...

Let me inform you that Mayor John V. Lindsay and Police Commissioner Patrick V. Murphy went to visit him at the hospital the day after the shooting.

The police department, in my opinion, was just putting on an act. They harassed him day and night with hourly bed checks. He later testified before the Knapp Commission.

The circumstances surrounding Serpico's shooting quickly came into question. Serpico, who was armed during the drug raid, had been shot only after briefly turning away from the suspect. That was when he realized that the two officers who had accompanied him to the scene were not following him into the apartment.

There were questions asked about the whole scenario. The media and the department were asking whether Serpico had been brought to the apartment by his colleagues to be murdered. Guess what? There was no formal investigation.

On May 3, 1971, New York Metro Magazine published an article about Serpico, "Portrait of an Honest Cop".

On May 10, 1971, he testified at the departmental trial of an NYPD lieutenant, who was accused of taking bribes from gamblers.

In October, and again in December 1971, Serpico testified before the Knapp Commission:

Through my appearance here today ... I hope that police officers in the future will not experience ... the same frustration and anxiety that I was subjected to ... for the past five years at the hands of my superiors ... because of my attempt to report corruption.

I was made to feel that I had burdened them with an unwanted task. The problem is that the atmosphere does not yet exist, in which an honest police officer can act ... without fear of ridicule or reprisal from fellow officers. Police corruption cannot exist unless it is at least tolerated ... at higher levels in the department. Therefore, the most important result that can come from these hearings ... is a conviction by police officers that the department will change. To ensure this ... an independent, permanent investigative body ... dealing with police corruption, like this commission, is essential ...

This was posted by "The New York Times", on December 15, 1971.

Serpico was the first police officer in the history of the New York City Police Department to step forward to report and subsequently testify openly about widespread, complete corruption payoffs amounting to millions of dollars.

Serpico retired on June 15, 1972, one month after receiving the New York City Police Department's highest honor, the Medal of Honor. There was no ceremony; according to Serpico, it was simply handed to him over the desk "like a pack of cigarettes".

Serpico decided to move to Switzerland to recuperate. He spent almost a decade living there on a farm in the Netherlands, as well as traveling and studying.

In 1973, he lived with a woman named Marianne, a native of the Netherlands, whom he wed in a "spiritual marriage"; she died from cancer in 1980. He decided to return to the United States afterward. They had one son, Alexander, who was born on March 15, 1980.

When it was decided to make the movie about his life called Serpico, Al Pacino invited Serpico to stay with him at a house that Pacino had rented in Montauk, New York.

When Pacino asked why he had stepped forward, Serpico replied, "Well, Al, I don't know. I guess I would have to say it would be because... if I didn't, who would I be when I listened to a piece of music?" He has credited his grandfather who had once been assaulted and robbed, and his uncle, a respected policeman in Italy, with his sense of justice.

Serpico still speaks out about police brutality, civil liberties, and police corruption, such as the attempted cover-ups following Abner Louima's torture in 1997 and Amadou Diallo's shooting in 1999.

He provides support to "individuals who seek truth and justice even in the face of great personal risk". He calls them "lamp lighters", a term he prefers to the more common "whistleblowers", which refers to alerting the public to danger, in the spirit of Paul Revere's midnight ride during the American Revolutionary War.

A policeman's first obligation is to be responsible to the needs of the community he serves ... The problem is that the atmosphere does not yet exist in which an honest police officer can act without fear of ridicule or reprisal from fellow officers. We create an atmosphere in which the honest officer fears the dishonest officer, and not the other way around.

In October 2014 interview published by Politico entitled "The Police Are Still Out of Control... I Should Know", Serpico addresses contemporary issues of police violence.

In 2015, Serpico ran for a seat on the town board of Stuyvesant, New York, where he lives, his first project into politics. He lost the election.

Among police officers, his actions are still controversial, but Eugene O'Donnell, professor of police studies at John Jay College of Criminal Justice, states that "he becomes more of a heroic figure with every passing year."

On August 19, 2017, Serpico gave a speech which was broadcast live on Facebook as he stood with NYPD police officers in New York City on the bank of the East River at the foot of the Brooklyn Bridge in support of Colin Kaepernick, for his protests alleging a culture of police brutality.

Serpico was quoted, "I am here to support anyone who has the courage to stand up against injustice and oppression anywhere in this country and the world."

As a result of Serpico's efforts, the NYPD was drastically changed. Michael Armstrong, who was counsel to the Knapp Commission and went on to become chairman of the city's Commission to Combat Police Corruption, observed in 2012 "the attitude throughout the department seems fundamentally hostile to the kind of systemized implantation that had been a way of life almost 40 years ago."

On June 27, 2013, the USA Section of ANPS, National Association of Italian State Police, assigned him the "Saint Michael Archangel Prize", an official award by the Italian State Police with the Sponsorship of the Italian Ministry of Interior.

Francesco Serpico is now an Italian citizen

During the same ceremony, he received his first Italian passport after extended research by the president of ANPS USA, Chief Inspector Cirelli, who established the Jus sanguinis, allowing him to gain Italian citizenship.

Update......

The legendary whistleblower isn't done calling out corruption

In his closing statement to the commission, Serpico called for a cultural shift that would promote good cops over bad...

In some ways, Serpico says, today's police are worse. "The brutality and shootings with cover-ups have intensified, I think, partially due to the changeover from a revolver to semi-automatic weapons and lack of training for proper use, such as in the case of Amadou Diallo," he says, referring to a 1999 shooting in which a West African immigrant in the Bronx was shot 41 times by the NYPD. "What has not changed, as I said in my closing statement at the Knapp hearings, is an atmosphere where the crooked cops would fear the honest cop, and not the other way around."

Powerful police unions assure virtual immunity for serious abuses; the Civilian Complaint Review Board, an independent entity that investigates police abuse and recommends disciplinary action, is virtually ignored.

The police commissioner has a final say on the punishment for wayward cops. Serpico says the culture of corruption goes up to the top. "It's the judges, the District Attorneys, the Mayors, the Governors, the police commissioner," he says, adding that every president, Democrat or Republican, should have ordered a commission to root out police misconduct.

He also believes that schools should teach kids about police abuse in school as part of their regular curriculum. "You've got to reach people when they are young," he says. "What I tell people is, we're treading water in a gutter. If you stop fighting, you're going to go under."

Serpico sees the potential for positive change. "We have to encourage young people," he stresses. "This is really needed.

Black Lives Matter...

All these young people are seeing it. It's being exposed, this police culture. A culture of cover up and brutality. Cops simply are not held to the same standards of the average person on the streets."

The movement seeks to reallocate money spent on policing to social services. Serpico says he gets where the movement is going and supports drastic changes to U.S. policing.

"Social services and other institutions that can address social and public health problems better than the police is always a priority, especially with drug enforcement and non-violent, victimless offenses.

Funding should also be used for better firearms training," Serpico says. "Too much seeing of guns where they don't, need, to exist."

Serpico also worries it might backfire by not fully addressing the culture of law enforcement. "It's not the individual cops as bad as they are," that's the problem, he says. "It's the culture. The police is a, quasi-military organization, just state instead of federal.

They are meant to enforce government rulings against the mostly poor and disenfranchised." And critics of the movement understandably worry that if departments start to lose funding, they may react by trying to bleed it out of the community however they can. "If we defund it may lead to more quotas, which they claim don't exist, petty enforcement, and fines to fill the coffers," he warns.

U.S. police culture gets the role of law enforcement all wrong, he says. "Police fail to grasp that they are public servants for peace," Serpico says. "They should provide a civil service, to enforce the laws equally, without bias and with discretion."

"They must understand that they do not have immunity or special privileges and most importantly, are just responsible for apprehending suspects, and should not act as judge, jury and executioner, which too many of them truly believe themselves to be," he adds.

Instead, they're encouraged to act like an occupying army. "The use of military hardware and body armor meant for combat in a war zone gives a feeling of being at war in our communities, and the enemy you must protect yourself against is naturally going to be the society you have sworn to protect and serve," Serpico says.

Fifty years after he was shot on the face, Serpico, who has received his share of death threats over the years, doesn't worry about speaking out. "I'm 84, why do I got to worry?" he says. He's careful, but not scared of getting taken out for his breach of the blue wall. "I protect myself. But if my time has come, there's no better way than taking out some crooked cops."

CHAPTER 52

DETECTIVE ROBERT LEUCI

Robert Leuci was born in Brooklyn, New York, on February 28, 1940, to an Italian American family. He is the son of James Leuci, a union official, and Lucy, a housewife.

Right after his birth, the family moved to Ozone Park, Queens, where he attended John Adams High School. After high school he attended Baker University in Kansas, and New York University, Fordham University as well as The New School for Social Research in New York City.

Leuci was married to Regina, a woman of Italian descent. They had two children, Anthony, and Santina, and divorced in 1990. Leuci married Kathy Packard in 2003, after he had moved to Rhode Island to pursue his writing and teaching career.

They lived on the Narragansett Bay. Leuci died on October 12, 2015, at the age of 75 after complications from surgery.

Robert Leuci was a detective with the New York City Police Department. He was known for his work exposing corruption in the police department and the criminal justice system.

After retiring from the NYPD, he wrote novels, short stories, TV episodes and a memoir of his years on the force. He taught and had residencies at over forty universities and law schools and lectured on morality and ethics erosion at many US police departments and the FBI academy in Quantico, Virginia.

Leuci knew Frank Serpico, known for being the first officer to expose corruption within the police department ranks. The book, by Robert Daley and the film Prince of the City are based on a portion of Leuci's police career.

At nineteen, Leuci took the test to enter the New York City Police Academy. At twenty-one, he graduated, becoming a member of the NYPD.

As a rookie, he was assigned to the 100th Precinct in Rockaway Beach, Queens.

In 1962, he was transferred to the Tactical Patrol Force, where he worked the Manhattan North and South Bronx precincts.

In TPF, he worked in the city's highest crime areas. Leuci established relationships with street contacts and became one of the top arresting officers in the division.

Leuci was then transferred to the Narcotics Bureau for undercover work when he was 24. He created a network of field informants that led him to work numerous important cases. One of his first assignments was as a student who bought drugs at a high school.

The late 1960s were times in which NYPD officers like Frank Serpico and David Durk began fighting widespread corruption within the NYPD.

In 1970s, Serpico and Durk came to believe that Leuci was the only honest detective in the New York City Police Department's narcotics bureau, though at the time, he was one of the corrupt.

In 1970, because of Serpico and Durk's revelations, New York City Mayor John V. Lindsay, along with a five-member investigative committee, created the Knapp Commission, named after its Chairman, Judge Whitman Knapp.

Soon afterward, the commission began questioning several members of the force, from patrolmen to high-ranking officials. Serpico and Durk both asked Leuci if he would speak to Assistant US Attorney Nick Scoppetta.

Leuci and Scoppetta developed a close relationship almost immediately. Leuci pointed out that the Knapp commission was focused only on the police and that was unacceptable.

The criminal justice system in New York City was corrupt as well. The police were working within a system that had been in place for fifty years or more.

Leuci told Scoppetta he would not be involved in an investigation that focused solely on the police department. Still, if Scoppetta was willing, Leuci would do the undercover work of an investigation into the entire system. Scoppetta agreed. Leuci was given a code name: Sonny.

Scopetta and his colleague Michael Shaw soon understood Leuci's emotional conflict about what he was being asked to do. They supported him knowing it would be the start of harsh times for law enforcement in the city.

From that moment on, Leuci wore a wire whenever he had to meet with any of the subject.

Future New York Mayor Rudy Giuliani was part of the investigation. It was a short time later that Giuliani became the U.S. Attorney for the Southern District.

Leuci's cooperation lasted two years, after which the SIU no longer existed. Detectives and other officers, along with lawyers and many who had tied into the dishonest criminal justice system, were tried in court and imprisoned.

Some of Leuci's colleagues committed suicide as the pressure mounted throughout the investigation. The investigation ended in 1972.

Ultimately, the Federal Government decided not to prosecute Leuci, noting his efforts and the risks he and his family had taken.

His experience inspired former NYPD Deputy Commissioner Robert Daley, who had become a writer since retirement.

In 1978, through Leuci's recount of this story, Daley's best-selling book Prince of the City was published. By that time, Leuci's work in the Department had taken a toll.

He continued working at the Academy as a lecturer, and in the Internal Affairs Division until his retirement in 1981. That same year, director Sidney Lumet and executive producer Jay Presson Allen adapted the book to a critically acclaimed though financially disappointing movie. Award-winning actor Treat Williams portrayed Leuci.

Leuci's desire to write grew after Daley's book was published, and thanks to an afternoon walk with novelist Robert Stone, a new career path began.

Leuci wrote seven successful books and continued to lecture at police academies and federal law enforcement agencies throughout the United States. Leuci's books have sold in the US, France, Spain, England, Germany, and Croatia. He also participated at several writers' conferences in Europe.

In 1999 he received the South County Center for the Arts Literary Prize. He was an Adjunct Professor of English and Political Science at the University of Rhode Island.

It wasn't long before Leuci entered the Special Investigative Unit, SIU, of the narcotics bureau, an elite unit formed by top detectives.

In SIU, street dealers' cases no longer represented his team's objective. Somewhat, the unit aimed to find the major sources of drug distribution in the country and make cases against South American or other foreign cartel operatives.

American hero or the biggest rat in NYPD history?

New documentary explores the controversial legacy of the late Robert Leuci, whose turn undercover led to more than 50 indictments of 1970s New York cops.

Brooklyn native Robert Leuci was a narcotics cop in the notorious Special Investigations Unit, which were known as untouchable 'Prince of the city'

He went undercover to expose dirty cops taking bribes, stealing drugs, and setting up businesses themselves.

He initially vowed not to implicate his friends and partners, but the investigation did so in the end'.

More than 50 law enforcement officials were indicted; two committed suicide and dozens of other lives were ruined.

Leuci remained conflicted until he died in 2015 about his role in the process.

He met Norwegian photojournalism student Magnus Skatvold at a Rhode Island barbecue in 2009.

The two became friends and filmmaker Skatvold, who was initially unaware of Leuci's past, became intrigued by his story.

He and co-director Gregory Mallozzi convinced Leuci and other people involved to sit for interviews for a documentary, though Leuci died before it was finished.

The unlikely duo met at a barbecue in Rhode Island, a young Norwegian student of photojournalism and a former NYPD detective who exposed massive corruption within the force in the 1970s.

Magnus Skatvold had no idea who Bob Leuci was when he was first introduced to him, considering the New York native a 'fast-talking … very kind, very charismatic grandfather that was just the center of attention and telling stories and being very interested in everybody.'

They struck up a friendship, and the more that Skatvold learned about Leuci, the more fascinated he became. Their relationship eventually sowed the seeds for a new documentary, which was just awarded the prestigious Pitch Perfect Award at DOC NYC film festival. This a prize given to a work-in-progress during a daylong pitch event.

His two years of work wearing a wire, under the code name Sonny, led to explosive prosecutions of dozens of law enforcement officials and at least two attempts on his life.

More than 50 men were indicted because of his evidence and lives were ruined. This left Leuci with a complicated view of his own involvement in the widespread exposure of police taking bribes, stealing drugs, and selling them themselves and other improprieties.

"I think there had been several, throughout the years, that had approached Bob and wanted to make either a documentary or a feature on him," Skatvold, 30, tells DailyMail.com. "He didn't want to open that chapter again about his life … but me being the outsider, not knowing anything about this case beforehand, kind of not being colored by prejudice or anything like that, I think he found that very fascinating."

"I was kind of like a blank page that could come in and maybe see this story in a different light, in a sense. It really started off as friends … and it kind of grew into the idea of making a documentary."

He adds: "I think also, with other people that have been involved with this story, this is very painful for a lot of people because what he did.

Essentially, it became a very big corruption scandal which implicated so many people. Over 50 cops were indicted for corruption because of his testimony, and two of his friends also committed suicide."

Some of the most interesting parts of this story is that this is a story that took place in the 70s; still, to this day, there has been so much pain and anguish in Bob's life. Talking to him, he had so much regret for what he really took part in not the corruption, not the misconduct itself, but kind of the betrayal of his friends and colleagues.

Skatvold says, "In today's society, I think we need stories about whistleblowers. We need stories about people who have really stood up against corruption. What's fascinating in Bob's story is that he isn't like a genuine hero. He's a very complex anti-hero, in a sense; he wasn't like the last honest cop like Serpico, who never took a dime. He was part of the same culture that he ... wanted to change. That's the kind of more of that Shakespearean undertone to this story."

"It's very much a tragic story. He kind of betrayed his friends and partners, which he kind of regretted his whole life after all of this."

Leuci was born into an Italian American family in Brooklyn on February 28, 1940, and graduated from the Police Academy when he was 21 years old. He was the first member of his family to graduate from high school.

"I found what I was looking for, acceptance, connection, kinship. Call it what you like. Belonging just to belong, that kind of thing," he wrote in his memoir, All the Centurions, about his feelings towards law enforcement membership.

He served with the Tactical Patrol Force and Narcotics Bureau before being assigned to the Special Investigating Unit, which focused on infiltrating drug cartels.

Former deputy police commissioner and journalist Robert Daley, who chronicled Leuci's career in a 1978 book, wrote of the SIU: 'Someone once called them the princes of the city, for they operated with the impunity, and sometimes with the arrogance, of Renaissance princes.

'They could enforce any law or not enforce it, arrest anyone or unite freedom. They were immune to arrest themselves.'

He explained, "After years of misconduct himself, he starts to have second thoughts. He was thinking, what kind of life was he really living here? He looked at himself more as a criminal than a cop … they were acting like gangsters, in a sense."

"By a couple of prosecutors, Bob is convinced to go undercover in his own department, in his own unit. He starts wearing a wire and collects evidence for almost two years."

Prosecutor Nicholas Scoppetta, in an interview following Leuci's 2015 death, said: 'I did something I never did with any witness.

"I brought him home, and we had dinner at my house. We began talking about corruption, and we talked through the night and into the morning. He had no stomach for what he was involved in."

"He wanted to get out from under it. He said: "Grabbing for cops is easy. If you investigate the whole system, that would be different." He took a chance; we took a chance. That there would be redemption and not retaliation."

Although Leuci did not initially want to implicate his friends and colleagues, the inevitable happened; of the 70 men assigned to the Special Investigating Unit, 52 were indicted because of his evidence including his former partner. The corruption was so widespread that dirty cops were taking bribes and stealing drugs.

Leuci became an incredibly polarizing figure. Many people either viewed him as a snitch and a traitor or a hero. He temporarily had to go into a witness protection.

"He didn't want to be treated as an informant,' Scopetta said, 'He wanted to be treated as an undercover agent."

After interviewing not only Leuci, but others involved, Mr. Skatvold said, he 'started to see that there were a lot of different takes on this story … I felt that was very intriguing, that there were so many different versions of what went on.'

He added, "All of the people I've talked to kind of rationalized a lot of their actions, as well: "It was a corrupt culture, it was another time, everybody was doing it, it was just a part of the job." I heard a lot of things like that."

After Daley published his book about Leuci, the cop was further immortalized in 1981 film Prince of the City; he later became a crime novelist as well as teaching writing and political science at the University of Rhode Island. He died in 2015 at the age of 75 while production of the documentary was already underway.

"That's probably the worst thing that can happen to a filmmaker – that your main character dies," Skatvold tells DailyMail.com. "Or me, he wasn't just the main character; he was a friend. So that kind of changed everything. But luckily, we had kind of what we needed, in terms of interviews with him and speaking with his family. We also decided we had enough to continue this journey … him passing away, it's going to be part of the story, in a sense."

Many of Leuci's relatives, he says, "were a bit skeptical, but they also knew my relationship [with Leuci]. And I have to say, my co-director and co-producer in the States also knew him personally, too; that was a big factor to the whole thing, is that they weren't working from random filmmakers that just wanted to do this."

CHAPTER 53

CORRUPTION
IN THE DEPARTMENT

All through the history of the New York City Police Department, several instances of corruption and misconduct, and accusations of such, have occurred.

Over 12,000 cases have resulted in lawsuit settlements totaling over $400 million during a five-year period ending in 2014.

In 2019, taxpayers funded $68,688,423 as the cost of misconduct lawsuits, a 76 percent increase over the previous year, including about $10 million paid out to two exonerated individuals who had been mistakenly convicted and imprisoned.

Criminal justice advocates report that public access to information about NYPD misconduct is increasingly restricted, particularly due to the department's controversial 2016 reinterpretation of section 50-a of the New York Civil Rights Law.

Molly Griffard, of the Legal Aid Society's Cop Accountability Project, has stated that "There's an epidemic of misconduct and the very taxpayers who pay these settlements don't have access to what's in these officers' misconduct records and how they're being disciplined."

According to data collected by the project, some individuals are permitted to remain in uniform following settlements of scores of lawsuits against these officers, which frequently total hundreds of thousands of dollars.

In June 2020, the Eric Garner Anti-Chokehold Act was passed, which repealed 50-a and made the use of certain restrictions by police anywhere in the state of New York punishable by up to 15 years in prison.

New York City has faced with the issue of police corruption for many generations.

Since the establishment of New York City Police Department in the mid-19th century, six high-profile commissions have taken their turn at holding hearings that made headlines by documenting widespread internal police corruption.

These commissions always stimulated calls for reform and, on occasion, urged the creation of a new agency aimed at improving police-community relations and accountability.

A few years ago, Police Commissioner Bill Bratton compared the internal department concern caused by an ongoing police corruption scandal involving high ranking officials to what was generated by the Knapp Commission in the early 1970s.

There have been calls for a similar self-regulating investigation of the department in the aftermath of arrests of veteran NYPD officers on corruption charges and the retirement of others who have been disciplined.

During the time of the Knapp Commission, the New York City Police Foundation was created as a nonprofit tax-exempt charity that could raise money to spend on projects supporting NYPD reform and modernization efforts as well as helping improve its relationship with the broader community.

Twenty years later, in the aftermath of the Mollen Commission, another body tasked with investigating the NYPD, Mayor Rudolph

Giuliani used an executive order in 1995 to create the Commission to Combat Police Corruption.

Both the New York City Police Foundation and the Commission to Combat Police Corruption are still in operation.

Yet, as evidenced by the recent arrest of an NYPD deputy chief, a deputy inspector and a sergeant, as well as the internal disciplining of several other officers, corruption within the department remains.

New York City's history of police corruption goes back more than a century. In the 1890s, Rev. Charles Parkhurst, described in the People's Almanac as "a scholarly Presbyterian minister," went on a fiery crusade "against police corruption, political connections and the underworld and all forms of urban vice."

Parkhurst went undercover to saloons and prostitution houses to validate his case that the city's police force was on the take. His campaign prompted Albany to form the Lexow Committee, named for Clarence Lexow, the state senator who led it.

The Lexow hearings generated a 10,000-page record that included testimony from saloon owners and prostitutes, who described a well-oiled machine that ran on paying off the police.

The disclosures set the stage for a defeat for Tammany Hall with the election of William Strong as mayor, who ran on a reform platform. Strong then picked a young Theodore Roosevelt to be police commissioner.

Roosevelt, who had already lost a bid for mayor before his appointment, spent less than two years on the job as police commissioner, but he had a major impact. His strategy of going out into the city during the overnight shift to catch sleeping police officers, who were supposed to be on duty, made him a tabloid sensation.

Roosevelt forced out one senior detective who had accumulated a fortune under the table from patrons on Wall Street.

Roosevelt ran into political headwinds when he tried to have the police enforce a Sunday closure law on the books for the city's popular saloons. Yet his decision to have police officers distribute ice to the families living in the city's hottest and most vulnerable slums during a punishing heat wave was an early example of what would become known as community policing.

Following police corruption panels after Roosevelt's brief time include the 1912 Curran Committee, the 1932 Seabury Investigation.

Also, the Helfand Investigation, which ran 1949 to 1950 was investigated. They were followed by the Knapp Commission in the early 1970s and the 1994 Mollen Commission.

The pattern has mixed little. Press reports of a major police corruption scandal forced elected officials to act. Sometimes arrests would be made, or implicated officers were forced to retire early.

Reforms would be implemented. Then, a few decades would pass, memories and resolve would fade. The self-correcting cycle would start all over again.

The Knapp Commission was established by Mayor John Lindsay after an exposé in The New York Times that reported police corruption was being ignored by the administration and by NYPD brass. The commission's star witness was Frank Serpico, a police officer turned whistleblower, who, along with Sgt. David Durk, had brought their well-documented claims of systemic police corruption to the Times.

Serpico and Durk had encountered resistance and hostility from within the NYPD. Serpico described a department in which 10 percent of the officers were corrupt, another 10 percent were honest, and the rest "wished they were honest."

It was the willingness of that 80 percent to remain silent about the misdeeds of the small percentage of their corrupt colleagues that defined the culture of what was shorthanded as "the blue wall of silence."

"Narcotics dealers, gamblers and businessmen make illicit payments of millions of dollars a year to the policemen of New York, according to police officer, law? Enforcement experts and New

Yorkers who make such payments themselves," the Times wrote in a story that rocked the city in April of 1970.

Perhaps even more worrying was Times reporter David Burnham's conclusion that the highest levels of the NYPD and the Lindsay administration had turned a blind eye to the corruption, even after it was repeatedly brought to their attention.

Almost a year after that bombshell series hit, Serpico was shot in the face while trying to make a drug bust in Williamsburg, Brooklyn.

According to his firsthand account in posted in Politico in 2014, Serpico had been abandoned by his fellow officers after he was shot by a drug suspect.

"I heard a voice saying, 'Don't worry, you be all right, you be all right,' and when I opened my eyes, I saw an old Hispanic man looking down at me like Carlos Castaneda's Don Juan," Serpico recounted. "My 'backup' was nowhere in sight. They hadn't even called for assistance. I never heard the famed 'Code 1013,' meaning 'Officer Down.' They didn't call an ambulance, either I later learned; the old man did."

Serpico says the officers were never called to account for their actions but were given awards for saving his life…

Years later, Serpico says he confronted the former Commissioner Patrick Murphy, whose tenure included that tumultuous period, but Murphy walked away. Murphy died in 2011.

Among the recommendations of the Knapp Commission was the establishment of special prosecutor to pursue police corruption cases. Such an office was opened in 1973, but it was abolished in 1990 by then-Gov. Mario Cuomo and the state Legislature.

On Mayor David Dinkins' watch, it was not a Serpico-type whistleblower from inside the NYPD who prompted the appointment of yet another panel to investigate police corruption.

It was the arrest in the spring of 1992 of NYPD officer Michael Dowd and five fellow NYPD officers, who were caught up in an undercover drug operation run by the Suffolk County District Attorney's Narcotics Bureau.

Dowd and his crew of fellow officers, operating out of the 75th precinct in East New York, Brooklyn, earned as much as an additional $8,000 a week targeting drug dealers for their money and drugs, while at the same time providing protection for other drug dealers.

In response to the screaming tabloid coverage of Dowd and his crew, Dinkins selected Milton Mollen, a retired state Supreme Court judge, to head up what would be the sixth independent panel to investigate internal corruption with the NYPD.

At the Mollen hearings, the public learned that Dowd had been on the NYPD's radar for at least six years prior to his arrest by Suffolk County police. Yet, despite being the subject of 16 complaints over that period for robbing drug dealers and selling cocaine, NYPD brass looked the other way. Internally Dowd was described in his personnel file as having "good career potential."

The Mollen Commission concluded that "while the vast majority of police officers" did not engage in corrupt behavior, there were pockets of corruption in 10 of the city's most crime-ridden precincts. In these areas, anywhere from a handful to as many as 20 officers were a law unto themselves.

The commission reported that for at least a decade, "from the top brass down to local precinct commanders and supervisors there was a persistent belief that uncovering serious corruption would harm careers and the reputation of the department."

"We find as shocking the incompetence and the inadequacies of the department to police itself," said Milton Mollen, the panel's chairman.

The Mollen Report's findings were rejected by then-Police Commissioner Ray Kelly, who at the time was serving his first stint as commissioner under Dinkins. "It defames the reputation of the department with a rather broad brush that I don't think is appropriate or warranted," Kelly said.

One of the key recommendations of the Mollen Commission was the creation of an independent agency with subpoena power to oversee how the NYPD policed itself internally.

The proposal gained control in the New York City Council, which moved to create such an agency with subpoena power that could legally compel the NYPD to produce documents.

The incoming of Mayor Rudolph Giuliani everything. He was a former federal prosecutor who enjoyed strong police support at the time. He succeeded in blocking the Council's move in the courts.

Giuliani right away substituted the used of an executive order to create the Commission to Combat Police Corruption. The commission had a handful of staff lawyers with a six-figure budget, but no subpoena power.

Ten years later, in 2005, Mark Pomerantz, the CCPC's chairman, and himself a former federal prosecutor, resigned because he said the volunteer post required more time than he could commit. He cited the difficulty the watchdog agency was having in getting documents from the NYPD without subpoena power.

Before he is leaving, Pomerantz testified before a City Council committee that his panel had been blocked by the police department in its efforts to examine issues like fraudulent NYPD overtime claims, allegations of sexual misconduct, and how domestic violence cases involving members of the department were handled.

Pomerantz said his agency also wanted to investigate allegations that supervisors within the NYPD regularly downgraded the seriousness of crimes that were reported to improve the department's performance statistics.

At that time, the NYPD denied Pomerantz's claims and asserted that the commission had gotten all the files in every case in which the NYPD thought that there was an instance of serious misconduct.

Three years later, the commission was once again in the headlines after Willa Bernstein, one of its four staff attorneys. She went public with claims… She was then terminated for having an anti-police bias.

During that time, the Daily News reported that Bernstein had called for an investigation into the decision of arresting officers to use a Taser on a teenage suspect who was already handcuffed.

Based on internal memos obtained by the Daily News, the commission leadership had determined that Bernstein had lost her credibility with the NYPD's Internal Affairs Division after she compared the Taser incident to the 1997 Abner Louima police brutality case. That case involved the brutal precinct house beating of Louima by one officer and the subsequent cover up by a handful of other officers.

The assaulting officer, Jason Volpe, was convicted and sentenced to 40 years in jail, while Louima was paid over $8 million by the city.

Despite the lack of subpoena power, the Commission to Combat Police Corruption's internal disciplinary process continues to play a role. According to the CCPC's last annual report in 2015, the panel conducted a detailed examination of 129 NYPD Internal Affairs Bureau cases and 540 disciplinary cases from 2014.

In the 40 cases involving allegations of domestic violence involving members of the department, the CCPC concluded that in seven of the cases the departmental penalties were too lenient.

Also, in two related cases described as "profit motivated misconduct" involving veteran officers who received a $100 gratuity for providing an off-duty police presence at the same contentious corporate board meeting the CCPC also found the NYPD's internal disciplinary response too light.

According to the annual review of the 32 instances in which officers were found guilty of department charges of false entries in NYPD records in the time under review, only two of those cases resulted in termination from the force.

The latest round of police accountability reforms has come in the wake of the political battle over the Bloomberg administration's reliance on the controversial stop and frisk policy.

At one point under Bloomberg and Kelly, police were making several hundred thousand stops a year, overwhelmingly of young men of color, while 95 percent of them did not produce an arrest or even a summons."

Eventually, a federal judge ruled the practice unconstitutional.

In the 2013 mayoral race, Bill de Blasio, the eventual winner, campaign against the tactic, which had become a defining issue.

In August 2013, the New York City Council voted to create the Office of the NYPD Inspector General, under the auspices of the city's Department of Investigation.

The new oversight office has subpoena power, and in its first two years has focused on issues like the NYPD's use of force on civilians and the efficacy of the strict enforcement of minor quality of life crimes to reduce the overall number of serious felonies.

In 1974, the Civil Service Leader reported on the Police Foundation's publication of a brochure entitled the "100 Hats of Officer Jones," which recounted how in one year, in addition to fighting crime, city police officers had delivered 46 babies and helped extricate 361 people caught in machinery and responded to over 1,500 stuck elevators.

CHAPTER 54

CORRUPTION
IN 30TH PRECINCT

The Dirty Thirty scandal took place between 1992 and 1995 in the New York City Police Department's Thirtieth Precinct. This was the largest collection of police officers charged with corruption in New York City in almost a decade.

A group of crook officers, led by Sergeant Kevin P. Nannery, participated in various unlawful activities, including civil rights conspiracy, perjury, extortion, grand larceny and the possession and distribution of narcotics.

The scandal led to several arrests of police officers and two suicides.

The "Dirty 30" were mostly stationed at the 30th Precinct in Harlem, Upper Manhattan.

During that time, the area was known as the "cocaine capital of the world" to locals and law enforcement.

Police corruption was extremely high around this time, and the Mollen Commission was created to help investigate and destroy corruption within the NYPD.

Corruption was so bad that although many supervising officers did not participate, they turned blind eyes to other officers committing unlawful acts.

Sergeant Kevin Nannery took the additional action and began participating. Soon his group of officers began calling themselves "Nannery's Raiders" and participated in "booming"

Nannery's Raiders began making bogus radio calls to cover up illegal search and seizures on known drug dealers' apartments. This is where they seized drugs and stole large amounts of cash.

They would then sell the seized drugs straight from the 30th Precinct itself at half-market price to profit from their loots.

A gram of powdered cocaine sells for $50 to $90. In the 30th Pct., the price was $20 to $25. An ounce, or a little more than 28 grams, goes for up to $1,200 elsewhere, more than twice what the best wholesale customers pay in the 30th Precinct. A kilogram which is 1,000 grams, 2.2 pounds, can cost up to $22,000. The 30th Pct. the kilos often went for $16,000 to $18,000.

In one case, the sergeant and two officers stopped a man in an apartment complex, took his keys and then robbed his apartment without a warrant.

They let the man go after taking several thousand dollars' worth of drugs and cash. They also participated in various extortions, with illegal drug wholesalers giving the officers weekly payoffs that ranged anywhere from $600–1,000 a week.

A squad car would pull up to a corner where these guys were working and just sit there," the investigator said. "Business had to halt.

Sooner or later one of the guys would start talking, feeling out the officer. Maybe they could work something out. Maybe the cop should stop by a certain "bodega". The cop goes away. He doesn't bother the corner again. At the end of the week, he goes to the "bodega" and gets his money.

In 1993, Dirty 30 officer "Otto", Barry Brown went undercover in an investigation against the Dirty 30. The two-year investigation included sting and surveillance operations.

On the week of Sept 28, 1994, 29 police officers were arrested, with five pleading guilty. A total of 33 officers were arrested.

The perjury committed by these officers also resulted in at least 50 of their cases being dismissed.

Names and Charges of the Dirty Thirty

Sgt. Kevin P. Nunnery 4 counts 1st deg. perjury, civil rights conspiracy

Sgt. Richard J. McGauley 1st deg. perjury, civil rights conspiracy

Officer D. Benitez extortion

Officer Edward M. Checke 1st deg. perjury

Officer George H. Eckerson civil rights conspiracy

Officer Justine A. Fazzini 1st deg. perjury, civil rights conspiracy

Officer Theodore Giovanniello 1st deg. perjury, civil rights conspiracy

Officer Kevin Kay civil rights conspiracy, tax evasion

Officer William H. Knox 1st deg. perjury, civil rights conspiracy, possession of narcotics, misprision of a felony

Officer Thomas J. Nolan 1st deg. perjury, civil rights conspiracy

Officer Armando Palacio 1st deg. perjury

Officer Steven L. Pataki 1st deg. perjury

Officer Blake C. Struller 3rd deg. grand larceny, civil rights conspiracy, narcotics distribution, tax evasion

Officer Joseph M. Walsh 1st deg. perjury, civil rights conspiracy, tax evasion

Thirty-three officers were arrested in a wide-ranging investigation of corruption at the 30th Precinct station house in Harlem.

The arrests, which implicated nearly one out of six officers assigned to the 30th Precinct station house, were the fruits of a probe began by an investigator, who worked for the Mollen Commission.

CHAPTER 55

CORRUPTION
IN 34TH PRECINCT

Federal investigators launched a probe over reports that some police officers were engaged in drug dealing.

At the same time, Mayor David Dinkins announced that he would "name a special investigator to look into the charges of corruption, as well as possible lapses in the Police Department's internal investigation methods.

Aides to the Mayor said the investigator would be Milton Mollen, the former Deputy Mayor for Public Safety," according to a report published by The New York Times, adding that the investigation by the U.S. Attorney's Office was focusing on the 34th Precinct, further noting that "The investigation is an unusual Federal intrusion into the workings of the city's Police Department, and it raises the specter of a departmental problem larger than that acknowledged by Police Department officials."

Among aspects or allegations triggering investigatory scrutiny was the fact that the 34th Precinct had the highest rate of homicides and that some 34th Precinct police officers were "overlooking drug dealing in exchange for money and drugs and acting as guardians for the dealers by protecting the buildings and stores where they live and work.

Other officers are suspected of buying and selling cocaine or crack."

Top NYPD officials stated that the Brooklyn cocaine ring and the 34th Precinct corruption allegations were isolated incidents, despite complaints of other wrongdoings.

Some complaints noted that officers with NYPD's Internal Affairs mishandled investigations.

In 1994, the 34th Precinct had the highest number of corruption complaints, according to statistics reported by The New York Daily News. The three-year federal investigation of the 34th Precinct ended with only one conviction of perjury.

A corrupt NYPD officer was caught delivering drugs, stealing evidence from an NYPD precinct, and offering to get a criminal case dismissed — all for a few thousand bucks and a bottle of good Scotch, prosecutors said Monday.

Johnny Diaz, a veteran NYPD officer working in Inwood's 34th Precinct, had been suspected of taking cash to "throw criminal cases" for the people he arrested for years, prosecutors said.

In May, he offered his services to a drug dealer he busted. Except that this time, the dealer turned out to be an undercover cop conducting a sting operation, according to prosecutors.

"I can do life for this," the 48-year-old cop was recorded saying at a Manhattan nightclub, prosecutors allege. "I should know better. I'm a cop."

Diaz was indicted Monday on first-degree drug possession charges, accused of helping shuttle a kilo of cocaine from the Bronx to Manhattan for $4,000. Assistant District Attorney Emily Farber said that there are more charges are likely coming.

He's been a police officer for 23 years. There have been allegations about his conduct going back years," Farber said.

Diaz arrested someone he thought was a drug dealer on May 23. The dealer was an undercover cop investigating Diaz, and the bent officer took the bait, prosecutors said.

Diaz seized a half a kilo of cocaine and $18,000 from the dealer, but only put $17,000 into evidence.

"After the arrest, he became friends the undercover cop. They began spending time together," Farber said.

They used WhatsApp to send encrypted messages to each other, and at one point Diaz stole the undercover's cell phone from the 34th Precinct's evidence room and returned it, Farber said. He received a bottle of Johnny Walker Blue Label Scotch as thanks, Farber said.

"Additionally, he accepted $7,500 from the undercover with agreement that he would help get the undercover's case dismissed. He was told that if he got it dismissed, he would get extra cash," Farber said.

He helped move a kilo of cocaine from the Bronx to the corner of W. 125th St. and Broadway. He started following the undercover officer with his own car and warning the officer to drive below 30 mph and stay off the phone to avoid getting pulled over.

When confronted by investigators, he said he knew the undercover officer was a cop but took the scotch and money anyway because it was offered to him, according to court documents. He also denied transporting the drugs, saying the cocaine was never in his car.

Diaz could face between eight and 40 years behind bars on the drug charge alone, Farber said.

His lawyer, Raymond Loving, asked for a low bail and argued he wasn't a flight risk.

Diaz lives in Yonkers with his wife and two kids. They've lived there for 12 years. His parents live in New York City.

Supreme Court Justice James Burke ordered Diaz to be held without bail.

The NYPD would not answer questions on how long Diaz has been suspected of offering to throw criminal cases, or how many cases he's believed to have gotten dismissed.

CHAPTER 56

CORRUPTION
IN 48TH PRECINCT

<u>In the News that all you see…..</u>
<u>nothing good about the department.</u>

Sixteen police officers, including three sergeants, have been indicted on charges of robbery, burglary, larceny, filing false police reports and insurance fraud…

Law Enforcement investigators are trying to clean up corruption in the New York City Police Department.

In addition, seven other officers assigned to the station house in the East Tremont section, including one sergeant, are to be suspended from the force and could face dismissal.

Although these officers were suspected of criminal wrongdoing in some cases, witnessing a crime and not reporting it.

The Bronx District Attorney's office told police officials that sufficient evidence to obtain an indictment had not been collected.

A senior police official said that officers from the Internal Affairs Bureau would begin taking indicted officers out of their homes in handcuffs overnight and would conclude the arrests this morning. The official would not say how many officers had been arrested last night nor release the names of the officers to be arrested and suspended, but shortly before midnight, at least 10 officers were taken in handcuffs through a side door at 315 Hudson Street in lower Manhattan, where the police Internal Affairs Bureau has offices.

A police barricade had been erected at the front entrance to the building.

The indictments handed up by two Bronx special grand juries in recent days are to be unsealed today, law enforcement officials said.

The indictments and administrative actions mark the second time in just over a year that large numbers of officers in a New York City precinct have been implicated in a corruption scandal. Last year, more than 30 officers were arrested in the 30th Precinct in Harlem on charges ranging from assault to drug dealing.

Senior police officials expressed dismay over the broad dimensions of the case. This involved nearly 10 percent of the officers in the 48th Precinct. Most of the offenses cited came since Mayor Rudolph W. Giuliani and Police Commissioner William J. Bratton took office.

"With all the major accomplishments we made in the reduction of crime in last year, I'm disappointed that some of that may be clouded by the alleged actions of a few," said Assistant Chief Rafael Pineiro, the Bronx police borough commander.

Police officials said the 16 indicted officers included 10 people who have already been removed from the field and placed on desk duty. Several of them, the officials said, have helped in the investigation by naming other officers.

The sergeants implicated include two from the 48th Precinct and one from the 40th Precinct, also in the Bronx, suspected of committing insurance fraud within the 48th Precinct.

Sixteen police officers from the 48th Precinct station house in The Bronx were indicted and arrested on corruption charges including larceny, filing false police reports, and insurance fraud.

Seven further officers faced disciplinary action, but not arrests, because there was insufficient evidence to lead to indictments. In total, nearly 10 percent of the police officers assigned to the 48th Precinct house were implicated in a corruption investigation that was inspired by pressure created by the Mollen Commission.

Reports also showed that a police union, the Patrolmen's Benevolent Association, undertook aggressive efforts to prevent investigations into corruption at the 48th Precinct.

A senior police official, who spoke on the condition that he not be identified, said he did not expect many more officers from the 48th Precinct would be implicated, although other officials said the Police Department was looking at many other officers in such adjoining precincts as the 46th, the 44th and the 52d.

"The people we are bringing in in the 48th are everyone who is known," the senior police official said, though he added that the suspects would be urged to name other officers believed to be involved in criminal activities after they are arrested.

At the precinct stationhouse yesterday and last night, there was more activity than usual, with police officers coming and going between regular shifts. Some of the officers wore grim expressions.

Police officials would not say precisely what the indicted officers were said to have done. But they did describe the insurance fraud case, saying that a sergeant had reported his car stolen, then dumped it at a car repair shop to be stripped for parts.

The investigation into the 48th Precinct was the first major corruption inquiry into a single precinct that was initiated by the Police Department itself. Under pressure from the Mollen Commission, which held public hearings in late 1993 identifying pockets of suspected corruption in the East Tremont, University Heights and Morris Heights neighborhoods of the Bronx, the Internal Affairs Bureau began a series of sting operations in the 48th Precinct to detect corrupt officers.

Mr. Bratton's aides said the Commissioner was clearly upset about the case. Speaking of the brutality and corruption found over the last year in the 30th Precinct in Harlem, one senior police official said, "We thought after the three-oh, it would have put a damper on it."

Mr. Bratton spoke with Bronx police commanders and police union leaders yesterday, and then taped a video to be distributed today to precincts around the city explaining what had happened in the 48th Precinct. Late last night, he toured the streets of the precinct.

Trying to find a silver lining to the crisis, police officials said they developed new investigative techniques in pursuing the 48th Precinct case that included more sophisticated sting operations and patterning types of arrests and complaints to single out suspected officers.

"I hope the message is learned that there are certain things this department will not tolerate," Chief Pineiro said, "and we have shown we are in the position to conduct these investigations to a successful conclusion."

The pattern of corruption found in the Bronx precinct was somewhat different from that of the 30th Precinct, where crews of four or more police officers were accused of beating up suspects, dealing narcotics and stealing drugs and guns from traffickers.

In the 48th, most of the offending officers worked either alone or with partners.

The differing patterns of police crime in the 48th and 30th Precincts reflected the differing patterns of the drug trade in Harlem and the central Bronx. Because upper Manhattan is a wholesale center where drug dealers from all over the metropolitan area shop for their drugs, the officers arrested in Harlem were often tempted by large sums of money or caches of the finest cocaine they found on the job.

The East Tremont section, by contrast, is dominated by small-time drug dealers hawking heroin and crack on the streets. Officers who stole did so for petty amounts of money.

Almost all the officers to be arrested or otherwise disciplined in the 48th Precinct worked on the overnight shift; the officers arrested in the 30th Precinct worked on all shifts.

Joseph Mancini, a spokesman for the Patrolmen's Benevolent Association, said he could not comment on the indictments.

Since brutality and corruption often go hand in hand, Police Department officials and outside investigators said patterns of abuse complaints in at least several other precincts in the city suggested the possibility of worse corruption problems than in the 48th.

Former staff members of the Mollen Commission said their preliminary investigations indicated severe corruption problems in a broad swath of the city stretching from Harlem to Washington Heights and into the central Bronx. They said there was another deep pocket of suspected police corruption and brutality in central Brooklyn.

CHAPTER 56

CORRUPTION
IN THE 40TH PRECINCT

In 2015, disciplinary charges were announced against 19 officers at the 40th Precinct station house in the Bronx.

These 19 officers failed to process crime complaints properly. During an audit of a four-month period in 2014, fifty-five instances of alleged discrepancies were discovered between radio call response activities and complaint reports that led to a deliberate misreporting of crimes.

After the discrepancies were corrected, it was discovered that crimes increased in the precinct from what had been previously reported for 2014.

CHAPTER 57

CORRUPTION
IN THE 67TH PRECINCT

There was pattern of arrests of individuals who were charged with gun possession, made by police officers in Brooklyn's 67th Precinct. It was reported that each case was apparently tampered.

According to many newspapers articles in 2014, the 67 Precinct was tampering with each arrest they made…

Lots of suspects stated that police officers had placed the guns on their person and even drugs. Each gun was found in a plastic bag or a handkerchief. The strange thing was that there was no trace of the suspect's fingerprints.

The defense attorneys have said in court filings that the arresting officers may have been inventing informers to satisfy arrest quotas and to collect $1,000 rewards from an anti-gun community safety program.

The questions raised about the arrests suggested the "pattern of questionable police conduct and tactics."

According to the report, after an inquiry by the newspaper, prosecutors admitted that they were going to review the cases of some of the arrests.

A couple of arrests were leading to gun possession charges. They were being dropped against at least two men.

There was a case against a third man that was eventually dismissed. This was at the request of the prosecutor. This was after the man's trial preparation had commenced.

A fourth man was acquitted at the conclusion of a federal trial after police testimony was found to be "inconsistent."

A trial against a fifth man arrested on gun possession charges was dismissed after police could not produce their informant before the judge.

Reportedly, an investigation is being conducted by the NYPD's Internal Affairs Bureau.

CHAPTER 58

CORRUPTION
IN 73RD PRECINCT

In January 1994, five NYPD officers assigned to the 73rd Precinct were removed from duty over allegations of extorting cash, guns, and drugs from drug dealers.

The investigation referred to the group of implicated police officers by the name, the "Morgue Boys," because the officers would sometimes retreat near an abandoned coffin factory. The police officers would go near the factory to divide the profits of their corruption.

One of the Morgue boys, a former corrupt police officer stated that protecting the public was the last thing on their minds.

Let me tell you that they were stealing from drug dealers while on duty. Guess what? They also made illegal arrests to gain overtime pay....

The former police officer, Daniel Eurell, began his testimony for the prosecution that led witness in the latest trial stemming from charges of major corruption at several New York City police precincts.

Law enforcement officials say that the group of 15 officers known as the Morgue Boys carried out a three-year reign of violence and fraud in the precinct.

The Morgue Boys conducted raids. They hit on suspected drug-dealing sites. They would steal money and drugs. Then, they made the unwarranted arrests.

All officers were tried in the Federal District Court in Brooklyn. At the trial of three officers who served in the 73 Pct., the truth came out. They were charged with conspiring to violate extortion and the civil-rights laws.

The three police officers were Richard Sanfilippo, 28, Keith Goodman, 29, and Frank Mistretta, 53. all of theme were accused of participating in the raids and sharing stolen money at various times in 1991 and 1992.

Keith Goodman was also accused of committing perjury at the trial of a person he arrested. The defendants were all placed on restricted duty. The three denied the charges.

Their lawyers argue that they are the targets of prosecutors working with Daniel Eurell and two other former officers, belong to the ring. The lawyers say the former officers have falsely implicated the men on trial to gain compassion.

In his testimony, Daniel Eurell, 29, painted a vivid picture of a band of predators in uniform, himself included. He testified that he took part in 200 to 300 illegal raids of apartments and bodegas while serving in the 73d from December 1988 until his arrest in May 1992.

Daniel Eurell explained that sometimes they got in buildings by verbally threatening people. There were other times when they would break in using any tools, we had such as battering rams and crowbars. There were nights when made two to three raids.

Daniel Eurell told the jury in Judge I. Leo Glasser's courtroom he made only 5 to 10 legitimate arrests in his entire time at the 73rd Precinct.

To guarantee overtime from processing the illegal arrests, Furell would try to make an arrest at the end of his tours.

On The Job in The Big Apple

The officers hid the raids from their superiors by avoiding radio communications that would give them away. Where arrests were made, they filed false reports to cover stories.

A spokesman for the Brooklyn District Attorney's office, Patrick Clark, said that a review of numerous cases handled by officers implicated in the ring had led to the dismissal of charges against 20 people. He said he did not know how many of the 20 had been convicted before the dismissals.

Officials say the ring at the 73d Precinct was exposed when Daniel Eurell was arrested in a separate drug conspiracy case in Suffolk County. He entered a plea deal requiring him to reveal all his other crimes.

In its report to the Mollen Commission, the panel that investigated police corruption in New York City, cited the 73d Precinct as one of several "pockets of corruption" that had existed for so long partly because of willfully blind supervisors who fear the consequences of a corruption scandal more than corruption itself.

Federal and state investigators worked in partnership to collect evidence for a federal grand jury, which included information that the implicated police officers would hold up drug dealers at gunpoint, usually while on-duty, netting up to $2,000 per night in criminal proceeds.

The investigation into corruption at the 73rd Precinct was made possible by information gathered at hearings held by the Mollen Commission.

Eventually, 15 police officers were suspected of having participated in the "Morgue Boys" ring, resulting in at least six arrests, three of which pleaded guilty, with the remaining three receiving either acquittals or mistrials by trial jurors with respect to criminal and civil rights charges, respectively.

CHAPTER 59

75TH PRECINCT COCAINE RING SCANDAL

In May 1992, five current and one retired NYPD officer were arrested and charged with trafficking drugs from Brooklyn into Long Island. Two of the officers were partners at the 75th Precinct, the other officers were from the 73rd Precinct.

Prosecutors alleged that one of the officers arrested, Michael Dowd, knew when he was under surveillance. He may have benefited from tips from department investigators.

The question is how Dowd may have managed, for some time, to evade investigation became a subject of inquiry by the Mollen Commission.

Officer Kenny Eurell, who also was one of the officers arrested at the same time as Dowd, tape-recorded Dowd plotting an elaborate plan to skip bail. His bail was revoked, and later Dowd was convicted of racketeering and conspiracy to distribute narcotics and served 12 years in prison.

CHAPTER 60

CORRUPTION
IN 77TH PRECINCT

In December 1986, 11 NYPD officers were arrested from the 77th Precinct in the first major instance of corruption after the Knapp Commission.

The investigation came to be known as the "Buddy Boys" case. The officers, "who knocked down doors, stole money and drugs from drug dealers and resold the stolen drugs," also "ran extortion operations within the precinct," according to a corruption timeline prepared by The New York Times.

Eventually, 13 officers were indicted, and all the nearly 200 officers at the 77th Precinct station house had to be transferred to other Brooklyn precincts, except for 1 union delegate.

A special state prosecutor, Charles Hynes, found later to be corrupt himself, had to present evidence to a special grand jury in the corruption investigation.

CHAPTER 61

CORRUPTION
IN 109TH PRECINCT

After the NYPD received complaints that police officers assigned to the 109th Precinct were using drugs, four officers were confronted. Three officers took drugs tests, failed, and were dismissed. One officer resigned.

The investigation of the precinct extended to at least 20 police officers, including a sergeant. Some officers were given desk jobs or transferred to other precincts. Three officers from the precinct were indicted for theft.

In its report about the investigations at the 109th Precinct, The New York Times noted that although the allegations were not as severe as those at the 30th Precinct, the investigation was notable, "because it demonstrates that major corruption exists in precincts outside the high-crime areas where the temptations for drug-related corruption are usually highest."

In the face of allegations that a police union, the Patrolmen's Benevolent Association, was undertaking "aggressive efforts to spoil major corruption inquiries," according to The New York Times, John

Miller, then the Deputy Police Commissioner for Public Information, said he found the actions "disturbing."

Efforts to root out bad cops were made difficult by the P.B.A., as that police union is known, according to officials and prosecutors, who worried "that they will have trouble rooting out substantial numbers of corrupt officers as long as the P.B.A. resists them," as reported by The New York Times. Indeed, the P.B.A. was shown to be a powerful organization with great influence. "Fortified with millions of dollars in annual dues collections, the P.B.A. is one of the most powerful unions in the city.

As an active lobbyist in Albany and as a contributor to political campaigns, the P.B.A. has enormous influence over the department and is typically brought in for consultations before important management decisions are made."

CHAPTER 62

ANTOINE POPPA

<u>This is his story…..</u>

"Truth, oath, honor, and integrity", are these just simply words? These are words that define and mold the character of an honest cop…….

"Corruption, deception, misconduct and cover-ups", these are words we should never use when speaking of law enforcement.

The following short story is made of fictional characters. They are real only in my imagination. I used to work for the New York City Police Department many years ago. Some of these writings are historical fiction from my past…

Twenty-five years ago, my law enforcement career came to a crying halt because I believed in the oath I swore to when I became a cop.

How did that happened is not a tale, but I believe that is worth telling, even though it occurred almost a quarter of a century ago.

Sometimes doing what is right and telling the truth has consequences.

You may ask yourself, "How can doing what is right end up so wrong?" I told myself that many times over the past two and a half decades.

This story is going to be a recollection of police war stories. There are hundreds of those I could tell.

To understand the cop, you first you must understand the woman or man behind the badge.

People become police officers for many different reasons. Many have honorable intentions and want to help keep their community safe. Others like the idea of the power that wearing a gun and a uniform project, which is the wrong reason to become a cop.

The reason why I chose to get into law enforcement was personal and profound.

Seventy-one years has passed since I was born in Brooklyn, New York. Life has taken me on many journeys. Some memorable and some I wish I could have forgotten, but that is life. You really can't remove from your memory events that have made a major impact on your life no matter how tragic they were.

As many t Americans, I am a descendant of immigrants. My grandparents on my mother's side immigrated to the United States from Italy. My father was born in Constanta, Romania.

I have very few memories of my father as he left my mother when I was just a small. As a result, I grew up without a father being present in my home.

I did have some French military medals that my mother had given me. They were from my dad. He received them during WWII, long since lost because of moving way too times in my life.

What I still have after all these years is a ragged faded Divisional Citation translated from French from the Free French Forces, 1st Free French Division, 13th Light Brigade, Foreign Legion 1st Battalion that reads:

By decision dated July 3, 1943, Major General Koenig, Commander of the First Division of the Free French, makes the following Divisional Citation: Antoine Poppa – Serial No. 80 – Private, "Participated on May 9, 1943, at Djebel-Garci in a difficult patrol within enemy lines which, in the full light of day, succeeded in capturing 14 Germans. Due to his discipline, daring and courage, he largely contributed to the brilliant success of this action."

I would like to think that I inherited from my dad the traits of discipline, daring and courage.

We had very little money when I was growing up. Fun for us was hanging out on the street, as it was for most kids in the city. Fate could have taken me down the wrong path, but that didn't happen. I guess my mother did a good job, looking back on things.

They say you are a product of your environment. I don't necessarily agree with that statement. I think what makes you a good person in life are the values that are instilled in you as you grow from a child to adolescent to adult. It doesn't make one bit of difference where you grew up or whether you were poor or rich.

They say we all leave this world with nothing, nothing materialistic anyway.

What you take with you is your character and your integrity. What made you the person in life that you were. And that is something that nobody can take away from you.

I have my mother to thank for that.

In Catholic elementary school I thought about becoming a Catholic priest, maybe because my mother was very religious or the books, I read that described how priests and missionaries help people.

Little did I know at the time that even a priest can disgrace his collar, just as a cop can disgrace his badge?

I also had an avid interest in science and loved the police dramas, western shows and war movies that were on television.

I never figured that one out. A priest on one hand, and a soldier and a cop on the other.

Every Sunday we attended church at St. Patrick's on 97th Street in Bay Ridge.

My mother's answer to life was that whatever happened either good or bad was what God wanted. She would always say things happen for a reason. They may not all be good, but there is a reason why God planned it that way.

Bad things may happen in your life, but it only makes you a stronger person, she would say. And bad things happen to good people.

As a child I really didn't understand what all that meant. Little did I know that many years later I would find out that what my mother had told me as a child, was right.

In September 1969 I ended up going to public high school, which was an eye opener for me, mainly because of the change in discipline. The Dominican nuns in elementary school were strict. By today's standard a lot of what they did back then would be considered child abuse. But no matter how bad it was sometimes; in the end I think it made me a better person in life.

Public high school was the other side of the coin.

Virginia driver's license with fictitious under cover name and identifiers.

Illegal drugs in the late sixties and early seventies were so prevalent on the streets and in the schools, it was no different. Barbiturates, amphetamines, acid, heroin, pot, and a host of other narcotics were easy to acquire.

I saw first-hand the destruction that drugs can do to young people. I saw the drug dealers making money off the junk they were peddling to the kids. When others would be taking the bus home, they would be driving home in their cars.

I never thought at that time that one day I would be going after them. Not them personally but other drug dealers in general.

There was the anti-establishment movement. The anti-war protests. Riots.

I remember watching the evening news, which showed the Vietnam War as it was happening. You could see the terror of war from the comfort of your own home. It was nothing like I had watched on television movies, it was real life with real soldiers getting killed or wounded.

Protesters against the war were mocking the soldiers who were fighting overseas and or coming home from the Vietnam War.

I never agreed with any of that. Too many John Wayne war movies I guess when I was growing up.

It was almost as if overnight respect for the police turned to hatred of the police.

What I saw was the police trying to keep a lid on things. Others saw it differently, but that didn't matter to me because all cops were the good guys, at least that is what I believed at the time.

Watching the police shows on television as a kid, it was always the good guys going after the bad guys. The good guys wore the uniform and carried a badge and arrested the crooks. In the back of my mind, I wanted to be a part of that.

So, after graduating from high school, I volunteered with the New York City Police Department's Auxiliary Forces Section. I wore a uniform and patrolled my neighborhood, directed traffic, and worked parades.

It was a little crazy, wearing a police uniform with no gun and not getting paid for it, but it got me closer to the real cops and I loved it, thinking that I would become a police officer with the NYPD one day.

One of my first jobs out of high school was working in a Radio Shack a few blocks from where I lived. I would see and talk to the beat cops who would stop in and say hello from time to time. Other times I would see the plainclothes anti-crime unit cops chasing down bad guys, which only strengthened my resolve to want to become a cop.

I remember one day when I was leaving the house, dressed in my auxiliary police uniform. My Uncle Joe was on his way out after visiting my other uncle upstairs. He had a permit to carry a gun because he owned a supermarket. He took off the holster with the gun in it and placed it on my side for a minute and said, "one day you'll have one of these on your hip when you become a real cop." His brother Frank was a NYPD officer who had passed away years before.

I never forgot that moment.

My uncle would never come to know that I became a police officer.

Tragedy struck my family.

One night after leaving his supermarket my uncle was making a night deposit drop at the bank at Hamilton Avenue and Van Brunt Street in the Red Hook section of Brooklyn. He was shot and killed during a robbery when some dirtbag grabbed the money bag from him.

My uncle who was a WWII veteran, had fought back and shot the suspect after he himself was shot. The suspect ran away, and my uncle died at the scene.

I remember receiving the telephone call from my cousin when he told me that my uncle was dead. My mother and my Aunt Lucy were standing next to me. When I told them that Uncle Joe was dead it was the worst scene, I have ever experienced in my life up until that time. I never seen anybody scream and cry like that before.

I left and we went over to my Aunt Nancy's house, my uncle's wife. It was terrible beyond belief. My uncle's daughter, my cousin Lynn and my aunt, they were going out of their minds. Such painful emotions of sadness and there was nothing anyone could do to make it go away.

All because one man placed the value of money over the price of another man's life.

When I was at the viewing at the funeral parlor, this elderly Italian lady came in and she went up to my uncle, looked at him and started crying uncontrollably. I asked who she was. My uncle for years would give her free groceries because she had no money, I was told.

And she wasn't the only one who benefited from his generosity. Every Thursday my uncle would drop off a free bag of meat to my mother.

My uncle was a good man, as all my uncles were.

The family was devastated and would never be the same after that. The holidays would never be as they were before, there was always someone missing from the table.

Reality hit me quick.

It wasn't like television where you see some actor getting killed and the next night, he is on another show doing a different role.

My uncle was gone forever.

I knew then that I had to be a cop more than ever. I had to go after the bad guys. I didn't want another family to go through the horror of what my family had gone through.

Then in 1975 New York City laid off thousands of cops.

I didn't want to hang around Brooklyn and wait to see when hiring would resume, years I heard it would be.

With no money and no prospect of a future I made a decision.

One that would change my life forever.

Less than a year later a friend and I went to see an Army recruiter who told us we could be cops in the military. Soldiers and cops at the same time. He said that would help us if we wanted to be civilian cops in the future.

We took the tests, passed and signed up. I didn't tell my mother I was leaving until two days before the recruiter was coming to pick me up for the short ride to Fort Hamilton in Brooklyn where we would take the oath into military service.

That decision would also strain the relationship I had with my mother. She never really forgave me for leaving Brooklyn.

My dream of being a cop had started.

That was 40 years ago.

As I get older in life, I face the prospect of my own mortality and lately often look back at my life. Police work was a major part of my life, and I did it with passion and pride. I wasn't one of those cops who just did what he had to do to get by on a shift. I was always looking for something to get into and many times I just fell into things.

I also learned that you had to communicate with the citizens. If you alienate yourself from them, you will never get any information or help when you need it.

I learned that a patrol officer can make plenty of cases if he keeps his eyes and ears open. Whether it was drugs or stolen property, having the contacts on the street is how you are going to make cases and arrests.

Police work cost me my marriage. I was married to my wife, but I was really married to the job, especially when I started to work undercover. I lost my marriage, my home, and a lot more than that.

Then a few years later I lost the job that cost me my marriage because all I did was tell the truth. I would often think over the years if it was all worth it.

I was a cop for almost 16 years of my life, up until 1992 when it all came crashing down. I sometimes find myself pondering what happened to my dream and why things turned out the way they did.

Why didn't I rise in the ranks or at least retire with a pension I would ask myself over the years?

After all I had years of experience and specialized training.

Doug Poppa when he was in the Loudoun County Sheriff's Office Motor Squad

Doug Poppa when he was in the Loudoun County Sheriff's Office Motor Squad

I had worked patrol, rode a Harley in the motor squad, was promoted to criminal investigator and did one of the most dangerous assignments in law enforcement, working undercover for many years.

I was one of the good guys, I would tell myself, I believed in the oath I took when I became a cop. Honor and integrity should be rewarded, not frowned upon, I would tell myself.

I never considered myself a kiss-ass either. I always said what was on my mind and sometimes I was called a rebel for it.

If someone had asked me a question, I gave them an honest answer.

My take has always been, don't ask something of somebody if you might not like their answer. If something was SNAFU, situation normal all fucked up, then that is exactly what I would tell them. I have been like that my whole life. A yes man I was not.

And I didn't cozy up to the boss just to make points with him.

Those that did really had no respect for themselves, because they couldn't exist just on the merits of their own abilities, so kissing ass was all they were good for.

Plenty of times though that would work to their own benefit. Everybody must live with themselves, so if that was the kind of insecure, losers they were then so be it. They must live with themselves, not me.

The downside of all that was in police work, that when the time comes to play ball with the team and something happens that needs to be covered-up and swept under the rug, you will do it, because now the boss has you in his pocket.

If you worked in law enforcement, you know the kind of cops I am talking about.

The ones who move up the ladder by having their noses so far up the brass' ass that if one stopped short the other would end up with a broken nose.

Those who would put a knife in your back just to make themselves look good.

Those cops who seem to get away with just about anything because they are close to the brass while others are disciplined and or retaliated against for doing the same thing.

They don't ever think about going up against the system and standing up for what is right, something you swore an oath to do. Telling the truth is sometimes a death sentence to your law enforcement career, at least it was in my case.

Hanging a cop out to dry because somebody less honorable must protect their own ass has occurred all too often in the past and way too many times in the present and that is a disgrace in police work and the criminal justice system.

I found out the hard way that not everyone who wears a badge is a good guy.

Not all cops are honorable and that goes for prosecutors also.

In my case when it came time to stand tall and do what was right, I was abandoned by not only my department, but the criminal justice system itself to some extent.

Good morals and ethics are inherent in good people. Pinning on a badge doesn't miraculously make you a better person. If you lack good character traits and you become a cop, you will end up being a bad cop.

And speaking of honor, honor is something that comes from the heart.

Good cops don't stand by and let a good cop get screwed. Good cops don't let bad cops get away with corruption and misconduct and disgrace the badge.

Maybe I should re-phrase that because, yes, they do.

In police work, integrity and honor many times takes a backseat to cowardice and complicity.

Cops are hypocrites, not all cops but many. Why? Because cops want criminals to inform on other criminals. That's how cases are made. That's how you move up the ladder in a criminal case.

But God forbid that a cop informs on a bad cop or stands up for the oath he swore to. Then he is a piece of trash, a rat because he broke that blue wall of silence.

I guess these cops think that wearing a badge gives them some God given right to break the law and or violate someone's rights and act like judge, jury, and executioner. What they do is spit on and tarnish the badge of every good cop and every cop who has given up their life on the job.

To this day I just don't understand why cops stand by and let these thugs with a badge get away with this kind of behavior. What bad cops don't seem to understand is that once they break the law, they have gone from being a cop to be a criminal.

And that goes for prosecutors also. It doesn't make a difference if the titles before their names are district attorney, commonwealth's attorney, or attorney general.

When it comes down to protecting their own ass they lie, cheat and do whatever they have to just to protect themselves and that is usually at the expense of another cop or a civilian.

That's not why I became a cop.

Standing up for the rule of law, defending the oath you swore to and not compromising your own principles.

That's courage, that's honor, that's integrity!

That's what wearing a badge meant to me.

I just didn't wake up one day in 1991 and decided I had to do the right thing. I had done it many times before in my life.

I learned the hard way that the strong-arm of the law has a long reach and sometimes that reach is deceitful and malicious.

When I was being methodically crushed by the same system, I gave my life to, it was devastating.

When they could find nothing else to attack me with, they did what any coward would do. They made up lies and defamed my character and integrity many times, and often behind my back. They embarked on a campaign of character assassination, making comments to the press off the record, because they were not man enough to say it outright.

I guess they thought that if they spread enough lies about me it would work to their benefit. How so wrong they were.

The truth does have a funny way of creeping out. In my case, it not only creeped out it poured out.

CHAPTER 63

DETECTIVES LOUIS EPPOLITO AND STEPHEN CARACAPPA

Who are Louis Eppolito and Stephen Carappa?

They are two former New York City Police Department detectives who worked on behalf of the New York City Mafia. They were principally the Lucchese and Gambino crime families. They committed various illegal activities.

In 2006, they were convicted of labor racketeering, extortion, narcotics, illegal gambling, obstruction of justice, eight counts of murder and conspiracy to commit murder, charges stemming from the 1980s and the early 1990s in New York City, and in the 2000s in Las Vegas. Both were sentenced to life in federal prison.

Let me tell you a little bit of each of these two individuals....

Louis Eppolito was born in 1948. He is the son of Ralph Eppolito, a member of the Gambino crime family. His paternal uncle and cousin, James Eppolito and James Eppolito Jr., were also both made Gambino members in capo Nino Gaggi's crew.

Growing up, he became acquainted with several other mobsters. His uncle and cousin were eventually murdered by both Nino Gaggi and Gambino family soldier, Roy DeMeo, with the permission of Gambino family boss, Paul Castellano. When he applied for the NYPD in 1969, Eppolito falsely stated that he was unrelated to organized crime figures.

Eppolito eventually rose to detective, a job which garnered him a few headlines. In 1983, he was suspected of passing New York City Police Department intelligence reports to Rosario Gambino, a distant relative of Carlo Gambino and Paul Castellano, the former leaders of the Gambino crime family. He was cleared in this case. Eppolito retired as a police officer in late 1990.

In his book, he cites his tarnished reputation over the Rosario Gambino corruption case as a reason for leaving.

Stephen Caracappa , 1942–2017, had worked in the NYPD's organized crime unit in Brooklyn, New York, since the late 1970s before he eventually retired on a disability pension in 1992.

He subsequently worked as a private investigator and retired in the mid-1990s, moving to Las Vegas along with Eppolito. Caracappa worked inside the Las Vegas Women's Correctional Facility as a correctional officer. While on trial in 2006, both he and Eppolito claimed that they were discriminated against during the proceedings

After meeting actor Joe Pesci in Cafe Central, a restaurant frequented by celebrities, he had a minor career as an actor, with small roles in movies including Lost Highway, Predator 2, Goodfellas, and Ruby.

In 1992, Eppolito wrote a book, Mafia Cop: The Story of an Honest Cop Whose Family Was the Mob, in which he of his attempts to avoid being dragged into the criminal life and having to fight for his reputation as a result of the Rosario Gambino corruption case. He moved to Las Vegas around 1994 and sold automobiles at the Infiniti dealership, where he would entertain fellow salesmen with NYC crime scene photos.

By 1985, Federal authorities recognized Eppolito and Caracappa as associates with the New York City Mafia. Caracappa was at this point a member of the Organized Crime Homicide Unit within the NYPD Major Case Squad based in Brooklyn. Both were known for using inappropriate methods to get results in their police work.

Anthony "Gaspipe" Casso role

According to Lucchese crime family underboss Anthony "Gaspipe" Casso, when trying to enroll in Witness Protection in 1994, he and his boss Vittorio "Vic" Amuso had paid Eppolito and Caracappa $375,000 in bribes. These payments were for murder contracts, since 1985.

Casso stated that in 1986 that, as retaliation for an attempt on Casso's life and on the orders of Casso and Amuso. The two police detectives kidnapped and handed over James Hydell, an associate of the Gambino crime family, to be murdered by Casso.

Again, on Casso's orders, this time with the assistance of Louis Daidone, Eppolito and Caracappa murdered Lucchese member Bruno Facciolo because Casso suspected him of being an informant.

Facciolo's murder is famous for the stuffed canary Federal agents discovered in his mouth at the crime scene; considered to be a message to other informants.

At least partially in retaliation for the 1985 murder of Gambino crime family boss Paul Castellano, arranged by John Gotti, Casso ordered Eppolito and Caracappa to kill Gambino captain Edward "Eddie" Lino.

On November 6, 1990, the detectives pulled Lino over in his 1990 Mercedes-Benz and shot him nine times.

On April 13, 1991, Caracappa and Eppolito provided information that led to the murder of Gambino crime family soldier Bartholomew "Bobby" Boriello on the orders of Frank "Big Frank" Lastorino, a captain in the Lucchese crime family. Lastorino was reportedly promoted consigliere of the family for this hit. As relations between the Gambino and Lucchese crime families worsened,

Lastorino reputedly ordered Eppolito and Caracappa to murder Lucchese "made man" Patrick Testa in 1992. Testa was a former Gambino mobster and Lastorino wanted to make it look like the Gambino's arranged the hit to start a war between the rival families.

After wholesale indictments came down for almost every crime family in New York City in the mid-1990s, Eppolito and Caracappa retired to Las Vegas. Casso later confirmed that both of the "Mafia Cops" were still involved in crime family business from Nevada.

They were contacted in 1993 by Lastorino to murder the new head of the Gambino crime family, John "Junior" Gotti, whose father was imprisoned for life in 1992. The plot failed.

Lastorino also wanted the detectives to murder the underboss of the Lucchese crime family, Stephen "Wonderboy" Crea. This plot failed due to indictments brought against the family.

In the late 1990s, both Eppolito and Caracappa conspired to kill former Gambino crime family underboss Salvatore "Sammy the Bull" Gravano, who had entered the Witness Protection Program in 1992 after testifying against his boss John Gotti.

A reward had been placed on Gravano's head by Gambino boss Peter Gotti. Gravano was later arrested and convicted of drug trafficking in 2003 and was sentenced to serve 19 years in prison.

Indictments

After a long investigation, highlighted by Burton Kaplan's decision to testify against his former confederates, both Eppolito and Caracappa were arrested in March 2005 and charged with counts of racketeering, obstruction of justice, extortion and eight counts of murder and conspiracy.

These included the murders of James Hydell, Nicholas Guido, John "Otto" Heidel, John Doe, Anthony DiLapi, Bruno Facciolo, Edward Lino, and Bartholomew Boriello and their involvements in the conspiracy to murder Gravano.

On April 6, 2006, Eppolito and Caracappa were convicted on all charges. Kaplan, a businessman and career criminal, who had been the link between Casso and the two policemen, was the chief accuser, giving two days of riveting testimony.

On June 5, 2006, Eppolito and Caracappa were sentenced to life imprisonment.

On June 30, 2006, the presiding federal judge, Jack B. Weinstein, threw out a racketeering murder conviction against the two detectives on a technicality. The five-year statute of limitations had expired on the key charge of racketeering conspiracy.

On September 17, 2008, their racketeering convictions were ordered reinstated by a federal appeals court.

On March 6, 2009, Eppolito was sentenced to life plus 100 years and Caracappa to life plus 80 years. Each was fined more than $4 million.

On July 23, 2010, their convictions were upheld by the 2nd Circuit. As of June 2018, Eppolito was incarcerated at United States Penitentiary, Tucson.

Prior to his death, Caracappa was incarcerated at United States Penitentiary, Coleman in Florida. Both are high security institutions.

Caracappa was transferred to a federal prison in North Carolina before dying of cancer on April 8, 2017.

CHAPTER 64

THE IMPORTANCE
OF LAW ENFORCEMENT

Law Enforcement plays an important role in our Society.

The tragic shooting death of Michael Brown and chokehold death of Eric Garner by police brought into focus the fact that many Americans simply do not trust law enforcement.

Recent polls suggest that most Americans do not feel that police are adequately held accountable for their actions, treat racial groups equally or use the right amount of force.

This lack of trust undermines the legitimacy of law enforcement and creates an unequal society in which some feel comforted by law enforcement while others feel suspicious and distrustful.

Members of the community are more likely to feel safe and cooperate in investigations if they trust law enforcement; thus, it is in the best interest of all stakeholders to understand and build trust in law enforcement.

Trust can be defined as the "belief that someone or something is reliable, good, honest, effective." High levels of trust promote healthy interactions, whereas low levels of trust undermine constructive relationships. Trust in law enforcement is essential for the belief in the legitimacy of law enforcement or feeling of obligation to obey the law and defer to decisions made by legal authorities.

Research shows that perceived legitimacy of law enforcement is crucial to effective law enforcement.

One study of 830 New York City residents who were predominantly either white, Hispanic or African American examined whether perceived legitimacy of police, which included measures of trust, obligation and confidence in police produced increased cooperation with police in law enforcement efforts e.g., reporting a crime, assisting law enforcement officers over time.

The results show that trust was significantly related to not only cooperation with the police but also to a lesser extent with the cooperation with others in the community. These findings have been replicated in other samples.

In a study of 300 Muslim-Americans, it was found that perceived legitimacy was associated with willingness to cooperate with police on terrorism investigations.

Further work suggests that it is trust that drives this effect. One study of 638 high school students ages 18 and older in Slovenia found that of the various factors that make up "legitimacy" it is trust in police that most predicts cooperation.

Research demonstrates that minority groups consistently show less trust in law enforcement. This difference in trust appears to be based on two things.

First, minority groups report having more direct negative personal experiences with law enforcement. Further, there is evidence of discrepancies in procedural justice outcomes.

Research shows that minority groups are disproportionately incarcerated; as an example, African Americans comprise 14 percent of drug users but 37 percent of those arrested for drug offenses. Even though minority groups make up a large percentage of people subjected to "stop and frisk," white people are more likely to have drugs or weapons.

In the most extreme cases, when lack of trust is so severe, perceived discrimination can be associated not only with poor cooperation with police, but also negative mental and physical health consequences. One recent meta-analysis of 134 studies found that perceived discrimination has a significant negative effect on both mental and physical health.

Perceived discrimination also produces significantly heightened stress responses and is related to participation in unhealthy behaviors and non-participation in healthy behaviors. There has been a call for looking at the public health effects of witnessing police misconduct and brutality.

Now, the question is, "What can be done?

Across the board, various entities have suggested that increased transparency is one of the best ways to build trust. There are several concrete ways that transparency could be increased. Perhaps most strikingly is the important need for data to be aggregated, organized, and shared across law enforcement and community agencies.

For example, research suggests that currently it is unknown how many people are killed by police each year. There have been similar calls for transparency in the results of evaluating rape kits.

These recent tragic deaths have ignited interest in whether police should be videotaped during interactions with the public. The debate has included calls for more flexibility allowing journalists and citizens to videotape police officers. Current state laws do not explicitly say whether this behavior is legal even though courts have upheld a person's First Amendment right to record public events such as protests or traffic stops.

More, evidence suggests that if police wear video cameras so that their behavior is recorded, everyone wins; studies suggest that complaints are radically reduced, and in the case of complaints police are exonerated far more often than if no recording existed.

There is a compelling need for more communication between law enforcement agencies and community organizations. This type of approach includes regular meetings with community leaders and law enforcement. Initial research suggests positive results in involving community leaders with cooperation, even for the smallest infractions.

There is also evidence suggesting that diversity training for police can improve relations with the community. Further, on a policy level, there must be examination of laws that result in unequal treatment.

Law enforcement agencies and the people that serve deserve our respect for putting their lives on the line to protect us. Similarly, our community deserves to exist in a context where everyone receives the same benefit from the legal system.

One of the best ways that we can show that respect is by being honest with ourselves and with others when trust has broken down and seeking ways to rebuild.

Why am I saying this? Because when trust is broken, everyone loses.

CHAPTER 65

BEING A POLICE
OFFICER IS AWESOME

There are many reasons why I believe that being a police officer is awesome. Sure, you have the chance to earn a good salary, excellent retirement benefits, and great health insurance for you and your family.

Then, there're those selfless reasons that come with the job. Such as public service, protecting your community and knowing that you're making a difference for the people around you.

The real secret is that, aside from all those practical reasons to becoming a police officer, the job is just plain fun. So, whether you're already on the job and just need a boost, or you're on the fence about whether to step onto that thin blue line, here are the 10 best things about being a cop:

Though mounted police were once a rarity, nowadays cops and cars go together like, well, like Starsky and Hutch. A lot of departments offer take-home cars, which is a huge plus, especially when you can check on and take a 10-8 right from your driveway.

Even if you work for a department that uses pool cars, there's nothing like patrolling the town in your mobile office. Not to mention, of course, that cop cars are just cool; the paint schemes, the body style, the emergency equipment and, of course, the police package upgrades all make driving so much more fun.

Just being honest here, a police officer's utility belt is as close to being like Batman as you can legally get. No, they don't get grappling guns and batarangs, but what we do carry are indispensable tools of the trade.

High-power flashlights, electric conductive weapons, better known as Tasers, higher-capacity magazines, and a well-performing sidearm, collapsible baton and, of course, handcuffs have all become part of the identity of the modern police officer. You must admit, most police belts just look cool.

Cops work hard and train harder. They learn to protect themselves and others - and safely control arrestees - through rigorous defensive tactics training.

It's hard work, but it's a lot of fun, and you get a great workout in the process. Besides "DT" training, we get excellent tactical and firearms training, pursuit driving, first aid and CPR, and all kinds of advanced training in several specialty areas.

In fact, ongoing training is so important that you can pursue an entire career path as a police instructor or training officer. Police training reinforces the skills we need to do our jobs, as well as skills that they'll never need outside of the training environment. The best part, though, is that good training provides all the fun and none of the paperwork!

Much is made of the so-called "brotherhood" of the thin blue line and the notion that cops band together and protect their own, allowing for corruption, a double standard and a "rules don't apply to us" mentality. While it's not a problem to be ignored, there's another, much more positive side.

Law enforcement is undoubtedly a unique profession, and few if any outside understands what it's like to spend a day in the life of a police officer.

Working as a cop offers a sense of belonging and family that you won't find in many other careers. When the chips are down, police do band together to help their fellow officers.

There is nothing like the feeling that you've done something to make someone else's life just a little better. True, if you encounter a police officer on the job, you're probably not having a very good day. Most cops know that they can affect the outcome simply based on what they do or how they treat you.

Whether it's by helping you change a tire on the side of the road, showing a little compassion and empathy on a traffic stop or at a crash scene, or helping you see that justice is done if you're a victim of a crime, officers rarely forget that most of us took the job because we wanted to help others.

Police officers save lives every day. Sometimes, it makes the news, like when a cop runs into a building to save a child, or when she puts herself in harm's way to protect the innocent or defenseless. Those are the lives saved that we know about.

In fact, there are countless others we will never know about, like the person who changed their driving habits because of a traffic ticket they got, the drunk driver who was taken off the road before he could crash into another vehicle or the would-be robber that changed his mind simply because he saw a patrol car drive by.

Even in the smallest things we do, police officers save lives every day, and there are few feelings as satisfying as knowing that fact.

Though they're often the heroes no one wants. It's often said that everyone hates cops until they need one. The fact is police officers still enjoy a measure of respect in their community.

Regardless of their rank or status in their department, among their circles of friends, church groups or other community involvements they are often looked to as leaders and examples to be followed. Not to mention the way kids look up to officers when they're around.

It's a tremendous responsibility, and officers often need to be reminded of the high ethical standard they are held to, but it's also quite nice to have a job for which people have such respect and appreciation.

Also, there's nothing like the way your kids look at you with pride when they see you in uniform.

A lot of people want a job that matters. They all must work, but if they're honest, most of them want that work to mean something and make a difference.

The incredible responsibility that comes with being a police officer - you always have a duty to act, whether on or off duty - is a reward in and of itself. It means that what we do makes a difference, and that's a great feeling, even if it feels like a heavy burden at times.

Don't take it the wrong way, but there's something to be said for being able to tell people to do something and have them listen. It's also nice to see a problem and be able to fix it. Obviously, there's a tremendous potential to abuse the authority police have, but when used properly and for the good of others, it's great to be able to be part of the solution rather than part of the problem.

CHAPTER 66

THE NEW YORK POLICE DEPARTMENT FRATERNAL ORGANIZATIONS

The NYPD celebrates its diversity through various fraternal organizations that emphasize pride in the many walks of life that make this department and the City of New York so great.

By joining a fraternal organization, it provides members of the service access to a swing of career-based and educational opportunities, as well as the opportunity to ramp up their social lives with ceremonies, dinners, and dances.

The following will show you how some organizations were originated and how it helps the city that is growing with the different ethics background.

<u>The Asian Jade Society</u>
<u>Promote tolerance and understanding of the different cultures</u>
<u>Their Mission</u>

They are teaching cultural diversity, tolerance and understanding of the different ethnicities. The Asian Society create a strong bond and working relationship between the Police Department and the Asian Communities

They work together to recruit talented, multilingual, and educated Asians to increase the number of Asian Police Officers in the NYPD. This will help, represent, and assist their communities by working in those Precincts.

This group is designed, devise and apply effective programs that will facilitate education of the public in such critical areas as officer safety, community police relations, crime prevention and personal safety with an emphasis on Children's Issues

The NYPD Asian Jade Society has worked hard towards this goal not only in New York City but also on a national level with the Federal Law Enforcement community as well as other states and local authorities.

The Colombia Association

From the 1890's right through the middle of the 20th century, despite the work of great cops like the legendary figure Joe Petrosino, Italian Americans were viewed as second class citizens in the NYPD.

The dominant ethnic group at the time, Irish Americans, did not readily accept what they perceived as an "influx" of "outsiders." Many Italian American cops believed they were subjected and held to a higher standard and faced vile sarcasm, unequal punitive action, and outright bigotry.

Sometime in the early 30's, several officers SECRETLY planned to start an Italian American fraternal organization, which would be the foundation of today's NYPD Columbia Association, officially organized in 1932.

The founding members were Police Officers, Maurice Sasso, Thomas Julia, and Captain James Giattini, who despite his rise through the ranks at a time when there were hardly any Italian supervisors refused to tolerate other bosses mistreating his fellow Italian Americans.

Giattini had to be particularly careful since he could lose his rank for the slightest infraction. You must keep in mind that Civil service was quite different during that time.

For approximately two years, these men would SECRETLY recruit members and hold meetings in basements and private residences to prevent detection by the brass, who strongly opposed the organizing of these "outsiders".

At one point when word of these "secret meetings" leaked out, Sasso was literally physically removed from his post by several ranking officers and brought to Bellevue Hospital for psychiatric evaluation. He was held there against his will for three days.

This incident only strengthened their founders' resolve to organize the department's first ethnic fraternal organization. Miraculously, then Mayor Jimmy Walker and Police Commissioner Edward Mulroney finally acquiesced when they realized the Italians simply would not go away.

Capt. Giattini would be appointed the first Columbia Association president, followed by Sassou, then Julia. One of the most decorated members in the history of the NYPD, Mario Biaggi, served as their 10th president.

Other ethnic groups would eventually follow their lead. Although the prominent ethnic group, Irish Americans, outnumbered Italian Americans by a very wide margin in those times, it was not until 1953 that the Emerald Society was formed.

Italian American police officers take equality, fair treatment, and upward mobility for granted today. However, they must never forget the sacrifices and miserable and unfair treatment that their founders and predecessors had to endure.

History of the NYPD Hispanic Society

On July 29th, 1957, the New York City Police Department Hispanic Society was incorporated, with Police Commissioner Stephen F. Kennedy's approval. The organizations founding fathers were William Rodriguez, Peter Rodriguez, Isabel Barber, Eric Seise, Ivan Marfisi, Eugene Calderon, Victor J. Ortiz, Alex Cuesta, and Thomas Martino. This indicated that the formation of the organization was "to promote and develop a friendly and fraternal spirit among all members of Spanish descent in the police force of the City of New York, and to create a more harmonious relationship within the police department and the City of New York.

Shortly before its inception, there were approximately 40 officers of Hispanic origin. These officers were apprised by Police Officer Victor J. Ortiz of the need to form a fraternal organization that would address and voice the concerns of Hispanic officers.

From its very beginnings, the Hispanic Society has been involved in enhancing the opportunities for appointments and promotions of its members. Hispanic Society members were not only concerned with the plight of the officers it represented, but they also set forth on an immediate recruitment drive to increase the number of Hispanic candidates taking the police entrance examinations. At that time, Hispanics did not join the Police Department for various reasons.

In 1954, there were only 20-30 Hispanics in a police force of 20,000. In their recruitment endeavor, the Hispanic Society members appealed to the Commonwealth of Puerto Rico to assist them in their recruitment efforts. To improve the prospective candidates' chances of selection, tutorial sessions were held. As a result of these attempts, the number of Hispanics joining the Police Department increased dramatically.

Throughout the years the Hispanic Society has been involved in challenging entrance and promotional examinations and assessing the status of Hispanic officers in the department. In the early 1970's, because of the recruitment drives, Society members discovered that many Hispanics were unable to realize their dream of becoming police officers because they did not meet the departments height requirement.

The Hispanic Society addressed the problem locally by attempting to have the Police Department change these criteria; this was an unsuccessful venture, but in 1972, congress amended the Civil Rights Act of 1964, prohibiting the height requirement as it was ruled discriminatory. This resulted in a change in personnel selection practices in the law enforcement field. The removal of this barrier substantially increases the number of women and Hispanics in the Police Department.

In 1972, the Hispanic Society joined the Guardians in contesting the entry-level examinations administered in 1968 and 1972. An injunction barred the selection of candidates from those lists. Subsequently, that lawsuit had an impact on those Hispanic and African American officers who were hired off that list. Those affected received retroactive monies due to their newly designated appointment dates.

On October 5, 1979, the Guardians Association and the Hispanic Society lodged a lawsuit, which challenged the June 1979, police examination as not being job-related and its format unlike that of previous examinations. Federal Judge Carter ruled on December 17, 1978, that New York City could not use its latest Civil Service Exam to select new police recruits until he decided on a plan to assist African American and Hispanic applicants to the Police Department. This lawsuit resulted in a hiring quota of 1/3 of the recruits selected being of Hispanic and African American descent.

In 1981, yet another challenge, the Hispanic Society mandated that the promotion of new police sergeants should be consistent with the number of police candidates competing for that position.

Not only is the Hispanic Society actively involved with issues relevant to its members, but it also engages in matters directly affecting the community. An example would be the significant role played immediately after the island of Puerto Rico's devastation by Hurricane Hugo in September 1989.

The New York City Police Department amassed personnel as well as heavy equipment from its elite Emergency Services Unit to assist the Puerto Rican government and the Red Cross in their post-hurricane assistance. To further these efforts, the Hispanic Society appealed to its members to volunteer their time and travel to Puerto Rico to help the many affected families. The officers that unselfishly left their families behind for three weeks provided diverse aid, some were translators for those Puerto Ricans who could not describe to Red Cross personnel the hardship suffered, others accompanied Red Cross staff to remote areas of the island that had not yet been assessed as to the damage incurred, and yet others distributed food and emergency supplies to non-for-profit organizations that is would in turn disperse supplies to the community.

The Hispanic Society also raised funds and provided aid for Hurricane George in 1998.

The Hispanic Society has helped during other catastrophic events, such as the tragedy of American Airlines Flight# 587 bound for the Dominican Republic, which crashed in Belle Harbor, Queens on November 12th, 2001.

The Hispanic Society raised funds, served as translators, and helped the families in the recovery effort. The Hispanic Society also participated in fundraisers for the victims of Hurricane Katrina in August 2005.

The Hispanic Society also held a fundraiser for the victims in the Dominican Republic of Hurricane Noel in October 2007 and for the victims of the floods in Mexico in October & November 2007.

On the local level the Hispanic Society has been involved in the restoration of a church in the Lower East Side in Manhattan. The Annual Christmas Party is dedicated to raising funds for sick or injured children who are spending the holiday in local hospitals. The

Hispanic Society has hosted and participated in vest drives, for law enforcement in Puerto Rico and the Dominican Republic.

The Hispanic Society pledges to continue in the tradition set forth by our Founding Fathers to assist our members, communities, and other countries.

Mission of the Hispanic Society

The Hispanic Society of New York Police Department was founded in 1957 to promote and develop a friendly and fraternal spirit among all members of Hispanic descent in the police department to create a more harmonious relationship between the department and those whom we serve, the people of the City of New York to promote full discussion and exchange of all ideas regarding the planning and conduct of such aims to disseminate the significant results of all these efforts and activities To improve the methods and activities. The Hispanic Society pledges to continue in the tradition set forth by our Founding Fathers to assist our members, communities, and other countries.

Emerald Society

The Emerald Society is an organization of American police officers or fire fighters of Irish heritage. The Emerald Society for firemen was founded by Michael C. Donohue in New York City on March 17, 1956, St. Patrick's Day, to preserve the music, culture, language, and traditions of Ireland, but primarily to protect Irish firefighters.

Emerald Societies are now found in most major U.S. cities such as New York City, Philadelphia, Milwaukee, WI, Jersey City, NJ, District of Columbia, Boston, Chicago, San Jose, San Francisco, Los Angeles, Saint Paul, Colorado, Baltimore, and Cincinnati.

Federal law enforcement officers such as Special Agents and Customs and Border Protection officers and who are of Irish/Gaelic descent are eligible to join the Emerald Society of the Federal Law Enforcement Agencies.

The organization known as the National Conference of Law Enforcement Emerald Societies, NCLEES, states that its objectives are:

To unite all public safety Emerald Societies to develop fraternalism amongst its members.

To preserve the Irish culture and to promote the contributions of our ancestors.

To recognize the accomplishments of Irish Americans in Law Enforcement and other public safety professions.

To exchange information and enhance communications among member organizations and to start new public safety Emerald Societies.

To provide a unified and effective voice for its member organizations to the Congress of the United States and other government institutions.

To work with civic and public safety associations on areas of mutual concerns.

While the organization is geared toward Irish American culture, Irish heritage.

The Pakistani American Law Enforcement Society

Pakistani American Law Enforcement Society , P.A.L.S, was founded in 2015 to develop and promote spirit of fraternity among all members of Pakistani descent serving in Law Enforcement Agencies in the United States.

PALS' aim is to create a harmonious relationship between Law Enforcement Agencies and those whom we serve, people of the City of New York and the United States. PALS will serve as an instrument for open discussion and better understanding of Law Enforcement policies, striving for a safer community.

PALS will also initiate and enhance contact between Pakistani youth and Law Enforcement Agencies, opening new horizons for a future in Law Enforcement.

RUSSIAN AMERICAN OFFICERS ASSOCIATION

The Russian American Officers Association, RAOA, is a fraternal organization of law enforcement officers. It was founded in 2003 by officers of the New York City Police Department.

In 2003, there were much fewer Russian Americans in the NYPD than there are now. The organization's founders decided that their bond of being from the same culture should become official. They hence established the Russian American Officers Association.

Membership in the Association is open to active and retired sworn law enforcement officers of the federal, state, or local government or its subdivisions within the United States.

Most of the members in the Association are Soviet-born and although the majority immigrated to the U.S. before their teenage years, nearly all speak Russian fluently. The Association is based in New York City; however, active law enforcement officers from as far as California, Nevada, Texas, Florida, Washington, and Ohio also hold membership. While most Association's members consist of officers from the NYPD, law enforcement officers from 32 other agencies are in the membership.

The Shomrim Society

The first Shomrim Society was established in the New York City Police Department in 1924. Capt. Jacob Kaminsky was the first president. It is rumored that a comment made to a young Jewish officer going on patrol was the spark that started this fraternal and charitable organization. It was suggested that he might feel more at home with a salami, rather than a nightstick, under his arm.

Well, he kept his salami, his heritage, and his police status. At that time only 1% of the department was Jewish.

Shomrim really blossomed in New York during the depression years. Civil service jobs provided the only secure means of making a living in those days. The civil service lists of 1935-37 added 400 new Shomrim members.

In 1939, 33,000 people took the test. Of that only 1440 passed and one third of them were Jews. Most of them were college graduates out of work teachers, lawyers, accountants and even two doctors.

Today, Jewish Police Officers hold many different positions, and almost every rank in the NYC Police Department.

The goal of the society appears atop its stationery "so that Law Enforcement Officers of the Jewish faith may join together for the Welfare of all."

By the mid-1960s this "class of 1940" had filled such positions as Chief Inspector, the highest uniformed rank, a female Deputy Chief Inspector, the Chief of Detectives, Chief of the Organized Crime Bureau, and Chief of the Narcotics Division; in effect, it was the class "the stars" fell on.

The Steuben Association

This is an organization representing uniformed members of the New York City Police Department who are of German or Austrian heritage. Members of the Department voluntarily join the organization to enhance and celebrate their Germanic heritage.

The organization conducts several events during the year including an Oktoberfest celebration, golf outing, a Family Christmas party, monthly general membership meetings, and other social gatherings to celebrate their heritage.

This organization is overseen by a Board of Officers which consist active members of the Department, three retired members representatives, and members who have previously served the organization in the position of President.

The organization provides High School and College scholarships for children and grandchildren of their members based on highest scores achieved during a testing process.

This group is a member organization of the Grand Council of Steuben Associations in Civil Service, Inc., and Committee of Police Societies.

The history of this association and how its acquired its name

Baron Von Steuben, as he was known in America, was literally born into the military. He was born while his father was an engineer lieutenant in the Prussian army stationed in the Magdebourg fortress.

He joined the Prussian army himself at age 17 and served on the staff of Frederick the Great during the Seven Years War. He was, for unknown reasons, discharged from the army in 1763, having only attained the rank of captain.

Von Steuben later served as the chamberlain at the court of Hohenzollern-Hechingen where he attained the title "Baron". When his prince went deeply into debt, Steuben was forced to seek other employment. He failed at several attempts to join foreign armies, France, Austria, Baden. Von Steuben traveled to France where he hoped to meet Benjamin Franklin and offer his services to America.

He was introduced to Franklin as having been a lieutenant general in the Prussian army, but he only a captain. He secured a letter of recommendation from Benjamin Franklin to George Washington. He was assigned by Congress to Washington's forces in winter quarters at Valley Forge in 1777.

Joining an army on the verge of dissolution, he set out to create an improved command structure, develop a training manual and establish a code of regulations.

Starting from scratch, he taught basic arms drill and formation movements. Through the winter and spring of 1778, he transformed the American army into a disciplined, effective fighting force.

When Nathaniel Greene was sent to command the Southern Department in 1780, Von Steuben was sent with him. He, however, stayed in Virginia where he helped organize recruits and supplies for Greene's army. Von Steuben went on to serve as one of the American divisional commanders during the Yorktown Campaign. He served in the American army until he was honorably discharged in 1784.

Sikh Officers Association

Sikh Officers Association is a religious fraternal organization. The purpose of the Sikh Officers Association is to create recognition of Sikhs in law enforcement by exhibiting the Sikh values of justice, equality, and selfless service.

Their vision is to create a fraternal bond among all Sikh law enforcement officers. Together they can make voices heard. They participate in charity work, hold recruitment events and seminars,

This association educate the youth and Sikh community by informing and teaching the value of law enforcement. The Sikh Officers Association serves the public with the teachings of their Sikh faith which is defend the weak and protect the innocent without fear and without hate.

The Gay Officers Action League

The Gay Officers Action League, GOAL, is a first of its kind organization that was formed in 1982 to address the needs, issues, and concerns of gay and lesbian law enforcement personnel and has since expanded to a nonprofit tax-exempt civil rights organization.

GOAL was founded by Charles Henry "Charlie" Cochrane, Jr. Who was born on August 5, 1943, and died on May 5, 2008. He was a sergeant of the New York City Police Department.

After delivering a public testimony on anti-gay discrimination legislation pending before the New York City Council, he became the first openly gay officer of the NYPD.

Since his founding, the fraternal organization has advocated for the rights of its members and has assisted them on matters of discrimination, harassment, and disparate treatment in the workplace.

GOAL furthers its mission by providing training at the NY Police Academy and Jersey City Police Department, among others.

This organization provides an arena for members to discuss their needs and concerns in a comfortable atmosphere without fear of job-related reprisals.

They provide a safe environment for a group of people who have been, and continue to be, victims of harassment and discrimination in the workplace. They also serve as a bridge between the law enforcement community and The LGBTQ Community at large.

They are the first organization of its type in the world whose objectives are to promote the establishment of other chapters, throughout the United States and around the world.

By striving for a high level of diversity and the inclusion of all people within the organization, they stimulate intellectual growth and self-awareness of their members.

In doing so, they aim to motivate their members to achieve a higher degree of efficiency in the discharge of their duties as law enforcement and criminal justice professionals.

While the Gay Officers Action League is a positive force within the LGBTQ community, it is also instrumental in attempting to change homophobic attitudes in the workplace and in the community at large.

CHAPTER 67

FAUSTO B. PICHARDO

Pichardo was born in the Dominican Republic, in a village called Dicayagua de Arriba. He immigrated to the United States when he was nine and grew up on the Lower East Side and attended public schools.

Attended NYC High School for the Humanities. Chief Pichardo holds a Bachelor of Arts degree in Criminal Justice from John Jay College of Criminal Justice, and a Master of Public Administration degree in Government from Marist College.

He is also a 2015 graduate of the Police Management Institute at Columbia University, and a 2008 graduate of the FBI National Academy at Quantico, Virginia.

Pichardo started his career in law enforcement as a patrolman in 1999 after graduating from the New York City Police Academy. [as the Executive Officer of the Patrol Services Bureau where he oversaw the department's 77 Precincts throughout the city.

On October 13, 2020, Chief Pichardo announced and filed for retirement. Retirement to take effect November 2020.

Fausto B. Pichardo is a Dominican American police officer, administrator and is the former Chief of Patrol Bureau in the NYPD.

In this capacity he oversees some 22,000 uniformed police officers in New York City and is the first Dominican American to reach his position.

The Patrol Services Bureau is the largest and most visible bureau in the NYPD, overseeing most of the department's uniformed officers on patrol.

As a Chief of Patrol, Pichardo still oversees more than 22,000 officers and 77 police precincts during one of the most turbulent times the Big Apple has endured in modern history with the convergence of a pandemic, racial justice protests and controversial police reform.

Pichardo, 43, was born in the Dominican Republic and migrated to the New York when he was nine years old. According to some of his Lower Manhattan neighbors, he was "well respected" from a young age for representing the ideals of self-improvement that characterize families who come into this country looking for a better life.

"He sets a powerful example for our youths. If you want to get on the right path, this city gives you opportunities," said Feliz Rosario, 68, also Dominican, who saw Pichardo grow up in the Lower East Side. Years later, Rosario was said to have been surprised to see him on TV turned into a "great police officer."

The first New Yorker of Caribbean origin named Chief of Patrol, Pichardo took the position in December. After having joined the department in 1997 and being promoted to different positions in an apparently unstoppable career, he unexpectedly requested to retire.

The reactions have flooded in. Raysa Gálvez, president of the NYPD's Dominican Officers Association, described Pichardo as a Hispanic man who will always be an inspiration and a positive influence for new generations in the police force, adding that he played a key role in creating bridges between the police and ethnic minorities in the city.

"This is a great loss," said Galvez. "Ever since he came to the institution as a cadet in 1997, he stood out for his talent, kindness, and high marks. Today, he is a model for thousands of aspiring officers who are taking tests to work in the NYPD. We hope that the commissioner will continue to consider Latino officers, who are now well prepared to occupy high-ranking positions. The NYPD must strive for diversity at this time."

In a press release, the Latino Officers Association also called to acknowledge the contributions of Latino leadership to law enforcement agencies.

"During these critical times, our priority is for the mayor and the police commissioner to recognize the need to protect Hispanic representation in policy-making positions," said Anthony Miranda, executive director of the association.

Police Commissioner Dermot Shea said he was "surprised" by Pichardo's resignation.

"He is a great asset to the department. He has really stood out in every one of the positions he has occupied. He will be missed," said Shea, who declined to comment on the ongoing rumors that the Dominican-born officer stepped down after a tense exchange with Mayor Bill de Blasio.

In the halls of One Police Plaza, the department's headquarters, and in the city's precincts, the resignation also came as a shock.

"He is a dynamo 24/7. Precisely because he belongs to an immigrant family, he understands every millimeter of the city. He is a professional police officer and has a contagious discipline. At the department, we used to see him as a future commissioner. He is not the only valuable loss we have had, but it's the most visible one," an NYPD source told El Diario.

Indeed, thousands of New York City officers have retired in the last four months. From May 25 to September 10, the number of officers who filed their paperwork to leave the force increased to 1,189, compared to 679 during the same period in 2019, according to NYPD statistics. That is a 75 percent increase.

"These anti-police climate and the budget cuts, and hearing politicians shooting down the entire institution day and night, they are doing terrible harm to New York City. This judgment will leave you without valuable professionals or youths coming from our neighborhoods, like Officer Pichardo, who love and respect the uniform," said another official who chose to remain anonymous.

Back in December, Pichardo's appointment as highest-ranked seat at the Patrol Services Bureau was considered progress for Latino officers, who occupy fewer than 10 percent of the top positions in the department.

Particularly in the last five years, Hispanics constitute more than 35 percent of graduates at the NYPD Police Academy. Most of them are of Dominican descent.

De Blasio categorically denied last week that the reason for Pichardo's resignation had to do with discrepancies or "disagreements" with his administration. He added that he spoke with the officer several times on the evening of his resignation and again the next morning.

"I am noticeably clear this was a personal decision, a decision based on personal and family factors. He is a very devoted family man. This was something he felt was important to do for his family," said the mayor in response to the stream of rumors that linked Pichardo's resignation with the mayor's interference in police leadership affairs.

CHAPTER 68

NICHOLAS ESTAVILLO

NYPD Chief of Patrol Nicholas Estavillo. retired, was born on March 13, 1945, is a former member of the New York Police Department.

In 2002, he became the first Puerto Rican and the first Hispanic in the history of the NYPD to reach the three-star rank of Chief of Patrol.

Estavillo was born and raised in the sector Hato Rey, a section of San Juan the capital of Puerto Rico. There he received his primary education at El Colegio del Espiritu Santo.

In 1954, when he was nine years old, he moved to New York City with his mother. They lived in the borough of Brooklyn, where he attended St. Peter's School. Estavillo graduated from Bishop Loughlin Memorial High School and was awarded the Puerto Rican Leadership Scholarship, making it possible for him to attend St. Francis College.

In 1968, Estavillo applied to become an officer in the New York Police Department and graduated from the New York Police Academy after six months of training. His first assignment as a Police Officer was at the 19th Precinct located at East 67th Street in the

Upper East Side of New York. The population density of the 19th Precinct is one of the highest in the United States, with residents estimated at 217,063.

In 1988, Estavillo graduated from the FBI National Academy at Quantico, Virginia. Back with the NYPD, he rose in rank throughout the years and served as Precinct Patrol Sergeant and Precinct Lieutenant/Platoon Commander at the 24th Precinct.

As Captain, he served as Commanding Officer of the 34th Precinct covering the Manhattan neighborhoods of Washington Heights and Inwood.

By 1993 he was promoted to Inspector and Deputy Chief, Commanding Officer Fifth Division, covering the Upper West Side of Manhattan.

In 1995 he was promoted to two-star Assistant Chief and designated Commanding Officer, Patrol Borough Manhattan North which includes the neighborhoods and 12 precincts north of 59th Street in Manhattan. There he served until promotion to Chief of Patrol in 2002. Most of the population in that district are of Hispanic origin.

Estavillo enlisted in the United States Marine Corps during the Vietnam War and was a member of the 3rd Force, Recon Co. of the Marines Recon Force.

After three years of service, 1964–1967, which included a tour of duty in Vietnam, Estavillo was honorably discharged with the rank of sergeant. He continued his education at the New York Institute of Technology where he earned a Bachelor of Science degree in Criminal Justice.

In 2002, Estavillo was promoted to Chief of Patrol, thus becoming the first Hispanic to reach the executive level of three stars Chief at N.Y.P.D. More than 20,000 Police Officers and 4,000 Civilian support staff of the N.Y.P.D. Patrol Services Bureau were under his supervision.

In 2003, Estavillo was named National Grand Marshal of the Puerto Rican Day Parade in New York City.

In 2006, he was the recipient of the Leadership Award, given during the Law Enforcement Explorer Awards ceremonies.

Estavillo is the father of four children and has six grandchildren. He is a member of the New York State Association of Chiefs of Police, the American Academy of Professional Law Enforcement, the N.Y.P.D. Marine Corps Association, the Marine Force Recon Association, the F.B.I. National Academy Associates, the N.Y.P.D. Hispanic Society and serves as advisor to the Association of Retired Hispanic Police.

The duties of a Chief of Patrol include the coordination and deployment of the Department's eight Patrol Boroughs which include 76 Precinct Commands.

The Patrol Chief is also in charge of the Special Operations Division, which includes the Emergency Services Unit, Mounted Unit, Aviation Unit, Harbor Unit and Canine Unit. Estavillo managed the resources to combat crime and support counter terrorism strategies; provided supervision to direct, observe and evaluate performance, equipment, and training of personnel. Estavillo retired in 2007 from the NYPD.

REFERENCES

Gaines, Larry. Victor Kappeler, and Joseph Vaughn, Policing in America (3rd ed.), Cincinnati, Ohio: Anderson Publishing Company, 1999.

Haring, Sidney, Policing in a Class Society: The Experience of American Cities, 1865-1915, New Brunswick, New Jersey: Rutgers University Press, 1983.

Lundman, Robert J., Police and Policing: An Introduction, New York, New York: Holt, Rinehart & Winston, 1980.

Lynch, Michael, Class Based Justice: A History of the Origins of Policing in Albany, Albany, New York: Michael J. Hindelang Criminal Research Justice Center, 1984.

Platt, Tony, "Crime and Punishment in the United States: Immediate and Long-Term Reforms from a Marxist Perspective, Crime and Social Justice 18 (1982).

Reichel, Philip L., "The Misplaced Emphasis on Urbanization in Police Development," Policing and Society 3 no. 1 (1992).

Spitzer, Stephen, "The Rationalization of Crime Control in Capitalist Society," Contemporary Crises 3, no. 1 (1979).

Pileggi, Nicholas (August 31, 1981). The Not Quite Prince of the City. New York Magazine.

Daley, Robert (November 20, 1978). Not Exactly The Perfect Crime. New York Magazine

Safety on the Fiscal 2022 Executive Budget for the New York Police Department" (PDF). New York City Council. May 11, 2021. p. 2. Retrieved October 13, 2021.

council.nyc.gov/budget/wp-content/uploads/sites/54/2021/03/056-NYPD.pdf

"QuickFacts: New York city, New York". U.S. Census Bureau. Retrieved August 17, 2021.

"Find Your Precinct and Sector - NYPD". www1.nyc.gov.

"Fleet Report - Mayor's Office of Operations". www1.nyc.gov.

"NYPD Crew: Meet the Mechanics Who Keep Police Cars, Boats, and Helicopters Alive". Popular Mechanics. February 28, 2018. Retrieved May 3, 2021.

"Bureau of Justice Statistics . United States Department of Justice. p. 34. Retrieved December 5, 2013.

Myers, Steven Lee (April 1995). "Giuliani Wins Police Merger in M.T.A. Vote". The New York Times.

"About NYPD - NYPD". www1.nyc.gov. Retrieved July 31, 2020.

"Microsoft Power BI". app.powerbigov.us. Retrieved April 8, 2021.

"NYPD Complaint Data Historic". NYC Open Data. Retrieved July 31, 2020.

Parascandola, Rocco. "Cops used more force in 2019 even as arrests fell last year: report". nydailynews.com. Retrieved July 31, 2020.

Akinnibi, Fola; Holder, Sarah; Cannon, Christopher (October 13, 2021). "NYC Cops Log Millions of Overtime Hours. New Yorkers Don't Feel Safer". CityLab. Bloomberg L.P. Retrieved October 13, 2021. The NYPD has blown past annual budgets every year for at least two decades, almost entirely due to overtime costs.

Kane, Robert J.; White, Michael D. (2012). Jammed Up: Bad Cops, Police Misconduct, and the New York City Police Department. NYU Press. doi:10.18574/nyu/9780814748411.003.0001. ISBN 978-0-8147-4841-1.

McArdle, Andrea (2001). Zero tolerance: quality of life and the new police brutality in New York City. New York University Press. ISBN 0-8147-5631-X. OCLC 45094047.

Hennelly, Bob (July 17, 2016). "New York City's cycle of police corruption: Do reforms stick, and does it matter?". City & State NY. Retrieved July 31, 2020.

The Wall Street Journal, May 13, 2017, p. C6

Browne, Arthur. "BOOK EXCERPT: First African-American to join NYPD suffered the silent hatred of his fellow officers". nydailynews. com. Retrieved August 3, 2020.

"Hearing and Markup Before the Committee on Foreign Affairs and its Subcommittee on Europe and the Middle East, House of Representatives, Ninety-ninth Congress, Second Session, on H.R. 4329, March 5 and 6, 1986", Foreign Assistance for Northern Ireland and the Republic of Ireland, U.S. Government Printing Office, United States Congress House Committee on Foreign Affairs, 1986

"Biaggi, Mario (1917-2015)", Biographical Directory of the U.S. Congress

"Mario Biaggi, congressman under the gun". UPI. June 3, 1987.

Williams, Mason B. (2021). "How the Rockefeller Laws Hit the Streets: Drug Policing and the Politics of State Competence in New York City, 1973–1989". Modern American History. 4: 67–90. doi:10.1017/mah.2020.23. ISSN 2515-0456.

"Shielded from Justice: New York: Civilian Complaint Review Board". www.hrw.org. Retrieved January 15, 2021.

"Police Unions Haven't Only Battled Bill de Blasio's City Hall". Observer. December 22, 2014. Retrieved January 15, 2021.

Oliver, Pamela. "When the NYPD Rioted – Race, Politics, Justice". Retrieved January 15, 2021.

"NCJRS Abstract - National Criminal Justice Reference Service". www.ncjrs.gov. Retrieved August 29, 2020.

Didier, Emmanuel (July 30, 2018). "Globalization of Quantitative Policing: Between Management and Statactivism". Annual Review of Sociology. 44 (1): 515–534. doi:10.1146/annurev-soc-060116-053308. ISSN 0360-0572. S2CID 150164073.

"What Caused the Crime Decline?". www.brennancenter.org. Retrieved January 24, 2021.

Retrieved April 10, 2021.

"About NYPD - NYPD (Demographics)" (PDF). www1.nyc.gov. Retrieved August 3, 2020.

"Keechant Sewell sworn in as NYPD's first female police commissioner". NBC News. Retrieved January 1, 2022.

"Juanita Holmes Named 1st Female NYPD Chief of Patrol". NBC New York. Retrieved January 1, 2022.

"A Majority of NYPD Officers Don't Live In New York City, New Figures Show". Gothamist. August 8, 2020. Retrieved December 7, 2021.

"This Interactive Map Shows You Where NYPD Officers Live". Gothamist. October 22, 2016. Retrieved December 7, 2021.

"Senator Parker Proposes Legislation Aimed at Improving Police Relations in NYC" (Press release). New York State Senate. July 13, 2020. Retrieved December 7, 2021.

"Document shows NYPD eyed Shiites based on religion". Associated Press. Retrieved September 27, 2013.

Hartmann, Margaret (January 27, 2012). "NYPD Now Has an Israel Branch". New York. Retrieved September 27, 2013.

"Crime Stats - Historical - NYPD". www1.nyc.gov. Retrieved August 29, 2020.

"An Updated Definition of Rape". www.justice.gov. January 6, 2012. Retrieved January 23, 2021.

Rivera, Ray (November 30, 2009). "The Officer Is Real; The Badge May Be an Impostor". The New York Times. Retrieved June 28, 2020. [S]some officers don't wear their badges on patrol...Instead, they wear fakes...[c]called 'dupes,' these phony badges are often just a trifle smaller than real ones but otherwise completely authentic. Officers use them because losing a real badge can mean paperwork and a heavy penalty, as much as 10 days' pay...Though fake badges violate department policy, they are a quirk deeply embedded in the culture and history of the New York Police Department. Estimates of how many of the city's 35,000 officers use fake badges vary from several thousand to several hundred roughly 25 officers are disciplined each year for using them...'lots of people have dupe shields,' said Eric Sanders, a lawyer and former police officer who now represents officers in disciplinary actions...Years ago...officers referred to a fake badge as a Pottsy, after the Jay Irving comic strip about a New York City police officer. They later took on the name dupes, for duplicates.

"Chief of Department - NYPD". www1.nyc.gov. Retrieved January 1, 2021.

"Chief who knelt with protesters retires in new NYPD shake-up". AP NEWS. February 25, 2020. Retrieved March 22, 2021.

"NYPD Chief of Department". Retrieved January 1, 2022.

"NYPD - Administration". nyc.gov. Archived from the original on September 20, 2016.

"Bureaus". New York Police Department. Retrieved May 18, 2017.

Dolmetsch, Chris (December 14, 2011). "Occupy Wall Street Judge Refuses to Throw Out Summonses". Bloomberg News.

Pinto, Nick (November 3, 2016). "Protesters Sue to Stop NYPD from Acting as Prosecutors". The Village Voice.

Michael S. Schmidt, have a Tattoo or Walk with a Limp? The Police May Know, New York Times (February 18, 2010).

Joseph Goldstein, If Son of Sam Were on the Loose Today, New York Times (March 10, 2011).

Ángel Díaz, New York City Police Department Surveillance Technology, Brennan Center for Justice (October 4, 2019).

"Developing the NYPD's Information Technology" (PDF). New York Police Department. Retrieved June 8, 2019.

Levine, E. S.; Tisch, Jessica; Tasso, Anthony; Joy, Michael (February 2017). "The New York City Police Department's Domain Awareness System". Interfaces. : 70–84. doi:10.1287/inte.2016.0860.

Richardson, Kemberly (December 11, 2020). "NY Police Department's new robot dog, 'Digidog', is already saving lives". ABC7 San Francisco. Retrieved April 25, 2021.

Cramer, Maria; Hauser, Christine (February 27, 2021). "Digidog, a Robotic Dog Used by the Police, Stirs Privacy Concerns". The New York Times. Retrieved April 14, 2021.

Dowd, Trone (February 23, 2021). "The NYPD Sent a Creepy Robotic Dog into a Bronx Apartment Building". Vice News. Retrieved April 14, 2021.

Richardson, Kemberly (December 10, 2020). "Exclusive: A look at the NYPD's new robot dog". WABC-TV. Retrieved April 14, 2021.

"NYPD robotic dog prompts New York Rep. Torres to draft legislation". PIX11. April 24, 2021. Retrieved April 25, 2021.

"A New York Lawmaker Wants to Ban Police Use of Armed Robots". Wired. ISSN 1059-1028. Retrieved April 25, 2021.

Zaveri, Mihir (April 28, 2021). "N.Y.P.D. Robot Dog's Run Is Cut Short After Fierce Backlash". The New York Times. ISSN 0362-4331. Retrieved April 29, 2021.

"QU Poll Release Detail". QU Poll. Retrieved October 18, 2020.

University, Quinnipiac. "QU Poll Release Detail". QU Poll. Retrieved July 31, 2020.

"Taking the City's Temperature: What New Yorkers Say About Crime, the Cost of Living, Schools, and Reform". Manhattan Institute. August 27, 2020. Retrieved October 19, 2020.

"AP series about NYPD's surveillance of Muslims wins Pulitzer Prize for investigative reporting". The Washington Post. Associated Press. April 17, 2012. Archived from the original on April 17, 2012. Retrieved April 17, 2012.

Belcher, Ellen. "LibGuides: NYPD - Historical and Current Research: NYPD Oversight: Excessive Force, Corruption & Investigations". guides.lib.jjay.cuny.edu. Retrieved June 5, 2020.

Rosen, Steven A. (1980). "Police Harassment of Homosexual Women and Men in New York City 1960-1980". Columbia Human Rights Review.

Gelman, Andrew; Fagan, Jeffrey; Kiss, Alex (September 1, 2007). "An Analysis of the New York City Police Department's "Stop-and-Frisk" Policy in the Context of Claims of Racial Bias". Journal of the American Statistical Association. 102 (479): 813–823. doi:10.1198/016214506000001040. ISSN 0162-1459. S2CID 8505752.

Eterno, John (September 20, 2017). The New York City Police Department: the impact of its policies and practices. p. 152. ISBN 978-1-138-45859-8. OCLC 1091191466.

Durkin, Erin. "NYPD, de Blasio blame bail reform for crime spike as defenders question police stats". Politico PRO. Retrieved June 5, 2020.

Goodman, J. David (September 29, 2015). "Officer Who Disclosed Police Misconduct Settles Suit". The New York Times. ISSN 0362-4331. Retrieved June 14, 2020.

"Right to Remain Silent". This American Life. September 10, 2010. Retrieved June 14, 2020.

Rabe-Hemp, Cara (2011), "Police Corruption and Code of Silence", Police and Law Enforcement, SAGE, p. 132, doi:10.4135/9781412994095.n10, ISBN 9781412978590

"About - CCRB". www1.nyc.gov. Retrieved April 21, 2020.

Freiman, Jordan (June 8, 2020). "New York lawmakers pass anti-chokehold bill named for Eric Garner". CBS News. Retrieved June 11, 2020.

"N.Y. Gov. Cuomo Signs Sweeping Police Reforms into Law, Says They're 'Long Overdue'". June 12, 2020.

Wilson, Michael (June 11, 2020). "Why Are So Many N.Y.P.D. Officers Refusing to Wear Masks at Protests?". The New York Times. ISSN 0362-4331. Retrieved June 13, 2020.

McCann, Allison; Migliozzi, Blacki; Newman, Andy; Buchanan, Larry; Byrd, Aaron (July 15, 2020). "N.Y.P.D. Says It Used Restraint During Protests. Here's What the Videos Show". The New York Times. ISSN 0362-4331. Retrieved July 16, 2020.

"'Kettling' of Peaceful Protesters Shows Aggressive Shift by N.Y. Police". The New York Times. Retrieved March 8, 2021.

"Protester Speaks Out After Mask Ripped Off by NYPD and Pepper-Sprayed in Brooklyn". WNBC. Retrieved March 8, 2021.

"George Floyd protests: Video shows NYPD vehicles driving into crowd". Global News.

"NYPD used excessive force during George Floyd protests, city investigation finds". NBC News. Retrieved December 18, 2020.

Thomson-DeVeaux, Amelia (February 22, 2021). "Police Misconduct Costs Cities Millions Every Year. But That's Where the Accountability Ends". FiveThirtyEight. Retrieved February 22, 2021.

"New York City Exploring – Discover Your Future". Retrieved April 16, 2022.

"The Officer Down Memorial Page (ODMP)". www.odmp.org. Retrieved April 11, 2021.

"New York City Police Department, NY". The Officer Down Memorial Page (ODMP).

"Fleet Report - Mayor's Office of Operations". www1.nyc.gov.

"NYPD Set to Retire Last of its Revolvers - The Firearm Blog". November 30, 2017. Archived from the original on December 1, 2017.

Parascandola, Rocco. "NYPD will issue easier-to-fire guns to new recruits, aiming for improved accuracy". nydailynews.com. Retrieved January 10, 2022.

"Training Bureau | Firearms & Tactics Section". nyc.gov. Archived from the original on March 12, 2009.

"Guide to Smith & Wesson Semi-Auto Pistols & Their Model Numbers". www.luckygunner.com.

"NYPD's Elite E-Men". Tactical Life. July 2009. Archived from the original on August 5, 2014. Retrieved July 26, 2014.

Further reading

Darien, Andrew T. Becoming New York's Finest: Race, Gender, and the Integration of the NYPD, 1935–1980. New York: Palgrave Macmillan, 2013.

Elliot, Bryn (March–April 1997). "Bears in the Air: The US Air Police Perspective". Air Enthusiast. No. 68. pp. 46–51. ISSN 0143-5450.

Miller, Wilbur R. Cops, and bobbies: Police authority in New York and London, 1830–1870 (The Ohio State University Press, 1999)

Monkkonen, Eric H. Police in Urban America, 1860–1920 (2004)

Richardson, James F. The New York Police, Colonial Times to 1901 (Oxford University Press, 1970)

Richardson, James F. "To Control the City: The New York Police in Historical Perspective". In Cities in American History, eds. Kenneth T. Jackson and Stanley K. Schultz (1972) pp. 3–13.

Thale, Christopher. "The Informal World of Police Patrol: New York City in the Early Twentieth Century", Journal of Urban History (2007) 33#2 pp. 183–216. doi:10.1177/0096144206290384.

Google (January 17, 2015). "Map of NYC Law Enforcement Line of Duty Deaths" (Map). Google Maps. Google. Retrieved January 17, 2015.

"With the Sky Police", Popular Mechanics, January 1932 article about the NY City Police Air Force and the Keystone-Loening Commuter in service at that time, photos pp. 26–30

NYPD Annual Reports 1912–1923 (digitized books) from the Lloyd Sealy Library on the Internet Archive

Historical images from the NYPD Annual Reports, 1923–23 from the Lloyd Sealy Library Digital Collections

Categories: New York City Police Department1845 establishments in New York (state)Law enforcement in the New York metropolitan area Municipal police departments of New York (state)Government agencies established in 1845

ABOUT THE AUTHOR

Norma Iris Pagan Morales was born in Ponce, Puerto Rico. She comes from a very lovable family. Her parents, Juan Jose Pagan Rodriguez, and Digna Morales Figueroa, now deceased, always helped her with her projects as a writer and teaching career. Norma had three siblings, Adelin Milagros Pagan Morales, Juan Jose Pagan Morales, and Julio Manuel Pagan Morales. Julio Manuel Pagan Morales died on September 19, 1998. He was also known for his writing / composer skills.

Norma did all her academic studies in New York City, Puerto Rico, and Canada. She worked in the City of New York Police Department. As an Educator, she worked in New York City Bd. of Education as an English Teacher, in Puerto Rico Bd. of Education as an English teacher and in the Puerto Rico Army National.

She has teaching certifications for English as a Second Language and Teaching English as a Foreign Language.

She has published five books: Proud of My Puerto Rican Bequest, Porque Soy Boricua? Poemas del Alma, Art in Written Form and A Baffling Short Stories Collection.